NIGEL TRANTER

SCOTLAND'S STORYTELLER

NIGEL TRANTER

SCOTLAND'S STORYTELLER

RAY BRADFIELD

First published 1999
by B&W Publishing Ltd, Edinburgh
ISBN 1 873631 98 7
Copyright © Ray Bradfield 1999

British Library Cataloguing in Publication Data:
A catalogue record for this book is available
from the British Library

Cover design: Winfortune & Associates

Printed by WSOY

CONTENTS

FOREWORD

I am pleased, indeed flattered, to have a biography published about me, the more so it being done by so estimable and talented a writer as Ray Bradfield. I cannot feel that I deserve this.

But, be that as it may, I greatly approve of the result, its thoroughness and scope, its accuracy and care and detail, all but an eye-opener for myself!

I cannot sufficiently thank and express my admiration for the compiler. The picture drawn, kind to me as it is, may give the reader some notion of the storyteller's life, whose aim has been ever to entertain and inform, as far as he is able, especially on his beloved land and its colourful and dramatic history.

My sincere thanks to Ray. I have enjoyed reading this, with its observations and conclusions drawn from my books. I hope that you do also.

Nigel Tranter

Gullane 1999

ACKNOWLEDGEMENTS

Many people have given generously of their time and delved deep into their memories to help me piece together my picture of Nigel Tranter, and it is a mark of the affection in which he is held that no one whom I approached for an interview was unwilling to talk to me. I am particularly indebted to his own close friends, among them Peter Gillies and Lin Dalgleish, Ian and Meta Gilmour, Dorothy Haddon, Jan Moffatt and Rosemary Pringle-Pattison. Kate Lyall Grant and Maggie Body gave valuable help on the books, and I am also indebted to the staffs of the National Library of Scotland Manuscripts and Rare Books Room, the Edinburgh Central Library Edinburgh Room, the Birmingham Central Library Local Studies and History Department, the Scottish Records Office and the Family Record Centre, London, for much expert help with research. I am particularly grateful to Maisie Tranter for help with research on the Tranter family, to Gordon Reid for help with theological points, and to David Skeoch for help with the history of the Order of St Lazarus of Jerusalem.

Special thanks are due to Maureen Stewart for much early interviewing, and to Liz MacLaren Innes for sharing with me her memories of the Corriemulzie Mountaineering Club and lending material on Philip Tranter. I am also grateful to Braemar Mountain Sports for lending material on Philip Tranter.

I am obliged to Hodder & Stoughton Ltd for generous permission to reproduce copyright material from Nigel Tranter's books.

I owe of course the deepest debt of gratitude to Frances May Baker for talking so generously to me about her mother and her brother Philip: her recollections of them both, and of her own childhood, are central to this book, a point of reference to which I constantly returned. I am also grateful to Alison Tollick for telling me how she remembers her grandmother and to Elizabeth Scott for her recollections of May Tranter and Hume Spiers Grieve.

My personal thanks go also to the close circle of friends who serve me in place of a family: they will know who they are. Their forbearance and support have been marvellous to see. Three friends in particular have helped cheerfully and unhesitatingly with abstruse aspects of research, badgering their own friends on my behalf: William Adams, Joyce Eveling and Richard Spear. Lastly, my thanks go to Joan Earle, to whom my debt is immeasurable and without whom this book might well have been begun but would certainly never have been finished.

The insights are theirs: the faults are mine.

R.B.
Gullane 1999

PROLOGUE

Out of the half-dark of a December noon he comes, a spare figure, head down against the wind, purposeful, preoccupied, absorbed, impatient at the break in his stride as he pauses to watch my car go by. He is dressed as a countryman in waxed cotton coat, breeches and stockings: his left arm swings free, a little out from his side, and his pocket bulges, but he carries no gun. Behind him stretch the mud-flats of Aberlady Bay, lacklustre on this dull day. I watch him in my rear mirror as he forges on across the road and disappears from view between the two little stone pillars splashed with white that guard his house. He is Nigel Tranter, coming off shift, back from his daily walk along the East Lothian shoreline, with another thousand words ready to type up before tea, another link in the long chain of writing about Scotland's past that has become his life work. For over fifty years he has walked this coast daily, winter and summer, in fair weather and foul. His imagination is as vivid as ever and he seems imperishable. He is our local celebrity, and a national phenomenon.

When I observed him that December day two years ago, I already knew him, though not well. I had met him for the first time in 1989 at a friend's house in Gullane, at a time when I was still living abroad. Two years later, I came home for good, and discovered that he sat in the pew behind me in church. I noted with approval a light tenor voice. Gradually, a dialogue developed and he discovered that I, too, had a passion for the past and, home in Scotland again after long absence, was now indulging it. I owned and greatly admired the five volumes of *The Fortified House in Scotland*, his great work on the little castles that dot our countryside, and that are particularly numerous in East Lothian. But the novels had largely passed me by: partly because I had given up novel-reading more than a quarter of a century before, when my life no longer held time for such indulgences. When the idea of this book came up, I was a clean sheet. But it faced me with a formidable challenge: reading the 130-odd books with the attention they deserved, while at the same time getting through them with sufficient speed to keep pace with the autobiographical material he was producing for me as we met week by week. Two years on, our friendship has deepened and we are both, in our separate ways, a day's march nearer home on journeys that seemed to be tailing off. For Nigel the journey has already been long, the companions he set out with long since gone on ahead; but he strides out full of hope, his appetite for life and for writing in no way diminished. This is his story.

I

GLASGOW

Glasgow. Mount Florida. 1911 or thereabouts. The back garden of a house in Brownlie Street. A small child stands rapt, in the middle of the drying green, gazing out at the field beyond, where there are cows and a wider view from the modest eminence to a hint of the city in the distance. But the child's horizons are more restricted and his eyes fixed on the cows: it is a treat of which he never tires.

Nigel Tranter was born on 23 November 1909 at 35 Brownlie Street, Glasgow. He was the son of Gilbert Tredgold Tranter and his wife, Eleanor Annie Cass, both Edinburgh people, and on the day that he was born, *The Scotsman* was reporting a constitutional crisis after the House of Lords threw out the Government's Finance Bill; Sir Arthur Conan Doyle was chairing a public meeting in Edinburgh on the Congo; Croall's were advertising the sale of "upwards of 120 riding and carriage horses"; a cook-general could be obtained for £18-20 a year and a "Footman 5ft 11ins" was advertising his services for £28. Ladies wore stays and ankle-length skirts and the turn-down collar for men was still a novelty. Nigel Tranter was an Edwardian, but born on the cusp of a new age: the first motor-cars were on the streets, Blériot had flown the Channel in July, and ragtime was all the rage in the United States.

His parents named him Nigel Godwin: Godwin after a Tranter uncle and Nigel for no reason known, at least to him. But in old age he recalls that Nigel is simply another form of the more familiar Scots Neil, and Neil was used interchangeably with Nigel in the immediate family circle. It may have been a haphazard choice, but it was to prove prescient and provide an unexpected link with the hero of his greatest novel, the novel that made him a household name: now he is proud to recall that it was the name also of Bruce's beloved younger brother. In *The Steps to the Empty Throne*, he gives the two brothers a strong family resemblance but makes Nigel, perhaps with some partiality, "the more nearly handsome", but with a certain "sensitiveness".

Eleanor was a second wife, Gilbert's first wife Hannah having died in 1901, and the household included the children of this first marriage, Gilbert John, always known in the family as Jack, born in 1896, and Dorothy Frances, born in 1897, both of whom were nearly grown-up by the time Nigel was beginning to be aware of them as individuals; and Phyllis Grace, born in 1901. Gilbert had married Eleanor in 1906 and she had had an earlier child, a boy they called Norman, who did not survive. She was 34 when Nigel was born and he was to be her only child: there can be little doubt he was anxiously watched over as an infant and greatly cherished. In his earliest years he never left her side and he remained exceptionally close to her all her life. Gilbert was another matter: 40 when Nigel was born, he was a distant figure, preoccupied with his own concerns and adhering perhaps to the practices of an earlier age, a solid Victorian *paterfamilias*. Nigel called him "Sir".

Gilbert Tranter settled in Glasgow sometime around the turn of the year 1905-6 and moved his family there shortly thereafter, on marriage to Eleanor. He was an insurance agent working for a family firm, the Scottish-National Key Registry and Assurance Association, long since subsumed in other companies. His position was relatively humble and involved a fair amount of pounding the streets. The house in Brownlie Street was comfortable but not stylish, on two floors, one of them a basement from which the ground fell away sharply at the back. The cows have gone now, but the fields where they grazed still present a pleasant open outlook over a shallow basin with football pitches and a scruffy little park close to the house. The entrance on the street side was tucked away under a short flight of stairs leading to the grander flats above. Brownlie Street lay on the edge of the exotically-named Mount Florida, a new suburb that had been opened up in the 1870s and which expanded rapidly after the completion of the Cathcart District Railway in 1886. The house is still there, and so is the railway, cowering at the bottom of a dank cutting that must always have attracted its share of urban detritus. Mount Florida is a windy spot. Just down the road, the roar of the crowd clearly audible on match days, was the splendid new Hampden Park football stadium, built on land first purchased by the Queen's Park football club in 1900: by 1910 it had an unprecedented capacity of 125,000, later increased still further, and it was to remain the largest football stadium in the world until 1950, when it was superseded by the Maracana stadium in Brazil.

The house in Brownlie Street was a little older than most in the area: the newer houses were solid stone-built blocks of flats, prosperous and dignified but not pretentious. These were the homes of the newly prosperous lower-middle classes, office workers, skilled artisans, teachers and the like, solid, respectable people, upwardly mobile but not yet property-owning: most houses were rented, not owned. In terms of male headgear, this was bowler-hat, not flat-cap, territory. There were busy shopping streets only minutes away. And of course, churches: this was still a church-going age. Not that the Tranters attended a local church: they went further afield to worship. The Queen's Park was also close by: a fine public park with ducks.

Glasgow's prosperity reached its apogee in those golden days just before the Great War, the "Second City" of a vast Empire, its undisputed industrial capital, and justifiably proud of it. It had been built on commerce and industry, the transatlantic trade that flowed in and out of the Clyde, the great ships that were built there, and the products of the mighty industries of Scotland's central belt. Clyde-built ships were to be found in every corner of the globe, and Glasgow-built locomotives could be found hauling trains everywhere from China to the Andes. Above all, it was a city of ships: masts, funnels and gantries lined the banks of the Clyde right up to the city centre. The product of business acumen, Scottish engineering genius and native brawn, Glasgow was the power-house of an Empire whose sun still seemed at its zenith. The ambitious scale of the Hampden Park football ground and the crowds that thronged to matches on winter Saturdays were indicative of the city's confidence: this was Glasgow's industrial working class flexing its muscles. In summer, they took to the seaways for their pleasure, surging down to the Broomielaw to board the *Ivanhoe* or the *Columba* for a blast of fresh air and a day out "doon the watter" in Rothesay or Dunoon. Football was beyond Nigel's comprehension at such a tender age; but he remembers the excitements of the steamers, just as he remembers another early treat—the bright blue engines of the Caledonian Railway Company he saw at Buchanan Street Station when the family sallied forth to visit relatives in Edinburgh. Despite the course his life subsequently followed, Glasgow was not an inappropriate place for Nigel Tranter to be born, for whatever lay ahead, Glasgow in 1909 had no doubts as to either its worth or its identity.

The Tranters made a brave show but they were not well-off and young Nigel's life was to be punctuated by developments that reflected the ups and downs, mainly downs, of his father's finances. When he was three, a downturn led to disposal of the house in Brownlie Street and a move round the corner to a less comfortable, top-floor flat (cheaper, particularly in those walk-up days, than the lower floors) at 93 Somerville Drive, newer property directly overlooking the football ground. The accommodation may have been less spacious, but the family's social circle expanded fast, as friends and relatives crowded in on Saturday afternoons to watch the matches, a circumstance not appreciated by Nigel, who didn't understand what was going on, and couldn't see beyond the forest of legs. Football holds little attraction for him to this day.

But the Tranters were not to be long in Somerville Drive either. A year later, following yet another crisis, they moved back to Edinburgh, where Gilbert took up a new appointment, this time as one of the Scottish-National Key Registry's insurance inspectors. It was a step up: an agent sells insurance, but an inspector examines claims. The First World War had broken out, insurance was booming, and staff were being shuffled as a result. As far as Gilbert and his family were concerned, the change was welcome: they would be slightly better off, and they were going back to Edinburgh, where they would have the support of family and friends.

The precarious nature of the family finances was to cast a long shadow over Nigel's life: it had seriously scarred his father and thus upset the natural balance of relationships within the family, and it would affect definitively Nigel's choice of a career. The fact is that Gilbert Tranter was not what he seemed. He is described on Nigel's birth certificate as an insurance official: but on the birth certificates of Jack, Dorothy and Phyllis he appears as a Minister of the Catholic Apostolic Church, residing at 20 Royal Crescent, a fashionable address in Edinburgh's New Town. To understand the cataclysmic nature of the disaster which intervened, it is necessary to go back well before Nigel's birth.

Gilbert Tranter had been born into comfortable circumstances, the son of an engineer who was also a minister of the Catholic

Apostolic Church, in his turn the son of another engineer. In the explosive expansion of the new industrial age in the 19th century, engineering skills turned over money. Gilbert seems to have attended the Heriot Watt College (now the Heriot Watt University) where he trained to be a surveyor. He worked for some years as a surveyor before being called to become a priest of the Catholic Apostolic Church. He was ordained on St Andrew's Day, 1894. This church, to which we shall return, is not to be confused in any way with the Roman Catholic Church: it did not require priests to be celibate and Gilbert married Hannah Andrew, the daughter of a prosperous Glasgow draper, the following June. The church had many part-time as well as fully-employed priests, but Gilbert became a "separated" or full-time minister. Within the four orders of the Catholic Apostolic priesthood, he was an "evangelist" or preacher. Hannah was a beauty, and well-to-do (she appears handsome, confident, and expensively dressed in the surviving photographs) and Gilbert, who was personable, lively and had a gift for words, was a catch. Jack was born the next year, and Dorothy shortly thereafter. Hannah died giving birth to Phyllis in 1901.

It is not clear what encouraged Gilbert to speculate in De Beers diamond shares. Possibly his unearned income, from whatever source, was declining, perhaps it seemed inadequate to support his life-style as his family increased, possibly he was looking for a suitable way to invest funds that came to him with Hannah or were left by her when she died. But speculate he did. The 1890s had been marked by a phenomenal rise in the value of South African gold and diamond shares, fuelled by the colossal dividends they were paying: diamonds in particular were booming. This was the age when every self-respecting middle-class girl expected to be given a five- or at least a three-diamond hoop to cement an engagement—a new idea—and the upper classes festooned their womenfolk with diamonds like so many Christmas trees. De Beers paid an astonishing 40% dividend in 1896. The London papers reported questionable dealings, and the South African market was insufficiently regulated, but as the shares rose and rose, it must have looked like a sure-fire investment. The get-rich-quick Darien Scheme which had so ravaged Scotland a couple of centuries before was long since forgotten and in any case irrelevant: Britain's industrial expansion appeared unstoppable and the wealth deriving from Empire inexhaustible. For many people investment on the Stock Exchange was a delightful novelty and the country was suffused with the kind of reckless optimism that would be repeated in the United States a couple of decades later.

For whatever reason, Gilbert plunged. With two Edinburgh friends, both professional men—which in Edinburgh tends to mean lawyers—he formed a syndicate to buy shares in De Beers. This in itself might not have been disastrous, but they committed themselves to an option arrangement whereby they would take up further shares at a predetermined price when the company called them in. The shares originally purchased formed the security for the call option shares. At this late date it is well-nigh impossible to disentangle the ins and outs of the affair, or its exact timing. But it is clear that the arrangement must have been entered into when the shares were at their peak. Then came the Boer War: Kimberley itself was besieged and production ground to a halt. To make matters worse, De Beers were implicated in the machinations that sparked the war, they were involved in financing railways, which also suffered, there was a tangle of inter-company loan transactions, some insufficiently secured, and De Beers shares dropped sharply. The coming of peace improved matters for a time, but a couple of years after the cessation of hostilities South Africa suffered a general recession and the shares dropped again. Sometime during this period, the options were called in, the shares fell due to be paid at their original inflated price, the original shares on which they had been secured had of course also dropped sharply in value—and ruin stared the trio in the face. The disaster took a little time to play out, but at the end of it—probably sometime in 1905—this already nightmarish situation was compounded for Gilbert by the defection of his partners: of the other two members of the syndicate, one fled to America and was never heard of again, and the other committed suicide. Gilbert was left to find the amount of the syndicate's net indebtedness, a very large sum of money, on his own. In those days, bankruptcy was not to be thought of—a man of honour paid his debts—and Gilbert's capital and the income arising from it were wiped out completely. To make matters worse, the Catholic Apostolic Church took an uncompromising view: speculation on the Stock Exchange was tantamount to gambling and incompatible with the priesthood. The upshot was that Gilbert was asked to resign and in so doing lost his licence as a minister. In one fell swoop, he had lost his fortune, his income and his position in life: it was a heavy price to pay.

Gilbert married Eleanor in the Mansfield Place Church in Edinburgh on 11 May 1906, giving as his address 40 West Campbell Street, Glasgow: he was not registered there as a householder, and it seems probable he was in lodgings. West Campbell Street is now wholly given over to commercial property and the house has gone, but it must have seemed a far cry from 20 Royal Crescent in Edinburgh. There must have been an understanding between the two before Gilbert left for Glasgow. Eleanor was the daughter of James Cass, another minister of the Catholic Apostolic Church, and she had been a member of his congregation in Edinburgh. More importantly, her brother Henry Cass was a successful businessman, who owned the Edinburgh-based Scottish-National Key Registry and Assurance Association, originally the Scottish Lost Key Recovery Association, and was a director of the Century Insurance Company Ltd, also Edinburgh-based: it was he who found Gilbert a job in Glasgow when disaster struck. There may have been some self-interest involved in finding Gilbert a job outside Edinburgh: given the nature of his business, Henry Cass may well have been as anxious as the Church to keep the couple out of the public eye for a while. Edinburgh is a city where respectability is all. But the fact remains that without Harry Cass, Gilbert and his family would have been destitute, and Harry was to prove a most devoted and loving brother who continued all his life to take a close interest in his sister's well-being and that of her family. Jack, Dorothy and Nigel were all provided with jobs in the family company, and as late as the Second World War, Nigel's wife May might be found taking over Nigel's files at the Scottish-National when he went off to the Army. At 31, Eleanor was no doubt glad to be settled: high levels of emigration had produced a shortage of men and though a gentle and charming girl, she did not have Hannah's looks. And Gilbert was glad to have her: there is no record of how he arranged for the care of his young family after Hannah died, but a wife in the house again must have taken some at least of the daily burden off his shoulders. Maybe a gentlemanly deal was struck, maybe not. But although the relationship between Gilbert and Eleanor never achieved the warmth and closeness Nigel would experience in his own marriage, the marriage was nevertheless a happy one, even though money was a constant source of anxiety.

His family background was perhaps less straightforward from the point of view of their only child. Scarred by the De Beers affair, Gilbert was always rather a remote figure to Nigel, coming and going about his own business, preoccupied no doubt with his own worries, semi-detached from the rest of the household. In any case, in his forties, he was on the old side to find himself the father of a young son and the novelty of fatherhood had perhaps worn off. Generally speaking, it was a formal household.

Perhaps unsurprisingly, Gilbert was reticent about the past as far as Nigel was concerned. It was Eleanor, not his father, who told

Nigel all he knows about the fatal speculation in De Beers and his father's sudden loss of status, and he never discovered where the money came from to repay the debt. All he was told about his forebears was that Gilbert was the son of William Tranter, a minister of the Catholic Apostolic Church (although even this requires some modification, for William is variously described on Gilbert's birth, marriage and death certificates, and his own marriage certificate, based presumably on information supplied either by himself or Gilbert, as a journeyman tool-maker, a civil engineer, a commercial traveller and a mechanical engineer), and that William's father, said to be another William, married a Frances Watt. The Tranters were believed to have originated in Galloway, but to have moved to the Birmingham area in the earlier part of the 19th century, for reasons unknown.

For the family historian, these are thin pickings indeed and as a child, Nigel was too much in awe of his father to ask more. By the time he might have plucked up courage, there was no one left to ask. But by and large, he seems to have been curiously uninterested in his own remoter origins. His lineage within the largely closed circle of the Catholic Apostolic Church, which constituted the social framework of their lives, was in any case impeccable: the son of a minister of the Church, however fallen from grace, and the grandson of two more ministers of the Church.

A strange, and in the event, cruel twist of fate appeared to shed some light on the past in 1980, just after Nigel's wife's death. He was working at the time on *The Patriot*, the novel he wrote about Andrew Fletcher, opponent of the 1707 Treaty of Union. In the book, Fletcher pulls out his pistol when threatened and shoots Alderman Dare dead where he stands. Uncertain whether this would have been possible with the pistols of the day, he sought out the firearms expert at the Royal Scottish Museum in Edinburgh for advice (and eventually solved his problem by having the pistol still primed from an earlier encounter). Intrigued by his name and errand, the man told him of a notable Birmingham gun-maker called William Tranter, who had perfected a single-trigger double-action pistol in 1856, and showed him an exemplar in the possession of the Museum: as the name suggests, the Tranter pistol was a percussion revolver with a trigger that both cocked the pistol and fired the charge. The dates seemed roughly right and Nigel recalled that when he was a youth, his father had given him "his grandfather's pistol" without further explanation: Nigel—a great giver of things away—subsequently passed it on to a friend "because he was interested in things like that". There was no way now of proving whether it was a Tranter pistol, but why on earth should his grandfather otherwise have owned a revolver? When Nigel confided that his grandfather and great-grandfather had both been named William Tranter (as he believed at the time) and had some sort of engineering background, and revealed further-more that the elder William had married a Miss Watt, the trail only became more exciting. What if Miss Watt was a grandchild of the great James Watt, also settled in Birmingham? For someone with a romantic bent it made a marvellous story: a reversal of fortune in the classic mould of the foundling who turns out to be a prince. Unfortunately, however, the facts didn't bear it out: the ground turned out be thick with William Tranters as leaves in Vallombrosa and the gunsmith married a different wife. Nigel's great-grandfa-ther's name in any case turned out to be Joseph, not William. The jury is still out on Frances Watt, but it doesn't look hopeful. It was great, though, while it lasted.

II

MANSFIELD PLACE

*Edinburgh now, a top-floor flat at 8 Eyre Crescent. It is Sunday and,
behind the front door, the family are getting ready for church. Gilbert is
dressed in frock coat and high collar and stands in front of the hall
mirror. Nigel, hair slicked down, gives Gilbert's gleaming top-hat a last
respectful polish with his sleeve and hands it to his father, who puts it on,
gives it a smart tap to settle it on his head, casts a quick glance round his
belongings and opens the door. The little procession sets off, Gilbert in
front, with Eleanor on his arm. Dorothy, Phyllis and Nigel bring up the
rear. Jack is in Gallipoli with the RAMC, for the year is 1915, Nigel is
five and Britain is at war. Army lorries line the other side of the street,
on the church side, many of the men hanging around, smoking. But the
Tranters are not stepping across the road to the Davidson Church, which
occupies the island site in the middle of the Crescent. As in Glasgow, they
are going further afield, and they turn left into Eyre Place. They are
bound for Mansfield Place, ten minutes' walk away, and the magnificent,
cathedral-like building erected thirty years before for the Catholic
Apostolic Church. Once there, the procession re-forms: Gilbert marches
up the centre aisle to his place at the head of a front pew while his family,
Eleanor included, scuttle up the side aisle to enter from the other end. The
Tranters are back from outer darkness, and if Gilbert is no longer robed
and in the chancel, he is not hiding in the back pew either. They will be
back for evening service and Nigel will be here for Sunday school in the*

afternoon as well. Whatever vicissitudes they may have suffered at the hands of the Church, there has been no falling off in faith. Judged by any standards, let alone those of the austere temples of the Church of Scotland where most people then worshipped, the interior of the Mansfield Place Church is magnificent, a riot of brilliant murals, picked out in gold, the soaring chancel arch covered with Phoebe Anna Traquair's serried ranks of saints and angels, with further murals under completion in the side-aisles. There are eight or ten clergy in the chancel, all gorgeously robed, and the congregation numbers hundreds: it, too, has an air of opulence. This is the Tranter family's spiritual home: this is where they belong.

Gilbert Tranter was the son of William Tranter, another minister of the Catholic Apostolic Church, and his wife Jane Lakin. The family originated on the Scottish side of the border, but married into local families in both Scotland and England: their family names include a scatter of Musgroves, Lakins, Metcalfs and the like. William's father had moved south to settle in England sometime in the early decades of the 19th century. They had been Methodists, and William had been a lay preacher in the Methodist Church as well as an engineer. In the 1820s and 1830s South-west Scotland experienced a number of prophetic manifestations significant in the development of the emergent Catholic Apostolic movement, and the Tranters may have been drawn in before they moved to Birmingham. Originally a movement within the established churches, and never intended to become a separate church, the hysteria surrounding some of the Catholic Apostolic preachers, in particular the charismatic Edward Irving, and rumours that Queen Victoria herself was coming under its influence, reputedly so alarmed the Archbishop of Canterbury that its preachers were eventually banned by the Church of England and other churches followed suit: in due course they established their own Catholic Apostolic Church. But—and this should be emphasised—it was never the intention that the Catholic Apostolics should form themselves into a separate sect. They were excluded: they did not exclude themselves. It was from these events that Gilbert's father William emerged as a priest of the new church.

The Catholic Apostolic Church, whose name derives from the passage in the Nicene Creed, "We believe in one Catholic and Apostolic Church", first began to emerge in the aftermath of the French Revolution as a result of widespread alarm at the upheaval of the old social order, deemed to stem from God, and parallel alarm at the equally disruptive effect of the industrial revolution. These developments seemed to be preparing the way for the cataclysmic events described in the Book of Revelation as the precursor of the Second Coming of Christ. The central tenet of the Catholic Apostolic faith was a belief that the Second Coming was imminent: the Book of Revelation was interpreted literally and was of central importance, and was understood to mean that God had communicated to the faithful enlightened certain truths, the infallibility of which was guaranteed. The characteristics of the Church are a sense that its members have been vouchsafed a special and privileged insight into the teachings of the Bible, an emphasis on the glory of God, a very firm belief in the continuity of life after death, and a commitment to pursue a moral and disciplined life in this world: strict tithing was imposed, and, since congregations were fashionable and well-heeled, the Church accumulated considerable wealth. Members exuded an all-pervading sense of joy, in marked contrast to the solemn gloom of, for example, the Church of Scotland at the time. Services in Catholic Apostolic churches were furthermore a feast of music and colour, and sermons inspiring and optimistic, infused as they were with the certainty of a glorious tomorrow. Congregations participated actively through "prophesy", sometimes "speaking in the spirit", as it was called, and there were few longueurs. Writing of a period only a few years later, the author Gavin Maxwell, who was born in 1914 and whose family on both sides were fervent adherents, tells in his childhood autobiography *The House of Elrig* of the infinite sadness of the services conducted by "tottering old men who had no power to ordain successors" and the "tired, trembling old voices—voices belonging, each one, to personalities of patently unusual saintliness." But this was not Nigel's experience. Nigel greatly enjoyed church from the word go: never having known any other, he had no idea how unusual the Mansfield Place Church was. He squirmed, though, when someone sitting behind him regularly launched into prophesy and all turned—as it seemed—to stare at him. Typically, prophesy occurred during the silence of the Communion, when some member of the congregation would go into a trance-like state, and start to orate in a loud voice. Gavin Maxwell found such behaviour "awe-inspiring and frightening", whereas the emotion uppermost in Nigel's mind seems to have been embarrassment. But "prophesy" played an important role in the Church: the process by which Gilbert was called to the priesthood must have started with an act of "prophesy" by a member of the congregation of the Mansfield Place Church. Speaking as the spirit moved them was taken literally by the Catholic Apostolic Church. The Church's practices were ecumenical and its liturgy eclectic, with elements taken from the Eastern as well as the Western churches, and there were branches in virtually every European country. A great hierarchy of bishops and clergy was established with unfamiliar names. Individual churches were run by teams of clergymen, some of them part-time, and William Tranter seems to have been one of these.

But the Church had one serious flaw, logical in light of its beliefs, but fatal nevertheless: thanks to its absolute faith in the imminence of the Second Coming, it had made no provision for renewal. When three of the original twelve Apostles, who stood at the apex of the hierarchy, died in 1855, the remaining nine decided that no replacement was possible. The Apostles alone could make "Angels" or bishops; the Angels alone could ordain priests, and after the last of the Angels died, there was no-one left to make priests; when the last Priest died in 1971 there was no one left to administer the Sacrament. Only a handful of members remain and the churches are closed, or given over to other purposes. The last service was held in the Mansfield Place Church on Easter Sunday 1958.

III

HERIOT'S

Eyre Crescent again, 1918-1927, any weekday morning in term-time, any time between half-past eight and twenty to nine. Halfway round the Crescent a door flies open and a human cannonball shoots out, clad in a blue school blazer, his school books on his back. Nigel is setting off on his daily race against the clock and his own previous best: he is on his way to school. Out into Eyre Place he goes, up Dundas Street, entering the New Town proper at Fettes Row, on past Great King Street and Heriot Row where Stevenson lived, across Queen Street and Queen Street Gardens, over George Street, on Hanover Street now, with its statue of George IV, across Princes Street, past the Royal Scottish Academy, up the steps behind the National Gallery of Scotland, with the towering mass of the Castle on his right, over the Mound, up into Lady Stair's Close, out into the High Street, with St Giles' Cathedral and Parliament Hall on his left and a view down the Forth on a fine day to North Berwick Law and the Bass, on up George IV Bridge, past the little statue of Greyfriars Bobby, stopping as a young boy to pat its head for luck, on into Lauriston Place, through the great ornamental gates and into the quadrangle of George Heriot's School in time for morning assembly. If he's late, he takes a short-cut through Greyfriars Kirkyard where the Covenant was signed. Nigel's daily school run cuts a swathe right through the very heart of Scotland's story. At the end of it, his day is spent in a magnificent Renaissance palace, with an astounding open, airy view of the south side

of the Castle from the school yard, so open and so extraordinary that,
standing there, the world seems to consist only of these two, the school
and the Castle, floating in space. His best time is an incredible twenty
minutes. Coming down again at the end of the day, he takes the steps
three at a time, and as he enters the home stretch at the top of Dundas
Street he looks across the glittering waters of the Forth to the green hills
of Fife. More prosaically, on rainy days his mother gives him a penny
for the tram and he buckets up the Mound, courtesy of an Edinburgh
cable-car. Otherwise, they can't afford the fare.

The Tranters moved back to Edinburgh in 1914, just after the start
of the First World War, when Nigel was four. It was a return home
for them, for Glasgow had been exile. Then, as now, Edinburgh
and Glasgow were different as chalk and cheese, Glasgow (in
Edinburgh eyes) all push and vulgarity, Edinburgh (in Glasgow
eyes) all prim pretentiousness. In fact, working people—insofar as
Edinburgh admitted to having any such—were much the same in
both cities, although a strong admixture of Irish immigrants had
perhaps rendered Glaswegians a little more rumbustious. The
accepted perceptions were accurate enough, though, even if they
related primarily to the more prosperous classes. The Tranters
and Eleanor's family, the Casses, both belonged to the moneyed
bourgeoisie, firmly established in the New Town, and with little
knowledge of, or, for that matter, interest in the world outside its
bounds. Brewery and insurance apart, Edinburgh was not, like
Glasgow, a commercial city. Nor was it a city dominated by
ships, although Leith, a couple of miles away and now part of the
general conurbation of Edinburgh, was still a thriving port. But if
it was not a city of ships, Edinburgh was most emphatically a city
of water. Built on one long spine and a multitude of smaller hills,
the Firth of Forth is a constant presence, and there are vistas of
water at every turn: from the Castle and the High Street, east to

North Berwick Law and the Bass Rock; from the tops of the grid of Georgian streets leading north across the New Town, to Fife and the Lomond Hills. It is also a city of green hills, with the great mass of Arthur's Seat shouldering its way into the Old Town, and the Pentlands a dozen miles away to the south-west. Above all, it is a city of panoramas, the creation of the great green saucer that replaced the old Nor' Loch when it was drained in 1820.

It was also rightly proud of its status as capital, and the seat of the great Scottish institutions that had survived the Union, whose continued existence was guaranteed in the Treaty of Union for "all time coming": the Law, the Kirk and the currency. Social stratification was very marked and underlined by address, the New Town proper being at the very apex, the preferred home of the aristocracy, the judges and advocates and ministers who were the leaders of society. Gilbert and Eleanor would both have expected to live their lives out within the elegant, dignified, well-to-do confines of this most fashionable of addresses. On their return from Glasgow their life was to be more circumscribed, and although they would spend the rest of their days in close proximity to this golden square mile, at Eyre Crescent they were in newer and less distinguished territory, unmistakably relegated to the fringes. But the fringes were still a cut above Broughton and Canonmills, further down the hill. In the first decades of the 20th century some made the experiment of moving out to the outlying suburbs, or further afield to villas in Portobello or North Berwick, but many of the *crème* came back to tread once more the hallowed streets trodden by Cockburn and Hume and Stevenson and Scott.

Nigel started school almost at once, and his parents enrolled him in the St James's Episcopal Endowed School in Broughton Street. Long since closed as a school, the little grey stone building can still be seen on the right-hand side as you go down towards Mansfield Place, gable-on to the street, its bell-tower perched on the rooftree, and it was here he learnt his three Rs. He remembers little about it, except that he was perfectly happy there. More vivid in his mind is the walk to school by the back-wynds and little alleys skirting the edge of Canonmills. He still delights in remembering the various landmarks like The Canonry and why it is important to get the spelling of Canonmills right—it is the ecclesiastical canon, not the martial cannon—and Captain Player's stables, a regular port of call, where he first learned to ride. He was taken to school at first by his mother, or Dorothy, but quite soon he was doing it alone: his first independent venture into a wider world, soon extended into exploration of the streets round about. The school walk was important, for playing in the street was frowned upon, and he and the other children played mainly in each other's houses.

The house was comfortable enough, although, like the houses in Glasgow, it had no garden of its own. Nigel had his own room, tucked away just off the dining-room where the piano was, and there was a little room, just off the kitchen, intended no doubt as a maid's room, to which Gilbert could, and did, retreat from his family. Brandon Terrace cut off the view of the Forth and the Fife hills at the back and the front windows overlooked only the Davidson Church, but from the window of Nigel's room, which overlooked the Crescent, you could see the Calton Hill if you twisted round a bit, and it was from this window that he saw a German Zeppelin one night, a huge, eery silver slug hanging in the sky, caught in the beam of a searchlight.

Back among old friends, the Tranters now did a little modest entertaining, musical evenings and the like, for both had good voices and were members of the Edinburgh Choral Union. Eleanor, Dorothy and Gilbert all played the piano, but it was Eleanor who usually accompanied the singers, breaking off from time to time to check whether Nigel was asleep. He liked the music and the voices, and would creep out of bed and open his door a crack to listen—and then give himself away by joining in the songs in his childish treble, so that Eleanor would swoop, and close the door firmly again. He had a good singing voice himself and remembers vividly the time he marched onto the platform of Edinburgh's Usher Hall at the age of eight to sing Schubert's *Serenade* and 'O Mary, go and call the cattle hame' in a school concert. Most of the friends who came to the house were members of the Mansfield Place congregation, and Eyre Crescent had been chosen for its proximity to the church, in those days when few people had cars. At the other end of the New Town other fashionable congregations gathered round Palmerston Place Church and St Mary's Episcopal Cathedral, also in Palmerston Place. Most church-goers lived close to their church.

Otherwise Nigel's entertainments were the same as those of most boys of the time: he had a wooden gun to shoot Germans with, and careered round the Crescent going "Bang, bang" until his mother caught up with him, cannoning into kindly old gentlemen who asked him how many Germans he had shot today. "Twelve" he would answer solemnly, or "Fifteen" or even "Thousands" when his imagination got the better of him. "All nonsense, of course" he says now, in case there should be any doubt. He had building bricks, and later graduated to Meccano. When he was very young his mother and Dorothy of course read to him, and told him stories: but he told them stories too and says "I suppose I got the storytelling bug early". Eleanor in particular was a great reader, and there were always library books around, mainly novels: Gilbert's tastes were more serious, and he was a member of The Philosophical Society. Nigel soon developed a possessive attitude towards books, though: if he liked a book, he wanted to have his own copy and saved up to buy it. Not unexpectedly in that household, the habit of saving was inculcated early. Nigel saved up for his books, he saved up for his motorbike, he saved up for his car, he saved up to get married, and he is still saving to this day. He has never taken out a loan in his life, nor does he dabble in the Stock Market, and he lives by the good old-fashioned rule of "Waste not, want not". He is a man for whom the word frugal might have been coined.

Otherwise, from his earliest years in Edinburgh, he remembers a succession of cats, the best-loved being Tippy, so-called for the white tip at the end of her tail. By now, even Phyllis was fast approaching womanhood and Nigel's life was beginning more and more to resemble that of an only child, so Tippy was an important member of the household. She must have been a resilient creature, for she slipped off the kitchen window-sill one day in a careless moment, fell four flights to the garden below, and walked away, "although," says Nigel, shaking his head over this domestic incident of eighty years ago, "she was never really the same cat again". Animals have always been a part of his life: as soon as he acquired a home of his own, he got himself a dog. And his mother took him occasionally to see the sights: they went to the Castle and gazed out from the Half-Moon Battery, and they paid their penny to climb to the top of the Scott Monument and admire the panorama of Fife and the Lothians. But he remembers no visits to the theatre or the circus. Most entertainments were home-made and money was short. The maid's room never held a maid, and Eleanor scrubbed her own kitchen floor. Nigel spent quite a lot of time in the kitchen, helping his mother, particularly after Phyllis was swallowed up by nursing training. They had a peggie-tub to do the washing, a tub with a three-legged wooden "peggie" in the middle which someone had to turn, and this was one of Nigel's tasks, along with "ca'ing" the heavy mangle, and lugging washing up and down to the shared drying green at the back. Nigel, if anyone, knew how hard his mother had to work and how weary she was at the end of the day.

Gilbert's financial situation eased a little with promotion and the return to Edinburgh, and, though there was no garden at Eyre Crescent, he took a cottage at Carlops. With it went the fishing on

an upper reach of the North Esk near the reservoir, and it was here
that the family, or some of it, repaired at weekends. Gilbert was a
keen angler and continued, right through Nigel's boyhood, to try
and interest him in the sport but without much success. There
were family holidays, too, from now on, usually in Elie or Crail,
where they would regularly take a house for two or three weeks,
travelling from Edinburgh by train, waiting for the roar and clatter
that signified they were crossing the Forth Bridge. Gilbert took
Nigel sea-fishing on these summer holidays and it proved more of
a success than angling, probably because it required less patience.
Dorothy and Nigel were both great walkers, however, and, as
soon as Nigel acquired his first bicycle, they would cycle out
regularly to Carlops and walk together in the Pentlands. Despite
the twelve-year difference in age, the two were "sib" and enjoyed
a close affinity, Dorothy perhaps playing the role of a favourite
aunt more than a sister. On these long walks together, she would
listen to all he had to say, and encourage him to note and observe:
the close association with two loving women all through his childhood no doubt compensated in part for his father's remoteness.
Possibly Dorothy, too, had an affection gap in her life, left by the
mother she lost at four. But Phyllis, who had never known her
own mother at all, was a more shadowy figure: maybe poor Phyllis
had never learnt how to show affection, maybe she was just the
wrong age. At any rate Nigel's memories of her as a girl are
scanty: she seems to have been characterised in the family as the
clumsy one, who could be guaranteed to break anything entrusted
to her. She must have overcome this clumsiness, though, for she
qualified as a nurse and rose to become a hospital matron.
Nevertheless it was Dorothy who was the most important person
in Nigel's life after his mother.

The first great adventure of Nigel's life was about to start
however when he entered Heriot's School in 1917 at the age of
eight. It is not certain where Gilbert went to school, but Eleanor

went to the prestigious Edinburgh Ladies College. Schools are important in Edinburgh, as they are in all aspiring societies, and whatever else they had to skimp on, the Tranters were determined that Nigel would have the best education they could provide. Edinburgh has more than its share of great day schools, deriving for the most part from past benefactions by prominent citizens. Of these, the earliest, arguably the greatest, and certainly the most romantic is Heriot's. Originally George Heriot's Hospital, it was founded as the result of a bequest from George Heriot, goldsmith and banker to King James VI & I and his Queen, Anne of Denmark, "for the maintenance, reliefe, bringing upp and educationn of poore fatherless boyes, freemen's sons of the towne of Edinburgh" and opened its doors on 11 April 1659. Fifty years later, the absence of any institution to provide similar benefits for girls was rectified when Mary Erskine donated money to found the Maiden Hospital for "the maintenance of burgess children of the female sex", transmogrified first into the Edinburgh Ladies College attended by Eleanor and now the Mary Erskine School. The Maiden Hospital was later joined by other schools founded for the same pious purposes to make up the Merchant Company Schools whose various uniforms still gladden Edinburgh's streets today. But Heriot's was the first, and the bequest on which it was founded so munificent that it has remained separate and a little apart from the others.

Heriot's was also blessed in possessing what the Edinburgh volume of *The Buildings of Scotland* calls "a prodigy of Scots Renaissance architecture", based, it is believed, on a plan for a palace from a sixteenth-century Italian architectural pattern-book, independently and inventively interpreted. Started for the school in 1628, it is 49 metres square with corner towers and a central quadrangle. It is one of the most important buildings in Scotland, built on a fine open site laid out in formal style, overlooked by the Castle and enjoying one of the finest views in Edinburgh, seldom seen except by pupils and staff. Cromwell used it as a military hospital after the Battle of Dunbar in 1650, and the first boys were eventually installed in 1659. The grounds back onto Greyfriars' Kirk and its kirkyard, where the Covenant was signed in 1638. Between the churchyard and the school runs a remnant of the Flodden Wall, put up by the citizens of Edinburgh to strengthen their defences after the disastrous defeat at Flodden in 1513. This then was where Gilbert and Eleanor sent Nigel: a place to conjure with, and it was to prove an inspired choice. It would be wrong to read too much into it, but one cannot help wondering what course his life might have taken, had he gone round the corner, say, to Edinburgh Academy and taken a more mundane route to school.

Although he claims to have been "no scholar" and was impatient of school discipline, Nigel retains the liveliest affection for Heriot's and his works contain a myriad of references to Heriot's and to Jinglin' Geordie Heriot (so-called because of the "siller jinglin' in his pooch"). Many of the heroes of his early, modern adventure stories are Herioters, but the major tributes will be found in the humorous and affectionate characterisation of Jinglin' Geordie himself and his relations with James VI & I in *The Wisest Fool* and *Poetic Justice*. Geordie Heriot is conveniently commemorated in more bucolic style in "Jinglin' Geordie's" halfway up the Fleshmarket Steps and the pub sign that hangs outside. It is not clear how much Nigel appreciated all this romantic grandeur at the time: he started at Heriot's after all at the age of eight, and soon took it all for granted, much as he took for granted Phoebe Anna Traquair's murals at Mansfield Place. But from then on, he knew Edinburgh, Old Town and New, in his bones.

In old age, he is proud of his school but remembers remarkably little about it. History lessons, focusing in those days largely on the mastery of dates, failed to grip, and English was too much concerned with reading dusty set-books and tiresome fussing over grammar. Already as a young boy, he knew he had a gift, and his essays were works of the imagination, whatever the subject. But instead of encouraging him, his English master lectured him about the importance of correct punctuation, sticking to the point and so forth. He has a natural talent for drawing, but art lessons, too, failed to inspire, and it was his mother's brother Harry Cass who taught him how to paint—so effectively that when the artwork on the dust-jacket of *Man's Estate* failed to please it was replaced by the author's own design. Maths was a closed book and was to remain so: years later, as a gunnery officer in the Second World War, he saw hostilities out with a light ack-ack unit, because he couldn't master the maths required for heavy artillery. As far as languages were concerned, his father put him down for German in preference to Latin, no doubt thinking he would have to earn his living and German would be more commercially viable. His German came in mildly useful when he found himself in charge of a German Prisoner of War camp after the end of World War II, but Latin would have been invaluable later on for poring over the historic documents in the Latin volumes of *The Register of the Great Seal of Scotland*, for example, never far from his desk. He has taught himself enough to get by (and rather enjoys scattering tags about) but admits it's a chancy business. Swimming in the school pool won his approval, though.

It seems unlikely that Heriot's was to blame: it was after all teaching the same subjects and employing the same methods as every reputable boys' school of the time, and probably doing so better than most. But Nigel is impatient by nature, always wanting to see what is round the next corner, what happens next, his quick intelligence leaping forward to conclusions without too much care for the way they are arrived at, and this trait, combined with the desire always to be outside in the open air, as far away as possible from human habitation, no doubt made him a difficult pupil. He was also precocious, accustomed from his home environment to receiving a lot of adult attention, and to the knowledge that he was

clever, accustomed probably to getting his own way as well.
Finding himself transported to a big school dedicated no doubt to
discouraging conceit must have been a shock: the race to school
was fine, but the race home at the end of the day was better. It
is perhaps significant that when asked now whether he did the
Scottish Highers exam, he isn't sure and says "I suppose I must
have. Yes, yes, I suppose I did." But however much of a penance
lessons seemed at the time, Heriot's left him with a sound
education, a powerful capacity for reasoning and a wide-ranging
vocabulary.

IV

SCOUTING FOR BOYS

*Heriot's yard, summer, any Friday evening in term-time. Out from a
shed comes a little gaggle of boys, in a different uniform this time, but
still with a distinctive Heriot's touch: their neckers are Heriot's blue
edged with white. They are manhandling a trek-cart out into the road,
with its burden of sooty kettles, stew-pans, kitbags, ground-sheets, sacks
of potatoes, poles and tents, all the paraphernalia for a weekend under
canvas. They are bound for Temple, and somewhere among them,
jumping around, is Nigel Tranter, now aged eleven and resplendent in
Scout uniform, drill shorts, bush hat, woggle and all. He is going to go
far in the Scouts, rising to become first patrol-leader and then Troop
Leader. He is following in a family tradition: Phyllis is Captain of the St
Serf's company of the Girl Guides.*

If Heriot's contribution to Nigel's scholastic education failed to
win his approbation, the school was to provide, in parenthesis as
it were, a much more far-reaching and enduring influence among
the extramural activities it offered. Friday evening was by tradition
the time for games practice, and the games were rugby football in
winter and cricket in summer. By the time Nigel went to school,
an alternative was available: the Heriot's 7th (Central) Scout Troop
had been formed a few years before and Nigel joined at eleven, the

moment he was old enough. The choice was significant in many ways: male school bonding in Edinburgh, with all its great public day schools, tends to be rugby-oriented, and the table of club fixtures is studded with the names of teams drawn from former pupils of the major schools, Heriot's among them. As far as Nigel was concerned, the pull of the outdoors decided the issue, and he is not in any case a team-player. But it is perhaps curious that Gilbert, with his experience of the dangers of being outlawed by society and his consequent care for the social network, appears not to have exerted any pressure on Nigel to go for the other option.

The Boer War, which had wreaked such terrible damage on Gilbert, had contributed to a new enthusiasm back home for the outdoors and a healthy way of life. Robert Baden-Powell had started his soldiering in India in 1876 and quickly realised, in frontier conditions, the importance of developing scouting as an integral part of Army training. He was detailed for "special services" in Ashanti and Matabeleland in the mid-1890s, and, after another spell in India, he was back again in Africa in July 1899, again as a special services officer, in effect a kind of supernumerary with specialist skills. He made his wartime name as the charismatic commander of the British garrison in Mafeking, successfully withstanding 217 days of siege (although the methods he employed to maintain supplies for the white population at the expense of the blacks would not be countenanced today). More importantly, he cemented his reputation for the skilled deployment of scouts. Back in England after the War, he found that his Army handbook *Aids to Scouting* was being used to train boys and, encouraged by this, he developed a more comprehensive programme and ran a first, experimental, camp for boys in Dorset in 1907. In 1908—the year before Nigel was born—he published *Scouting for Boys,* sub-titled *A Handbook for Instruction in Good Citizenship through Woodcraft* and the Scout movement was born. The Girl Guides were founded in 1910 and both movements expanded rapidly. By the time Nigel was offered the choice in 1921 between rugby football and scouting, scouting was in full flood.

Not, however, at Heriot's, where the troop never numbered more than 70 in all Nigel's time at the school. It is clear, furthermore, from the jocular comments in the school magazine *The Herioter* that the Scouts were regarded with some amusement by their heartier colleagues. A Sixth form column in the July 1925 edition notes with Olympian amusement that the Scouts are rumoured to be learning how to make their own breeches and looks forward to inspecting the result. The Scouts' own reports of their activities are more sober and record "taxing the trek-cart to the utmost" collecting goods for hospitals on a Day of Chivalry, and a summer camp at Douglas, in Lanarkshire, where they were flooded out and compelled to attend church minus their stockings: Mark Stewart was to be similarly embarrassed by bare legs due to wet stockings in *Mammon's Daughter*, published in 1939. Nigel also went with the Scottish contingent to the Imperial Jamboree held at the new Wembley Stadium in London in August, 1924, when the Scots, Nigel among them, danced the fearsomely complicated sixty-foursome reel in the presence of Their Majesties King George V and Queen Mary. He is still ready to dance Scottish country dances at the drop of a hat, and even attempted, as President of Scottish PEN, and heroically seconded by his Secretary, the novelist Lavinia Derwent, to teach the eightsome reel to the assembled delegates attending an international conference in Oslo in the 1960s. The Prince of Wales attended the Jamboree, too, and took part in the campfire sing-song, and sing-songs were an important part of the ritual. When asked to contribute an old toy to a charity auction some years ago, Tranter replied that none of his old toys had survived but sent them instead the words of 'Paddy McGinty's Goat' as a memento of his childhood: the words of 'Delaney had a Donkey', another song learnt round the campfire, found their way into *Trespass*.

The Scoutmaster was one of the masters, a Mr Middlemass, whom Nigel liked, and it was from him that he learned skills and imbibed principles that have stood him in good stead to this day. Baden-Powell's "Good Citizenship through Woodcraft" was a simplification: what was offered was good citizenship, measured by an austere Victorian standard and practised in all aspects of life, with a strong emphasis on a healthy outdoor way of life and an understanding of and respect for the natural world. Its precepts were the precepts of the English public schools as they prepared their boys for a God-given role in the Empire: the Christian virtues of faith, hope and charity, expanded to embrace loyalty to the Crown and to the team, discipline, honour, fair play, and all "the simple truths" as Baden-Powell puts it, "of honesty and charity and helpfulness and self-reliance". It was of course essentially a middle-class movement, and one particularly suited to boys attending day schools. Another boys' movement flourished in Scotland at the time—the Boys' Brigade, also Christian in its ethics but less muscular in their expression, and more directly connected with the churches, particularly perhaps the Church of Scotland. But, says Nigel, "We were inclined to look down our noses at them in the Scouts. We thought they'd got it wrong."

Specifically, *Scouting for Boys* abjures its readers to be cheerful, thrifty and independent, to start earning money as soon as possible in order not to be a burden to others, to think things out for themselves before acting, to be helpful and courteous to all classes, and in particular to ladies, to be obedient to command and to be alert and observant at all times. The skills Nigel learned with the Scouts included map-reading, drawing sketch-maps, calculating distances, observing wind-direction, assessing terrain, tracking, practical countryside skills like fire-building and living off natural resources, practical domestic skills like simple cooking, sewing on your own buttons, generally looking after yourself. After nearly eighty years, most of them with a wife or mother at home to do these things for him, he can still sew on a button and darn a sock, and still keeps his Scout mending roll ready to hand in a drawer. He's a dab hand at making his own porridge in the morning, too. But, although helpfulness, thrift, cheerfulness and a certain sense of chivalry are still his hallmarks today, these are matters he might well have learnt at home. More important are the outdoor skills: it was the Scouts that laid the foundations of the later writer's masterly grasp and understanding of his native terrain.

For Nigel, the Scouts were an escape, not necessarily from the confines of home or classroom (although home could be oppressive, with Eleanor overworked and Gilbert a brooding presence). It was the chance to get out into the countryside that was the attraction. The 14-mile hike out to Temple on Friday evening (with 14 miles back again on Sunday) was a small price to pay for the freedom at the other end, the excitement of sleeping under canvas or, when the grudging Scottish summer permitted, under the heavens, singing round the camp-fire at night, eating curious stews out of a billy-can. Once he became a patrol-leader, with badges up and down his arms and a green-and-yellow cord, he revelled in taking charge and passing on his skills. Because they were accustomed to take a house in Elie each year, he would sometimes take his patrol further afield in summer, in the school holidays, loading the trek-cart onto the *William Muir*, the paddle-steamer that plied between Granton and Burntisland on the far side of Forth. He knew the usefulness of caves from the Pentlands, and they would seek out caves to sleep in at West Wemyss or Pittenweem. Once he negotiated successfully with the minister of Elie Parish Church to let them sleep in the graveyard, hitching the guy-ropes of the tent to a convenient gravestone. "Most people were quite happy to let us onto their land," he recalls. "They knew we wouldn't do any damage, would leave the place the way we found it . . . it encouraged independence, you were on your own, and if anything went wrong, you had to take the responsibility. I never had any regrets about joining the Scouts. And for city people, you know, it was a good thing, we learned a lot about the countryside." Extraordinary to think that Nigel Tranter, so essentially a countryman now, once thought of himself as a townee.

A less successful exercise in self-reliance and using the materials to hand, pursued at an earlier age, was sledging at Hillend in the Pentlands. Aged fourteen or thereabouts, four of them decided to try sledging one snowy day using a ragged old piece of corrugated iron they found lying about and launched themselves down a steep slope. There was a convenient escape spur halfway down, but the craft slewed round and pitched them over the fifty foot drop into a quarry, where they landed in deep snow and a flurry of limbs, Nigel taking the brunt and gouging large lumps of flesh out of both legs in the process. He carries the scars to this day—worth remembering when reading the accounts of the thrills and spills and tactics of hurley-hackit, a "grass-sledging activity . . . played by sliding down the hill on the skulls of cows or oxen, steering by means of the up-curling horns", as practised by the young King James V on the slopes below Stirling Castle in *The Riven Realm*. Another example of misplaced confidence in his own practical skills occurred on a holiday visit to a friend at Lunan Bay. The two of them decided to build a boat from orange-boxes: they knocked it together, launched it, christened it the *Tarry Ann*, climbed aboard, pushed off, and promptly sank. Fortunately Lunan Bay shelves almost as much as Aberlady Bay. Fifty years or so later, the friend, "Browno", turned up at a lecture Nigel was delivering to a local history society and said, "I was the boy who . . ."

The Scouts also provided an entrée into a male world not connected with the classroom. Nigel was happy at home but his father was always an ambivalent figure, living at home but somehow apart, in the household but not of it. He was prepared to unbend at Carlops or Elie and take the boy fishing, but did not really provide the constant day-to-day male presence that was needed to maintain the balance in an otherwise female household. Where other boys had fathers who took an active interest in their doings, retreating only occasionally into their own affairs, Nigel had a father who was immersed in his own affairs most of the time, with only occasional bursts of geniality (although an interesting, and accomplished, piece of nonsense verse has survived, in which Gilbert teases "Mrs T" over her enthusiasm for the new fad, Vitamin C). And while other fathers were prepared from time to time to talk to their sons man-to-man as they grew older, Nigel was never admitted to this kind of intimacy. Just as Gilbert never dandled him on his knee as a baby, so he never offered a confidence—or admitted one. Jack, who might have provided a male stepping-stone into the adult world, had not returned home after coming out of the Army and was lost to Nigel for all practical purposes. It was Mr Middlemass and the Scouts that taught him many of the things a father might have taught, and more: Mr Middlemass and the Scouts provided important male role-models with whom to identify.

Henry Cass, Eleanor's brother, was another. Harry Cass was a man of parts, in the old phrase—a successful entrepreneur, a gallant soldier (he also appears in the family albums in the uniform of a Captain in the Royal Scots), and a talented amateur artist, who painted a battered portrait of his maternal grandfather still in Nigel's possession. Despite having sons of his own, he seems to have taken a particular interest in Nigel, perhaps sensing that he wasn't getting enough attention from his father. Uncle Harry was a large-hearted man, as his rescue of Gilbert and his family in 1905 made plain (and his generosity extended also to Hannah's children, for jobs were found for Jack and Dorothy as well). He was the rock on which they all depended, and he eased their return to Edinburgh and its sometimes narrow society: he was to remain a prop to the end of his life and beyond. As far as Nigel was concerned, he was a source of the occasional tips that were the pocket-money of the day, he was the first member of the family to acquire a car, his home in Eildon Street, with its two maids, provided a glimpse of comfort and ease lacking at home, and he found the time to teach Nigel to paint. His family's dependence on Eleanor's brother might well have soured relations for Gilbert, but this was not the case: Gilbert was grateful, not bitter. Harry Cass was the stay on whom they all relied.

They were soon to need this steadying presence behind them again, for when Nigel was 12 or 13, Dorothy, in her mid-twenties by this time, fell ill. The diagnosis was tuberculosis, then greeted with the kind of horror that would greet cancer a generation later. Its origins were imperfectly understood and there was no known cure: treatment consisted by and large in exposure to large quantities of fresh air, and special sanatoria were built with long balconies open to the weather, where the patients were put out in often freezing conditions. Dorothy's tuberculosis was a terrible blow to them all, for all shared the unspoken belief that it was a death warrant. At first she was treated at home, and Nigel was warned not to get too close. Although he missed her presence at home, matters eased a little for him when Dorothy was in hospital, as she was recurrently: he reckoned that there should be no risk of infection in a hospital, and people went into hospital to get better. When she failed to get better, he nurtured a deep anger against the doctors, who he thought didn't know their job. Although never mentioned at the time, it seems possible that this illness of Dorothy's influenced his parents' attitude to Nigel's passion for the Scouts: they certainly believed it to be a healthy pursuit. It also seems possible that some of the love of walking he shared with Dorothy is traceable to the same tragic circumstance.

From then on, Dorothy had periodic bouts in hospital. She continued however to work (she was a clerk in the family insurance company) and she had admirers, to one of whom she eventually became engaged: cruelly, he vanished like smoke when he discovered she had TB and his name is graven forever in Nigel's heart as a result, one of the few betrayals in his life he is unable to forgive. By 1926 her condition was serious and she eventually died in the Royal Victoria Hospital, Edinburgh on 11 July 1930, aged 33, when Nigel was 21.

V

CASTLES

A quiet scene, sometime in the early 1920s. A bike leaning up against a wall, a little castle in the middle distance, partly ruinous. A boy, bobbing up and down, peeping furtively over the wall at the castle, pad in hand, then crouching down under cover of the wall, apparently to scribble. Nigel has embarked on one of the great informing interests of his life: he is thirteen, and he has discovered castles. Take a good look at him: from these schoolboy beginnings will grow the great data base from which sprang the historical novels.

Nigel acquired his first bicycle when he was about 13: his licensed independence had already been established with the Scouts, and the bike gave him wings, extending his range of operations far beyond Carlops and Scout expeditions to Temple. He was a good draughtsman, the Scouts had taught him to be observant and he was fascinated by the little castles or fortified houses that dot the countryside in the Lothians and Fife in such abundance, so many of them dating from the 17th century. Later he would learn the reason why: as he writes in *Nigel Tranter's Scotland*, they were built in fulfilment of one of Mary Queen of Scots' canny son James VI's ideas for policing the country and bringing in a little ready cash at the same time. James "made it a condition of every grant of land worth £100 Scots that the new owner built a 'tour of fence' upon the said land for the weal of the kingdom and the shelter of the lieges from attack by the lawless". He once calculated that there must have been as many as seven thousand of them at one time.

He set about recording every little castle within reach, sketching it accurately as it stood, and writing it up in his schoolboy jotters with a full description of all the architectural features. With the help of MacGibbon and Ross's *Castellated and Domestic Architecture of Scotland* and his own keen eye, and with Eleanor's active encouragement at home, he gradually made himself an expert. He was crouching under the wall out of diffidence and unjustified guilt: he was convinced that any owner or estate employee who spotted him would smartly chase him off. It did not occur to him to go boldly up to the door and ask permission. But he did not share the Gilbertian view that "There's a fascination frantic in a ruin that's romantic". On the contrary, the ruinous state of many of these buildings, particularly those which lay south of Forth, right in the path of invading English armies, notably Cromwell's in 1650, distressed him. Much of Nigel's adult life sails under the flag of "I wanted to get something done" and the little castles were his first, and most enduring cause. He could see that they were deteriorating fast, falling under the weight of neglect as well as war, and that many of them would soon be no more than an anonymous "rickle o' stanes". His first object was to record them, his second, formulated only gradually, a burning ambition to become a restoring architect, and at least help halt the decay.

What put the idea into his head? Restoration of the grander historic buildings had begun with the increase in wealth in the 19th century and the national romanticism generated by the Scottish novels of Sir Walter Scott. What was new and much-discussed in the 1920s, when Nigel was growing up, was the restoration of historic properties in city centres. This was particularly true in Edinburgh, where the Old Town was still largely the verminous slum it had degenerated into in the 19th century. In this, as in so many other respects touching on national sentiment, the Great War was the watershed: there was a sense that when the men came marching home again, it should be to homes fit for heroes to live in. Scandalously, urban overcrowding in Scotland, particularly in Edinburgh, where it was endemic in the soaring tenements that lined the High Street, was four or five times higher than it was in England. Serving together in the kilted regiments had moreover given many Scots a new sense of identity, which generated in its turn a new interest in the monuments of the past. Although it took time to come to fruition, an ambitious restoration programme was drawn up in the 1920s under the supervision of Edinburgh city architect John MacRae, a man of foresight. These were also the years in which Kellie Castle in Fife was being restored as his family home by Sir Robert Lorimer, famous as the architect of the Scottish National War Memorial in Edinburgh Castle. The profession of restoring architect was now an exciting practical possibility, which, when associated with castles, would provide an opportunity to combine his talent for draughtsmanship with ample opportunities for getting out into the countryside.

These early notebooks bear all the characteristic marks of Tranter's later work. The drawings are meticulously executed, a pencil sketch made on the spot, then carefully gone over again at home, only an occasional error of perspective or misjudgement of scale betraying the artist's youth and inexperience. The notes which accompany them are equally meticulous and remarkably mature and detailed: he made good use of *MacGibbon and Ross*. Both drawings and writing are small, going right up to the margins, with no space wasted—another distinguishing feature. The writing has not yet acquired its adult spikiness but is easily recognisable nevertheless. These early castle notebooks were to be the first of a long series covering several decades, the first documentation of material he would use for the rest of his life, and the first writing done out in the open air. The notes were already appearing in their characteristic pocket-size format and were originally made in pencil, the only practical solution, before the coming of the Biro, to writing in all weathers in a climate like Scotland's. By the time he had turned twenty, there was enough material to consider a book and in 1935, it came out: *The Fortalices and Early Mansions of Southern Scotland 1400-1650*. "Terribly pretentious and pretty amateurish," he says now, "but then I was very young." 1933 had marked the publication of the final selection from the National Art Survey whose detailed drawings of historic Scots building techniques provided such an impetus and inspiration for all with access to them. The five volumes of *The Fortified House in Scotland* appeared thirty years later, but adhere closely to the pattern laid down in the early notebooks. There was one difference however: as an adult, he walked up and rang the bell. A very few proprietors showed him the door, but as the books began to come out, they recognised the potential benefit to themselves. In time, *The Fortified House* series came to be seen as a standard work, and inclusion in it an accolade. In the late 1960s, the data base would be expanded still further in the four volumes of *The Queen's Scotland*, a detailed gazetteer covering every parish in Scotland. Readers and researchers alike avid to know on what historical material Nigel Tranter relies in his work should start here in this huge self-generated data bank to which he is still adding: his first inspiration stems not from the ancient chronicles but from the ancient stones of Scotland, and the terrain in which they are set. Many other weighty historical, genealogical and legal tomes and much close personal analysis and interpretation of course contribute to the fine detail, but the castles are the bedrock.

VI

THE RABBIT-FARMER

A field on the banks of the Water of Leith, Redbraes House in the background. A summer evening. A boy is energetically engaged in cleaning out rabbit hutches of which there are a great number, some more substantial-looking than others. A girl with long legs and a pretty heart-shaped face comes down the path from the direction of Edinburgh and stops to watch. He picks up a rabbit and gives her the fluffy bundle to stroke. Nigel has found a new enthusiasm and with it, love. From now on, he will have a willing partner in all his enterprises; from now on, May Grieve will be at the centre of his life.

The next great leap forward in Tranter's life sprang from unlikely beginnings. Powered no doubt by an urgent desire to start saving up for something else, and obedient to Baden-Powell's teachings about the desirability of earning money young so as not to be a burden to other people, Nigel conceived the idea of becoming a rabbit-farmer. It was not quite so extraordinary an idea as it appears, for rabbit-farming was a mild craze at the time. Rabbits are famously fecund, they don't cost much to feed, you can keep them in hutches, and if you go in for the right kind, you can sell their pelts to make fur gloves or turn the wool into knitting yarn. You can also eat them. No-one had yet heard of myxomatosis, no-one had read Maurice Pagnol's terrible tragedy of Jean de Florette's failed attempt at rabbit-farming in the foothills of Provence. It was an odd idea nevertheless and stuck in people's minds: fifty years later an old Heriot's schoolfellow, writing to him out of the blue, says "I seem to recall that your main interest . . . was angora rabbits . . ." He has no idea what put the idea into his head, but, curiously, there may have been a link with the Catholic Apostolic Church. Gavin Maxwell relates in *The House of Elrig* that Lady Victoria Percy, his "Aunt Victoria Northumberland", who used to sit behind Nigel in church and tap him sharply on the shoulder when he shunted the hymnbooks along the book-rest to make them fall off at the other end, was a chinchilla farmer. (The Mansfield Place Church was the nearest Catholic Apostolic Church to the ducal seat at Alnwick.) Wherever the idea came from, he decided he would keep a few chinchillas for their pelts but go in primarily for angora rabbits, because of the wool: he would look after them and harvest the wool, and Eleanor and Phyllis would knit it up into baby garments which they would then sell. He eventually had about 120.

First, however, it was necessary to find somewhere to keep them. He could hardly start a rabbit-farm in the New Town and yet it had to be close enough for him to go and attend to the rabbits before and after school. The policies of Redbraes House on the banks of the Water of Leith, where there was already a nursery garden, seemed a possibility, so he went to see the nurserymen, whose name was Grieve, and persuaded them to let him have some ground. He fenced off a little patch of land with chicken-netting, knocked together the hutches, installed the first rabbits and he was in business. Gilbert was less than enthusiastic when he realised what Nigel was up to, but Eleanor was supportive and in any case it was too late to do anything about it. The rabbit farm was up and running. Nigel, in his matter-of-fact way, killed the rabbits when the time came, skinned them and took the carcases

home for the pot. He exhibited at the annual shows in the Waverley
Market, sold the baby clothes and the knitting wool and even took
along a spinning-wheel to demonstrate the spinning process. He
made friends at these shows with another boy who had been in the
business rather longer and gave him tips on how to clip the rabbits
instead of laboriously plucking the wool. He even made a little
money—enough to give some to his mother and keep a little for
himself. And all went merry as a marriage bell (although it seems
likely that lessons, never one of Nigel's top priorities, must have
suffered).

Marriage bell, indeed. The rabbits at the bottom of the garden,
and the lively and energetic young man who had set up this
curious new business under their very windows, so to speak,
attracted the attention of other members of the Grieve family, who
lived in Redbraes House, now demolished and even then divided
up into two separate dwelling-houses. They included May, one of
the daughters of the house, a pretty girl with long legs and brown
hair just eighteen months younger than Nigel, who walked past
each evening, when he was feeding the rabbits and cleaning out
hutches, on her way home from her first job. He gave her one of
the fluffy bundles to hold and her fate was sealed. It was to be love
at first sight and extraordinarily enduring. They were seventeen
and sixteen respectively. In less time than it takes to tell, May had
taken her place at the spinning-wheel.

May Jean Campbell Grieve was the daughter of Thomas Grieve
and his wife Hume Spiers Gray. Thomas, in his turn, was the son
of James Grieve, the choleric man and gifted gardener responsible
for breeding and developing two notable eating apples: the James
Grieve and the Cox's Orange Pippin respectively, both long
household names. The apple which bears his own name is today
little seen in Britain outside private gardens: apparently it bruises
easily and doesn't travel well enough for commercial growing.
Nigel and May grew James Grieve apples in their garden at

Aberlady, though. The story of the Cox's Orange Pippin, very much an English favourite, is rather more complex. As Nigel tells it, Grieve trained originally as a gardener at the Royal Botanic Gardens in Edinburgh, then entered the employment of a London business magnate called Cox, who owned the island of Rum in the Inner Hebrides, and it was while he was in Cox's employ that Grieve bred the Orange Pippin apple. As far as the name was concerned, Cox appropriated the apple for his own, with the result that Grieve, who was a short-tempered man, resigned on the spot and returned to Edinburgh, where he later created a variant of the Pippin and named it the Cutler Grieve. He was also reputedly the creator of the viola. He eventually set up in business at Redbraes on his own account. When he died, the business was taken over by his sons Thomas and James.

The family into which May was born was comfortably-off, but by the time Nigel met May, Thomas Grieve was dead, and the business was being carried on by the surviving partner, his brother James. Thomas's widow was however still occupying the upper half of Redbraes House with her daughters, May, then sixteen, and Ailie, who was "just a lassie, ten or so". An older daughter, Daisy, was already married to a Grieve cousin who was a schoolmaster. There were also two brothers. Thomas's death altered all their circumstances considerably. The business was already going downhill, and as a direct result of the settling up of partnership affairs following Thomas's death, the cash-flow became inadequate to sustain it and James was forced to sell up. Hume Spiers' share of the proceeds was much less than she bargained for, and she never forgave him.

Hume Spiers Gray, Thomas's widow, whom Nigel calls "the most formidable woman I ever met", was reputedly a beauty and at the same time an oddity for her age—a woman who regarded with more pride than shame the noble blood she claimed to have inherited on the wrong side of the blanket. Certainly her name (by which she liked to be known, although Nigel called her "Humey" behind her back) was distinctive and presumably commemorated a connection with someone of that name. At any rate she was registered when she was born in 1875 as the child of Adam Gray, and his wife Mary Campbell, who were married in Dunbar in 1868. The tale behind her singular name was not the only one of alleged lofty connections she was addicted to telling in order to give a little relish to life: she had another such tale to account for the proliferation of the Scott name among members of the Grieve family. In Hume Spiers' eyes, these supposed connections gave her children and herself an extra distinction. May herself was less impressed, and the story has interest only in its suggestion that she came of a line that seems to have produced some unusually attractive girls.

Certainly Nigel found May unusually attractive, and the course of their love affair may be followed in literally dozens of his books: the protagonists are very young; the girl is pretty but has a mind of her own; the boy is a little solemn, thoughtful, clever but becomingly modest; they take one look at each other, they fall in love, the boy is unbelieving, the girl encouraging, romantic love is matched by physical passion, they plight their troth, there are obstacles to be overcome, but eventually they marry, and live happily ever after. The girl always has long legs and the unions are always blessed. The girl is fearless, and a partner, a helpmeet, determined to be included in every enterprise. Neither of them ever looks at anyone else. Anyone who finds the love stories—and there are many of them—in the books too fairytale, too simple, should know that this was Nigel's own experience: it is his own story he is telling over and over again, with minor variations. Nigel and May fell in love in their teens, they never had any doubts, and it was mutual. It was the happy-ever-after story, and it was his: he was exceptionally lucky, and he knew it.

At sixteen May was still a girl, tall, long-legged, quite well-built, with a pretty, heart-shaped face, broadish across the cheekbones but with deep-set blue eyes. She had the typically Scottish colouring of fair, creamy skin combined with darkish hair. She had left school early in the aftermath of her father's death and had recently started work in an office. After Thomas Grieve died, the business was carried on by his surviving brother and partner James and Thomas's widow and her family remained for a time at Redbraes. But with a difficult and dissatisfied mother May, too, had problems at home. At any rate, their heads met over the rabbits, and soon May was helping to look after them and taking a hand in the little home industry that carded, spun and knitted the wool. It was some time before her mother realised that this friendship was something she was going to have to take seriously. Both were so young when it started that she probably thought it would wear off. At any rate, it was innocent enough and they seem to have been allowed a fair amount of licence.

By this time however the clouds were gathering again over the Tranter household. Gilbert was beginning to seek solace in alcohol, straining finances still further, and causing concern to Eleanor, who sometimes smelt the whisky on his breath and was afraid that others would smell it, too. It was Gilbert who put Nigel off smoking for life by giving him a puff at a cigar, but it was Eleanor who made him promise never to touch alcohol, a promise he regarded as sacred. Dorothy was getting no better and was costing money rather than bringing it in. At 17, Nigel would shortly be leaving school and the time had come to think seriously about his future. He was still dead set on becoming a restoring architect (and busily filling his castle notebooks to that end), but this required some preparation. Apprenticeship with a reputable firm would cost money and would call for some proof of aptitude. It was eventually agreed that Nigel would go as a clerk to J W Matthews & Company, a firm of accountants in George Street, for a couple of years to get a grounding in accountancy, attending evening classes in architecture in the meanwhile at the Heriot Watt College, where Gilbert had trained as a surveyor. Successful completion of the Heriot Watt course would qualify him to be articled to an architect, and Aldjo, Jamieson & Arnott had agreed to accept him on this basis. Whatever happened at the end of the day, a training in accountancy would come in useful. As at every turn in this story, the practical side of the Tranters asserts itself: Nigel accepted the arrangement without enthusiasm but without demur. He found accountancy exceedingly boring but he learned to be patient, as far as in him lay.

But disaster struck again. In January 1929, Gilbert, then aged 59, suddenly contracted erysipelas. This is a particularly unpleasant disease, dreadful for the sufferer and very distressing for the family, an infection affecting the skin and the tissue immediately beneath the skin which swells and erupts. Nowadays it can be controlled and is seldom life-threatening. Gilbert's head was affected and his face and neck quickly swelled to become unrecognizable. Within ten days he was dead, and Nigel, now nineteen, had overnight become his mother's sole support. As might have been expected, but was not in fact foreseen, Gilbert had nothing to leave, his income died with him, there was no pension provision for Eleanor, and apart from her own small savings, she had no funds. There was furthermore a rent to pay. Although both Eleanor and Nigel were of course well aware how straitened the family's circumstances were, the discovery after Gilbert's death that he had left nothing at all came as a shock. Neither had been initiated by Gilbert into the real state of his affairs, and almost all Nigel's information about Gilbert's financial position and his family background in general has been gleaned by him since his father's death and from other sources, some quite random.

A quick survey of the situation made it perfectly clear that any thought of becoming an architect must now be abandoned. Aldjo, Jamieson & Arnott would require payment of a £400 fee before

Nigel could become indentured. The money simply wasn't there, and, furthermore, it was now essential for him to earn a proper income. A seven-year apprenticeship with no money coming in was not to be thought of. Harry Cass was dead by now but Nigel was found a job in the family business—possibly at the behest this time of Jack, now rising rapidly in the hierarchy in the London office of the Century Insurance Company—and he was taken on as an insurance inspector, a better position than Gilbert had had to start with, but perhaps justified by the fact that Nigel already had some experience of clerical work at J W Matthews & Co. It had never been his intention to work in an office—the call of the outdoors was far too strong for that—but he had no choice. It is tempting to speculate what his subsequent career might have been, had that fixed intention to become a restoring architect been fulfilled. He believes himself that the urge to write was so strong that he would have wound up writing anyhow. But would he have turned to historical novels? Might not his urge to recreate the past have been satisfied instead in stone? There is no way of knowing.

For Eleanor, Gilbert's sudden death and the discovery that she was now wholly dependent on Nigel was the most appalling shock. Dorothy was still living at home, but Dorothy was already ill, and not likely to live long, her contribution to the family income meagre and sporadic. Phyllis was off nursing. From now on, Eleanor turned more and more in on herself and became subject to depressions which added further to Nigel's own distress. Whatever role he may have played in bringing Nigel into the family business, Jack had disappeared to London for good in 1925, before Nigel left school, and was by now in effect no more than a semi-detached member of the family. He was also married, with responsibilities of his own. Possibly he never wholly understood the situation: possibly Nigel—never lacking in confidence—told him, "I'll manage." Eleanor was furthermore Jack's stepmother, not his mother. For whatever reason, Jack was not directly involved and Nigel was left to get on with it on his own. Meanwhile, Dorothy was sinking and required repeated hospitalisation, which did not always come free in those days. Nigel had to be ready at any time to bear the costs, and, when this dearly-loved sister was in the Royal Victoria Hospital, where she eventually died in 1930, he had to visit. Dorothy and Eleanor had been close and her death, coming so soon after Gilbert's, was hard for Eleanor to bear, too. Indeed the whole of Dorothy's illness had imposed a severe strain on the family. Although the situation altered radically with the discovery of streptomycin in the 1930s, when Dorothy contracted tuberculosis the nature of the illness was imperfectly understood and its cure uncertain. Diagnosis was still popularly regarded as tantamount to a death-sentence, and since it was known to be highly contagious, the infection carried in droplets of moisture on the breath, all the members of a victim's family were liable to be affected. Nigel remembers standing in the open doorway of Dorothy's room at Eyre Crescent trying not to breathe, and Eleanor would have had to keep all Dorothy's bedding, and the implements she used to eat with, separate from those of the rest of the family. Worse than that, there was the risk of social ostracism: witness Dorothy's rejection by her fiancé. Although never mentioned, the shadow of TB in the family may have affected Hume Spiers' attitude towards Nigel.

As this tragedy developed, May became his refuge. School and rabbits now behind him (the rabbits were abandoned soon after he started work) Nigel was saving up again: he had marriage on his mind. But this was a long-term goal, something they spoke of and felt sure would happen eventually, but still some way off, a distant dream. Most young people in their position would have expected to have to save up to get married; for one thing, it would be assumed that even if the girl had a job, she would give it up on marriage. By now their relationship had developed from wandering around the policies of Redbraes House together to walking further afield and outings to Carlops at weekends. As an interim solution, Nigel acquired first a motorbike and then a car. He had his first car at 19. A pattern developed whereby they would go off on longer and longer expeditions into the country, there to walk and talk and look at castles. May, like Nigel, was a dedicated walker, and it was a way to be together. Nigel had already formed the habit as a schoolboy of going off on long solitary bicycle expeditions to the Highlands in the school holidays, taking a sleeping bag and sleeping rough, and eventually he and May reached the stage of going off together, sometimes to Elie and later further afield up to the Highlands, staying away overnight. All above board, separate rooms and so on, says Nigel: but it was a miracle that her mother agreed. May was, after all, under age. And Hume Spiers, having finally woken up to the relationship, was now implacably opposed to it. Not that she disliked or disapproved of Nigel *per se*: but he was distinguished neither by birth nor by prospects—as had become abundantly obvious following his father's death—and she was convinced her daughter could do better. It seems possible, at least, that Hume Spiers was just a little bit fixated on her supposed lofty connections: Nigel's background was after all as good as May's by any rational calculation, and his prospects, in the event, better. But she was not to be swayed. One of her surviving grand-daughters remembers her as a strict disciplinarian and is inclined to think it wouldn't have mattered to Hume Spiers very much who May wanted to marry: she wanted to keep her at home. The youngest daughter, Ailie, eventually filled the role of daughter-in-residence and never married.

Nigel settled into insurance work and, the castle notebooks apart (May now actively encouraging him), put architecture resolutely out of his mind. They were happy together, and, insofar as he could raise his head above his immediate responsibilities to his mother, he was beginning to think—again encouraged by May—that all these careful notes about castles might one day be turned into a book. In the meantime, Eleanor's state of health was deteriorating: the depressions continued and became more frequent. May came frequently to the house now and proved her solid worth by sitting with Eleanor and encouraging her to talk and start playing the piano again. All her life, she would show concern and compassion for the old or ailing. But Eleanor, who had become attached to May, now began to need hospitalisation from time to time for another condition. By the beginning of 1933, she knew she was dying. She was concerned that Nigel, who had already had so much to bear, would now be left alone, and knew how much he needed affection and a secure home life. She knew and approved of May, she was now anxious to see them settled before she died, and this was the reason they married so young.

With Eleanor's encouragement they became engaged at the beginning of the year. Nigel took May out to Habbie's Howe at Carlops, a suitably romantic spot, believed to be the "verdant green" of Allan Ramsay's pastoral comedy *The Gentle Shepherd*, and proposed. He was pretty sure she would say Yes. He had provided himself with three different rings from a Princes Street jeweller and she chose a square-cut sapphire set with little diamonds, a typically modest little ring, now in the possession of her grand-daughter Alison. Blue was her favourite colour and gentians, so like a sapphire in colour, her favourite flowers. May herself was over the moon and danced home down the Granton Road hugging her news to herself and saying, over and over again, "I'm engaged, I'm engaged, I'm engaged!"

VII

THE THIRTIES

High summer, a sunshiny day, a garden. Nigel and May's wedding day. They are posing for photographs, the bride and her bridesmaid in flowery, floaty, ankle-length dresses and pretty, shady hats, the groom and his groomsman in lounge suits. There will be no larger group photograph, and there are few guests. In particular, no mother of the bride. But there was one little niece there that day who remembers it and says, "I thought it was all lovely".

They were married in Athelstaneford Kirk on 11 July 1933: Nigel was 23 and May 22. The ceremony was performed by May's parish minister from Pilrig Street in Edinburgh and the local Church of Scotland minister in Athelstaneford, and there was a third minister present in the person of the best man Eric Stevenson, son of the "Angel" or bishop of the Catholic Apostolic Church in Edinburgh and himself a part-time minister. It was the first wedding to be performed in Athelstaneford Kirk in a quarter of a century, everyone else having elected to get married in the manse, as the custom then was, and the local laird was so delighted to see a wedding in the Kirk again that he filled it with flowers in their honour. Eleanor was in hospital, too ill to attend. They went on honeymoon to Elie, close enough to visit her, but five weeks after the wedding she was dead and Nigel was organising the funeral. May records in a manuscript note that the honeymoon was "spent in the usual Honeymoon way" but Eleanor's impending death must have cast a shadow. They had a second, proper, honeymoon in Rothiemurchus in the autumn.

Sadly, Hume Spiers found herself unable to give her blessing to the match. She had set her heart against it and would not be moved. She refused pointblank to attend the wedding, which was organised instead by May's elder sister Daisy and her husband Tom Grieve, now headmaster of the village school in Athelstaneford. To her dying day, although May and Nigel visited and, once their children were born, took the children to visit, May's mother never set foot in their house.

The wedding itself was a low-key affair, less in deference to Hume Spiers' wilful boycott than to the fact that Eleanor was on her deathbed, but the sun shone and the photographs of the lounge-suited groom and the bride and her bridesmaid in their flowery ankle-length dresses and pretty hats are suffused with the air of optimism that marked that brief period between the Depression and the realisation in 1938 that, with the failure to stand up to Hitler on Czechoslovakia, Britain was facing the threat of war once more.

Nigel had bought a house at 19 McDonald Place: as always, he paid cash, and it cost him £500, five years' savings. It was a modest row-house in a little oasis of new building tucked away on a patch of land in the Bellevue district of Edinburgh and close to Mansfield Place. The household at Eyre Crescent was broken up and it was into McDonald Place that Nigel and May moved when they got back from their honeymoon. They took the spinning-wheel with them. The houses themselves look as if they would be more at home in the suburbs, but this is by no means a suburban area: quite the contrary. Hume Spiers, who had moved from Redbraes to Wardie, now settled into an equally modest establishment round the corner in West Annandale Street: the keen-eyed can still distinguish the name Hume in faint brown lettering above the front door—an odd arrangement since her married name was Grieve and her maiden name Gray. Nigel's daughter Frances May Baker remembers visiting her grandmother as a child and her recollection is somewhat different from Nigel's: where Nigel found Hume Spiers by turns a tartar, a trial and a joke, at the very least a highly singular figure, Frances May says "She was just Grannie, you know, I didn't know any other grannies. She used to give us sweeties: there was nothing odd about her." She remembers her dressed in black and wearing a lace widow's cap, though, surely somewhat unusual at the end of the 1930s. Another grand-daughter who used to be sent as a child for holidays in the household did not greatly enjoy the experience however: she remembers her grandmother as being very difficult when thwarted, a woman not to cross with impunity, and says she was a woman of strong likes and dislikes. Her own mother Daisy, May's elder sister, had encountered opposition when she married a few years earlier, and the old lady comes across as an autocrat who would have objected to any marriage not arranged by herself. Hume Spiers relented when it came to her will, however, and all of them eventually benefited. The surviving pictures show a woman with an extraordinarily piercing gaze, so there may be some truth in the sterner version.

But here we come up against a recurrent problem: Nigel has kept no diary and decided some twenty years ago not to write an autobiography on the grounds that no autobiography was likely ever to be wholly honest. Nevertheless, apart from his daughter Frances May, he remains the prime source of information concerning his early adult as well as his younger years. All of us subconsciously re-write our memories with the telling of them and a novelist, who exercises his imagination daily as part of his stock in trade, is perhaps more likely than most inadvertently to re-cast the patterns of the past. To him, the raw material of his mother-in-law presents certain traits which have come, by reason of their unusual nature, to obliterate the more straightforward aspects of her character: his novelist's transforming imagination, highly developed over the intervening sixty years, has got to work on her, and where Frances May sees a Grannie in a white lace cap pulling sweets out of her pocket for the children, Nigel sees something quite different. Both versions are equally true; but for each of them—the child Frances May and the young husband with a mother-in-law problem—the salient points about Hume Spiers Grieve are different. The problem crops up again and again when dealing with aspects of a life for which there is no written record: best to imagine different people's versions as so many transparencies to be laid over Nigel's core version—since it is how his early past appears to him that is important—until more light and shade emerges.

The next few years were spent nest-making in McDonald Place, an occupation for which May was to show a real talent. They were blissfully happy together, released from the strains of the recent past, enchanted with each other's company and highly delighted with themselves for having stolen a march on their contemporaries. Nigel was still working in insurance, but the hours were flexible— in examining claims, he had to interview policy-holders who were often at home only in the evenings—he had acquired a Baby Austin, and the expeditions into the country continued, as did the castle notebooks. The wedding behind him, and his domestic situation settled to his satisfaction, he started work on the castles book in earnest, doing the initial planning on his honeymoon. It was to be his first published book, *The Fortalices and Early Mansions of Southern Scotland 1400-1650*, and it came out in 1935. Roughly speaking, 1400 marks the point at which gunpowder and the cannon were coming into more general use: roughly speaking, 1650 marks the point at which fortification was no longer a necessary adjunct of house-building. Good use was made of both in the intervening years. Tranter is described on the title page as FSAScot (Fellow of the Society of Antiquaries of Scotland) and another FSAScot, W Mackay Mackenzie, author of *The Mediaeval Castle in Scotland*, provided a generous and astute introduction in which he drew attention to the way in which the drawings (all Nigel's own, except for a frontispiece by his best man, Eric Stevenson) brought out the character of the buildings, giving a "clearer impression . . . of the native qualities of the old Scottish tower-house, its frequent picturesqueness rooted in details of utility . . . that reflect modest living in not too favourable circumstances of wealth or weather." The point about modest living is well taken: Nigel's glimpses of "modest living" as the background to stirring events are one of the charms of the historical novels. The reviewers praised his ability to distil an immense store of knowledge into so few words, revealing a capacity for getting to the heart of the matter without a surfeit of detail.

Read now, the book is a prentice work, painstaking and accurate but smelling slightly of the student's lamp. Probably he was out to impress a little, and make his number among those whom he had hoped to join. With the five volumes of *The Fortified House in Scotland*, published in 1962-70, behind him, Nigel himself is deprecating now and calls it pretentious and incomplete. Nevertheless, it represents a considerable achievement for a young man of only 25. The plan of this early work echoes that of the manuscript notebooks and foreshadows that of *The Fortified House*: short descriptive pieces of around a page in length, illustrated with his own drawings. The main difference perhaps is that *The Fortalices* was not written with the general reader in mind. The drawings in *The Fortified House* are in most cases identical with those in *The Fortalices and Early Mansions* and the text closely related, but an easier read. Tranter has never been averse to recycling material and in this case we are in his debt, for copies of

The Fortalices are now rare indeed. The book went well, and he was extremely pleased with himself, as well he might be. Indeed, the evidence suggests that he was getting a little above himself, and, to take him down a peg or two, May challenged him to write a "real" book, by which she meant a novel. It is a Tranter characteristic, manifested again and again throughout his life, never to resist a challenge, and he took this one up without delay. He set about writing his first novel on holiday that same year. By way of explanation, he says the weather was poor and he had nothing much to read. Perhaps it was the summer he described in *Mammon's Daughter,* when "Day after day the rain fell, steadily, remorselessly, with a dreary persistence that levelled all the colours of the land to a grey tonelessness. And when the rain faltered, a chill mist came down . . ."

Publication of *The Fortalices*, momentous as it was, was however topped soon after by an even more notable event. The nest made, their first child, a daughter, was born on 12 February 1936. They christened her Frances May Scott, combining family names on both sides with her mother's name: Frances after Nigel's great-grandmother Frances Watt, Scott for the Grieve connection. She was to bear a striking resemblance to her mother, in looks, style and character, although Nigel never saw it. Perhaps, having the original already, he looked no further.

Having sold his first book to the first publisher he offered it to— The Moray Press—Nigel anticipated no trouble with the next. He called it *In Our Arms Our Fortunes* and he gave it everything he had. The only trouble was he gave it too much and the ark was overloaded. The name alone is an indication of what was wrong with it: the Arms of the title is heavy with meaning, arms entwined, coats of arms, military arms, and much, much more. The Moray Press, to whom he offered it, sat on it for a long time and then, in the kindest possible way, told him it was no good: a novel should tell a story, not provide a vehicle for the author to show off. *In Our*

Arms Our Fortunes was never published, but Nigel was determined to succeed and he took the lesson to heart. When he offered them a new book, *Trespass,* a year later, it was a much more workman-like affair, and they accepted it. It was published in 1937, but The Moray Press went into liquidation shortly thereafter and he was never paid. Ward Lock & Co however took it over and re-issued it under their own imprint in 1940. *Harsh Heritage* and *Mammon's Daughter* followed in 1939.

These early novels were modern adventure stories, set in Scotland and with some admixture of romance, and they set the pattern for a whole series of similar books over the next twenty years or so. They owe a little to John Buchan, whom Tranter admired, and echo faintly the world of Dornford Yates. Viewed post-Fleming, they are of course dated, but they reflect the same confident society of public schoolboys and emancipated young women as *Berry & Co,* young people with money and leisure, ready for anything, and positively relishing the opportunity to flout authority—although always in the best of causes, to do down villainy of some sort—falling in and out of love, but not yet paired off. They have however humour and great period charm, the stories swing along against their background of hills and peat-bogs and lochs; and they are more readable now than Dornford Yates, mainly, perhaps, because the central character is the sort of stolid reliable Scot who has a quality of timelessness. Quite quickly, they began to show a charming humorous bent. He had found a niche which suited him, and the elastic hours he worked for the two insurance companies (he now had accounts for both the Scottish-National and the Century) enabled him to exploit it. It was a further bonus that he was employed in a family firm, which perhaps allowed him more licence than would have been allowed an ordinary employee, and he was ideally placed to wind down his insurance activities as he established himself as a writer.

The 1930s slipped easily by for the Tranters, happy in their marriage and excited by Nigel's early success as a writer. Political crises at home and abroad left them comparatively unmoved: Nigel is interested in causes not politics as such, and domestic rather than foreign affairs. As the 1930s wound to a close, however, developments in Europe could no longer be ignored and after the cave-in over Czechoslovakia in March 1938, the alarm sounded at last in Britain. That summer the first trenches were dug in London parks and families with young children were advised to get out of the cities in case of air-raids: official evacuation plans were drawn up for those without the means to make their own arrangements. Nigel and May were living in Edinburgh, Frances May was just two, and May was expecting another child. It was clear they must take stock of their own situation. By this time Nigel's sister Phyllis was matron of the Children's Village in Humbie, twenty miles or so south-east of Edinburgh, and had her own house there: she suggested they move in with her as a temporary measure, and they were there for six weeks. When Neville Chamberlain came home from Munich in September 1938, waving his piece of paper and crying "Peace in our time", the country heaved a collective sigh of relief, and returned to normal for the moment, and Nigel and May went back to McDonald Place. But it was only the lull before the storm. By December the government had started registering men of military age and the following year Hitler was ready, and there was no longer any way out. In January 1939 a son was born, whom they named Philip Nigel Lakin. By the summer, it was time to draw up contingency plans again and Nigel's wildfowling friend, Harry Brydon, who had a holiday house in Aberlady, offered to lend it to them for the winter. By summer 1940, they had arranged, as a temporary measure, to take a two-year lease on Cross Cottage in the centre of the village. They were to stay there for eleven years.

Nigel was twenty-nine when the War broke out in 1939 and,

like all men of military age, he had been reviewing his position. *Trespass* had been followed by *Harsh Heritage* and *Mammon's Daughter* and he was busy with another novel: as an established writer, he had been approached, like other writers of his acquaintance, by the Royal Air Force, which had decided that professional writers could usefully be employed turning the intelligence gleaned from returning air-crews into a coherent narrative. They offered a niche in intelligence, carrying Squadron-Leader's rank, which sounded attractive. Unexpectedly, however, insurance work turned out to be a reserved occupation, and, however little insurance work Nigel might now be doing, he was still officially employed as an insurance official: to his chagrin he was left behind, ingloriously, a civilian. It was a sore point, since by now he was giving at best half a day to insurance.

He was anxious nevertheless to do what he could on the home front: he joined the Local Defence Volunteers (later the Home Guard) when they were formed, and he became a Special Constable. Service with the Home Guard was to prove a frustrating experience, at any rate in the early days when Nigel was a member: they exercised with pikes round Aberlady Bay on Sundays, marching parade-ground style, and playing "pass the parcel" with their one rifle at the old butts constructed in the dunes at Kilspindie for target practice by Boer War volunteers. To begin with, they didn't even have a uniform, only an arm-band. A police uniform with silver buttons and powers to arrest people went with being a Special Constable, which made it seem more serious. But the incident that sticks most vividly in his mind from his stint with the Police was pure farce: detailed to rendezvous with an army convoy in the black-out and pilot it through the centre of Edinburgh, driving his own little car, he inadvertently led them in the pitch dark up onto the broad pavement at the West End of Princes Street, and bumped them along, up and down, over the kerbs, all unwitting, scattering pedestrians like chaff, and coming to his senses only when he nearly ran down a pillar box at the bottom of Hanover Street.

It was not until insurance work was taken off the reserved list in 1942 that he was called up, and, in the event, it was as an Army private—although the RAF continued to pursue him off and on for years, without success. At 19 shillings a week, it was an unpleasant surprise. Although he had half a dozen books in print by this time, his income from royalties could not be guaranteed to make up the shortfall from insurance work. Women were being encouraged to replace men wherever possible, and May took over the insurance clients: she didn't drive, however, so she moved back up to Edinburgh with the children, taking a couple of rooms in town, where they stayed during the week. Cross Cottage was kept on for weekends, school holidays and Nigel's leaves.

He went for basic infantry training to the Durham Light Infantry barracks at Brancepeth Tower in County Durham as the only Scot in the intake, another disappointment because he had of course hoped for a Scottish regiment. The other men in his hut were mostly Durham miners, the first time he had ever been thrown together with ordinary working men. He got on well with them, but remembers how they snored. His first posting thereafter was to the Royal Army Service Corps. At a loss what to do with a self-confessed writer, they put him in a mobile printing unit—one sees, without admiring, the logic—where his duties consisted mainly of turning the handle on the duplicating machine. On this slender evidence, the Army decided that he was potential officer material and he went from there to an Officer Cadets' Training Unit at Llandridnod Wells in Wales. At 32 he was considerably older than most of his colleagues and found the course pretty demanding. But when it came to survival exercises, he shone. The Scouts and years of scrambling over Scottish hills had taught him how to live off the land, make a fire without a bundle of kindling from the local shop, and sleep rough, and he could read a map like the back of his hand. He came to the Army fully equipped to join the partisans or the maquis. Not that it was required of him: once commissioned, he went into the Royal Artillery, and spent most of his army service in East Anglia and in or around London with a light ack-ack unit, living grandly for a time at Kensington Palace, but more often sleeping in a tent on a bomb-site in the East End. To his disappointment he never went overseas, although his kit went—with the manuscript of a book—never to be seen again, after one of his many embarkation leaves. A stubborn medical problem kept him in and out of hospital at the crucial time when he might have gone to Normandy with the invading armies: he did not enjoy the experience and bitterly recalls being ordered by a draconian Matron to "sit to attention" in bed. As far as embarkation leave was concerned, he was not alone in having this experience: there were times when many were called but few were chosen, and in one of his wartime novels, *Delayed Action*, when Philip Lakin announces that he is on embarkation leave, and Margaret says "Oh, Phil—I'm sorry", the hero David Scott says "He's not away yet . . . I had three embarkation leaves before I actually sailed—remember?" Tranter neatly sums up the mood of the moment in Lakin's laconic telegram home: "Hold everything. Embarkation cancelled. New job. More leave. See you tomorrow. Bringing my sugar . . ." But when his regiment landed in Normandy, Nigel was left behind in command of the aptly-termed "residue": a collection of elderly vehicles not up to the rigours of war and 200-odd other ranks, deemed not up to the rigours of war either. At the end of the war in Europe, when he might have been sent to the Far East, his hopeless maths decided the issue: only heavy anti-aircraft units were going and his maths wasn't good enough to calculate the aim-off necessary for heavy guns. Total war in the Far East was a far cry from the "duck and a half ahead of a duck" formula he rehearsed to himself wildfowling in Aberlady Bay.

His late call-up meant he had a low priority as far as demobilisation was concerned when Victory in Japan Day eventually came in August 1945, and he found himself posted to Greystoke Castle five miles outside Penrith in the Lake District, in command of a Prisoner of War camp. Although in no sense an exacting posting, in command of a mixed bunch of nondescripts fit for little else, he made the most of it, choosing—unlike his colleagues—to live in the deserted 75-room castle and imbibe the atmosphere: it was reputed to be haunted. When he left, Colonel Howard, whose home it was but who did not expect ever to live in it again, gave him as a keepsake a Hepplewhite chair that had somehow been left behind when the place was requisitioned. His prisoners of war were German other ranks and a lot easier to deal with than the inmates of the nearby officers' camp. They worked on the local farms and, since many of them came from what was now East Germany and were unwilling to go home, they were intent on finding the means to stay: the preferred technique was to get the local farmers' daughters pregnant and so have to marry them, and one of Tranter's jobs was to try and protect the girls' virtue by frequent visits to the farms where they worked. He was eventually demobilised in September 1946.

One of the great advantages of a relatively humdrum war was that Nigel's young family did not grow up strangers to him. He got regular leaves and travelled up from London by train, discovering in the process an old railway instruction introduced to accommodate A J Balfour when he was Prime Minister and came north to holiday at Whittinghame, in East Lothian, for the golf, whereby a word to the guard would ensure that the London train stopped by request at any of the little stations between Dunbar and Edinburgh. There was no carriage waiting for Nigel when he stepped off the night express at Drem or Longniddry in a grey dawn, however: he walked the three miles or so home to Aberlady, hefting his bag, and, being Nigel, made short work of it. His democratic Scottish soul revolted, though, at the conditions of travel, the officers, of whom he was one, travelling First Class, with many empty seats, while the men sat on their kitbags in the corridors of packed carriages, or tried to sleep standing up, which he thought very wrong. Later, coming home from the POW camp, he carried treasured booty in the shape of packages of butter, eggs, honey and the occasional chicken pressed on him by the Cumbrian farmers' wives.

His children Frances May and Philip were at their most enchanting in those wartime years, six and three respectively when he went off to the Army, and *Delayed Action*, one of the first of five novels he wrote on the King's time, contains a delightful portrait of them. *Delayed Action* carries forward into wartime conditions the story of David and Margaret Scott, the lovers of *Trespass.* This tale of a Home Guard platoon—which bears a close resemblance to the Aberlady platoon, and caused some merriment in the village—chasing German spies over the Border hills, contains countless markers put down like talismans that the war would be over again some day, or perhaps—who knows?—as a kind of posthumous message of love to his family and friends, should it be needed if he didn't come back. The hero's friend and boon companion, also a carry-over from *Trespass*, is Philip Lakin: the child Philip in the book is the adult Philip's godson and his sister is Susan, one of the names Nigel and May had considered for Frances May. Susan and Philip Scott (another family name) are the same ages as the real Frances May and Philip. He has Susan saying "D'you think they'd let me into the Home Guard?" and demonstrating how well she can salute, and he gives the young Philip "a noble forehead—as yet productive of promise only" just like his own Philip's at home. May is there, too, in the hero's pretty, sensible, game-for-anything wife, and when he tiptoes back to the beckoning comfort of their bed after a night-time foray "with a little sigh of content Margaret's arm encircled him, in a gesture that was welcoming, cherishing, the more adorable in that it was subconscious . . ." And the hero, like his friend Andrew Haddon, is a Border farmer and a lawyer. He even gives his hero a cocker spaniel bitch like his own at home in Aberlady: he calls her Beauty, though, not Gyp. The whole book is redolent of the nostalgia he was experiencing for life at Cross Cottage and the unquestioning values of peace: one of the most striking passages describes the sense of well-being and elation when "the harvest was over, cut and in-gathered".

They kept in touch as best they could with letters and leaves to look forward to and the occasional telephone call. Frances May was beginning to read for herself by the time he left and the letters to May enclosed letters for her, too. In them, he told her stories of a Grumpy Bear she only later realised was himself, and a Little Blue Fairy who could work magic and all would come right. They came embellished, too, round the edges of the pages, with the Beatrix Potter-like drawings of little furry animals, rabbits and the like, that he still occasionally produces to this day, crawling on the floor to amuse a child.

VIII

THE WRITER AT WAR

*Dark of night, mist seeping relentlessly up from the river. An eery
silence, with few cars and those, lights dowsed against the black-out, with
only a thin line of light crossing their headlamps, hooded and sinister as
lizards' eyes. A solitary great-coated figure walks, pauses, walks again, a
tiny pinpoint of light winking sporadically waist-high. Out of the deeper
darkness of a doorway the watchers emerge to bar his way. " 'Allo, 'allo,
'allo," they say, or the Air Raid Warden's equivalent. "What do you
think you're doing with that torch? Put it out at once." "I'm writing a
book," he says. Resourceful as ever, the writer has gone to war.*

It has to be admitted that Tranter was a bit of an oddity among his
brother officers. In the first place, he was older, by a good ten
years, than the run of subalterns; in the second place, he neither
smoked nor drank nor played games; and in the third place, he
was a writer—writing had supplanted insurance by now as his
principal civilian occupation. May was already noting, before he
was called up, that the money coming into the house was "very
small" and the sudden reduction to a private's pay when he was
called up was an unpleasant surprise. It was clearly going to
be necessary to supplement his Army pay and, as a published
novelist, he had the means to do so. Army life notoriously

involves long periods of waiting about, and he reckoned it should be possible to go on writing. In any case, writing had by now become an emotional as well as a financial need. There was a problem however. Whereas his brother officers could support life smoking, drinking, arguing and reading the papers in the Mess, and could tolerate, if they did not exactly embrace, the lack of privacy that went with it, Tranter needed solitude if he was to write. With two small children in a tiny house, he had already established a habit of writing out-of-doors: in clement weather he wrote in the walled garden of nearby Luffness House, where he kept a folding stool, and the six gardeners treated him with a kindly if uncomprehending tolerance, as one might an invalid; when the weather was poor, he crouched over an Aladdin oil-stove in a wooden hut at the bottom of the Cross Cottage garden, and May summoned him to meals with a penetrating coo-ee that could be heard out in the village street, to the deep embarrassment of her young daughter.

It was in the Army that he hit upon the practice that has since become his hallmark. Only by walking could he be sure of the privacy and peace he craved, so he would write as he walked. But since his walking and writing frequently had to be done in the black-out when not only car headlamps but street lamps as well were extinguished, he needed some form of portable illumination to enable him to see. With her hospital experience, his sister Phyllis came up with the answer: a pencil-torch—which actually had a pencil built into it—such as doctors and nurses use to examine patients. Mindful that batteries were scarce, he of course switched it on only when he wanted to write something down and the sporadic flicker soon attracted indignant attention. He managed to evade arrest successfully enough to write four and a half books on these solitary peregrinations in uniform.

By the time he was demobilised, his children were older and, though well-trained, even more of a disturbing element in the tiny

Cross Cottage, so he continued the practice. Since 1946, he has walked ten to twelve miles daily along the East Lothian coastline, writing as he goes. The local population ignore him, but know that when he stops to scribble, inspiration is flowing and all is well. Visitors take him for a bird-watcher or a Countryside Ranger. He takes with him a minuscule note of dates, events and personalities, often including a genealogical note, covering the next 1200-odd words he expects to get down on his walk, and he composes directly onto the postcard-sized slips of paper he carries in his pocket. Serious walking, like jogging, is known to be beneficial mentally as well as physically, aiding the flow of oxygen to the brain. But it is not walking alone that gives Tranter a "high": it is the combination of walking and writing. If he works his way through all his notes and runs out of material two or three miles from home—which seldom happens—he is miserable until he can get home and replenish the supply.

IX

HALCYON DAYS

Aberlady Bay, a summer evening. The tide is out and the winding course of the Peffer Burn clearly visible among the mud-flats. There was a haar here earlier and a haze still hangs over the Firth, so that sea and sky melt into each other without a break. In the burn, a man and a couple of children bend to their task, sleeves and trousers rolled, a pail by their side. Most of the time they are twiddling their toes: every so often, one of them pounces, picks something up and turns in triumph to show it to the others. Westward from here, this coast once abounded in figures picking sea-coal or gathering winkles, but the Tranters are engaged in a nobler pursuit: as the afternoon sun warms to gold, they are spearing flounders, a sport as old as man himself. It is a scene straight from the elder MacTaggart.

When Nigel came home for good in 1946, Frances May was ten and Philip seven. For the past four years, their time together had been strictly circumscribed and punctuated by farewells, and May and the children had had, perforce, to function as a family unit without him. Now at last he could taste again the full joys of fatherhood. The picture he painted in *Delayed Action* makes clear how much he missed them: now he could enjoy again on a daily basis the fascination of watching his children grow up.

Frances May, at ten, was very much the older sister at this stage, keeping her younger brother in order when called for. They were constantly together, and although Frances May would marry young and follow the fleet with her naval officer husband, brother and sister continued to be close, slipping back easily into the old relationship on their rare meetings and corresponding sporadically. Like her father, she was not greatly interested in lessons, and her memories of her schooldays are mainly memories of girlish giggling and naughtiness. She attended the village school only briefly and was launched early onto the business of travelling daily to school, inhibited always as far as after-school activities were concerned by the need to catch the bus home to Aberlady. It was an experience she shared with her brother. Philip, too, moved on at an early age, going first, as one of very few Protestants, to a Catholic prep school in North Berwick, where he startled the Fathers, accustomed perhaps to think of Protestants as devoid of theology, by taking them to task on the subject of transubstantiation. Nigel conducted family prayers at home, usually in the kitchen, the hub of the house, always certain to be warm. They all attended church every Sunday, and Sunday afternoon walks were devoted to improving conversation, when Nigel would expound the meaning of what they had heard in church that morning or the mysteries of science, depending on circumstance, and young Philip was well up in these things.

The child Frances May appears in different guises in the early modern novels, and she continued as a young woman, with her mother, to inform the portraits Nigel draws of girls in the modern novels of the 1950s and 1960s. But when he turned to historical novels, the picture altered. Little girls figure rarely in history, except as lay figures, pawns in the marriage game, and Nigel's starting-off point in developing character in the historical novels is always the facts as far as he can ascertain them: in most cases he has names but no facts to support them when dealing with the girls. At the same time, he already had his model for the older girls in the young May: it is May he portrays, over and over again, in all her aspects. As a result, the traces of Frances May largely disappeared. In any case, she turned into a very womanly woman, retiring like her mother, and bent on creating the kind of warm, family background her mother had created, happiest perhaps with her husband and children. But history is made of sterner stuff, and it is for his historical novels that Nigel will be remembered.

It was a different matter with Philip. Scottish history abounds in boy-kings and Philip was made to be a model for them. At eight, when Nigel came home, he was a continual source of fascination to his father. Lively, intelligent, irrepressible, it was Philip who provided the blueprint for the long succession of little boys his father does so well: Prince Henry in *Poetic Justice*, the "ever-inquiring" Mungo in *Druid's Sacrifice*, Alexander II in *Crusader*. But it was the Stewart dynasty in particular, with its short-lived kings, that offered a rich harvest: the young James III in *Price of a Princess*, the young James IV in *Chain of Destiny*, the young James V in *The Riven Realm* and *James By The Grace of God* and the young James VI in *Lord and Master*. It is *Crusader* however that was written "remembering Philip" years after he was dead. The name mystifies readers who rightly point out that Davie Lindsay does not go on crusade until the end of the book, and then does not return. And the book is most memorable for its portrayal of the young Alexander II and the relationship between the two. The portrait of Alexander, spirited, headstrong, impatient, inquiring, of course suggests the young Philip; but the real Lindsay was the crusader in the stone coffin in the chapel behind Quarry House, the Tranters' "special place" which meant so much to them all.

Nigel came home to the little cottage by the Cross in Aberlady they had taken on a two-year lease in 1940. It was cramped with two growing youngsters and not particularly comfortable, but they were used to it, and it had a long garden behind. They moved to Quarry House, round the corner, right on the Bay, in 1951. It is a story he never tires of telling, for they almost missed it. They had considered various other places but failed to find anything that justified a move. But they came home from Rothiemurchus in 1951 to learn in the village that Quarry House, which they had long coveted, had been vacated by its long-term tenants, the lease had been advertised and over a hundred people had expressed an interest—all during their absence up north. The opportunity to live in their dream house had come and gone, without their even knowing it. But they reckoned without Mrs Hope of Luffness, to whose family the house belonged and who had given Nigel the run of her walled garden to write in when the weather was fine. She expressed surprise that they had not applied, they explained the reason why, Colonel Hope came round to see Nigel and the whole matter was settled on a shake of the hand. He would be there for 47 years.

In recompense for the tyranny of the bus home, the two children now had the run of the Quarry House garden and the wood beyond, with its romantic ruined chapel and stone crusader's coffin, into which they had poked bits of biscuit when they were young to sustain him on his journey. Above all, they had the run of Aberlady Bay and the marine wilderness beyond. For them, too, the timber bridge to the salt-marsh, about which their father would later write in *Footbridge to Enchantment*, was the doorway to an enchanted world that seemed peculiarly their own. And the household always included a dog and always included cats. Frances May can still reel off their names and describe their various fates. They grew up like farm children, though, with a matter-of-fact attitude to animals and no false sentimentality. But though Nigel wrote children's books about the Bay, he does not seem to have written about the house and the wood.

Spearing flounders in the Bay was to be a regular pursuit for years, until May put a stop to it, ostensibly on grounds of pollution, but probably because she feared one of them would come home one day having speared a foot instead of a flounder, for it involved feeling your way along the sandy bottom with bare feet, keeping a sharp eye out for the tell-tale little flurry of sand that announced a fish had been disturbed and then pouncing, quick as light. Like everything Nigel enjoyed, spearing flounders found its place in the books: the tinker brothers McPhail in *Ducks and Drakes* are armed with spears for an afternoon at the flounders and Sorley Matheson, hero of the same book, brings home a string of "stickily-congealing flounders" for his supper. A much later book, *The Marchman*, opens with a splendid glimpse of John Maxwell triumphantly spearing a salmon in the Solway, a rather more taxing affair. But it was reserved for the young Alexander II of *Crusader* to learn, like Philip, to spear flounders in Aberlady Bay, and it was Davie Lindsay, hero of the same book, who went wildfowling there with Pate Dunbar and saw "the geese flighting over in their wavering ribbons night and morning . . ." He even puts the footbridge into *Crusader* and has the young Alex complaining that it was "shoogly".

Spearing flounders wasn't the only thing he taught his children round the Bay: he taught them too about the rich local flora and fauna he hymns so fondly in *Footbridge to Enchantment*, they learned to swim at Jovey's Neuk, and in due course Philip joined him wildfowling. There was rock-cod to catch, and always there were birds to watch going about their business: terns, gannets and even solan geese diving dramatically for sprats. There was human drama, too: the woman Nigel came across, bent apparently on suicide, who changed her mind and walked off home dripping wet, and the boy Frances May found too late, suffocated by a sand-fall while trying to retrieve a ferret. And Nigel contributed his own drama. Like Eleanor with Vitamin C, Nigel embraced with enthusiasm the new fad for tearing off your clothes, and in the summer, he would stow his clothes under a convenient stone or stuff them down a rabbit-hole when he got to the beach and continue on his way in bathing trunks, startling the elderly ladies out walking their dogs. "There's a man down there without any clothes on," they would warn each other, and change course. As one interviewer wrote in 1971, "His office dress is a little unconventional—shorts, shirt, rucksack and a plastic bag." May was not so keen and can be seen looking distinctly shy about her bathing suit in contemporary photographs. They found a punt in the garden at Quarry House when they moved in and launched it occasionally, but it was heavy to lug across the road and languished for the most part unused, even for wildfowling. There were bathing picnics in the summer when the Haddons or their other friends the Jupps came for the day or Phyllis was staying, and in the winter there were family evenings round the fire, playing board-games. In winter, the sound with which they went to sleep was "the high-pitched, incessant gabble, honk and bugling" of the thousands of pink-foot geese out on the sand-bar that crossed the Bay. An added bonus was the constant fascination of flotsam and jetsam, which Nigel, for one, found well-nigh irresistible, coming home with now a kitten or a leveret (which Frances May took to her Edinburgh office in her handbag), now a useful stool or chair or plank, only resisting, with some regret, the 50-odd fathoms of serviceable fire-hose he stumbled across one morning. It came to be a family joke: whenever May said she wanted something for the house she couldn't afford, like a new cooker or a new fridge, the children would say, "Just you wait and see—some fine day Father will bring you one home from Jovey's Neuk". The Bay was theirs, the dunes and the salt-marsh, and the larks "shouting their heads off, rocketing up on all sides . . . like celestial spiders on invisible webs": they had taken possession of it and it was a golden time.

Nigel himself was supremely happy: he was doing what he wanted to do—writing—and he was doing it in the ideal place for his purposes. Quarry House, with its isolated situation, the wood behind, the fields on either side, the Bay and the wildfowling in front, and no domestic neighbours, had an expansive feel to it that they all relished. Almost, he might have been a bonnet laird, living, as he did now, more or less permanently in tweeds. It suited him down to the ground. For there was another point about Quarry House. Although he never owned it, Quarry House represented a subtle change in status: like his father at Mansfield Place in 1914, he had come home. This was where he belonged.

With war and the Army behind them, they settled down to re-discovery, and a new routine, but money was a problem with all now dependent on the income from Nigel's writing. Unless you enjoy phenomenal success—and phenomenal success did not come to Nigel Tranter until he was entering his sixties, his children long since grown-up and gone—life on a writer's earnings is a life of constant juggling with funds that are uncertain of arrival. As far as your income is concerned, the final arbiter is the public: if you get the formula wrong, they won't buy the product and there is no support group to pick up the pieces. May, like Eleanor before her, was to worry constantly about money and scrimp and save to make ends meet: she turned into a most economical housewife but she longed at times to be able to afford extras for the children, a bike, for example, for Frances May.

It was around this time that the education problem began to loom large. There were never any doubts in their parents' minds that Frances May and Philip must have the best education available and that this meant fee-paying schools: they had both attended fee-paying schools themselves. The question of sending them away to school, not in any case much favoured at that time by native Scots, did not arise. But the Tranters went for expensive options among the Edinburgh schools, sending Frances May to St Hilary's and Philip to Edinburgh Academy. The Edinburgh Academy in particular is Edinburgh's Establishment school, with a distinguished academic record, and fees half as much again as those at Heriot's, Nigel's own old school. But they were determined that Philip should have the best, and their faith was justified for he did well, emerging with a string of academic medals: had he not changed course in his final year to get the qualifications necessary to become a civil engineer, he might have done even better.

By the time he returned to civilian life in September 1946, Tranter had published a dozen or so books. He wrote easily and was reasonably confident he could earn a living as a writer. He discussed the matter with May, and they agreed that he would not go back to insurance or any other form of paid employment: from now on, he would go it alone. "It took a lot of faith and courage on her part," he says now, "but that was never lacking." There was never any question after the war of May taking a job, but commitment to a decade of school fees imposed a serious burden. In the case of Philip, at least, there was the probability that he would want to go on to University. To cope, his father's output quickly assumed extraordinary proportions, and there was a sly story current at the time among his fellow-writers that if recession struck in the book trade and there was a shortfall in royalties, Tranter would simply step up production and write an extra book a year: he did better than that, for he added two or three, and he did it by expanding his range to include Westerns. Right through the 1950s and 1960s, he was publishing an astonishing three or four full-length books a year. He was also churning out a constant stream of articles for the Scottish daily and periodical press, notably *The Scottish Field* and *The Scots Magazine,* producing on average four or five thousand-word articles a month, none of them very deep, and most of them based on matter already in his head in connection with a book, but a huge additional burden nevertheless. And by now he was heavily involved in the first of the public campaigns which would occupy so much of his middle years. One of the most extraordinary things about Nigel Tranter is his enormous capacity for work and apparent total immunity to anything resembling writer's block.

The Westerns are not great literature and were not intended as such. They were pot-boilers in the most literal sense. Western films were enjoying a huge popularity at the cinema and Western tales and novels followed in their wake. Tranter's were written at speed, taking him only six weeks on average, and he sold the manuscripts to Ward Lock & Co outright for £100 apiece. Prudently, he published them under a pseudonym, Nye Tredgold. But he cannot have intended them to disappear completely without trace, for Tredgold was a family name and Nye pretty close to Nigel; and he confided to a friend that he hoped the alias might be useful to Philip some day. This was taking the long dynastic view and never came to pass: but Philip, too, wrote easily and would supplement his income with his pen. For the moment, the Westerns helped pay the school fees, and he managed to fit in some children's books as well. But the wonder is that he managed to write the Westerns at all: by his own admission an indifferent horseman, he had never set foot in the United States, much less worked as a cowherd or ridden shotgun on a Stage. His technique was simple: he got a Western out of the library, soaked up the atmosphere, mastered the lingo—up to a point—and he was off. Without the Westerns, the post-war years would have been a lot leaner. He wrote ten of them, all told.

The children's books, of which he wrote a dozen in the decade between 1958 and 1968 (by which time he had grandchildren coming along) were also written fast. They are aimed at 8-10 year-olds, beginning to read full-length books for themselves, and are by and large junior versions of the adult books, adventure stories, mainly in Scottish settings, much of the action taking place outdoors. Like the adult books, they contain many cross-country chases: like the adult heroes, the boys in particular are resourceful and inventive. His straightforward, page-turning storytelling technique, without too much in-depth exploration of character, was well-suited to youthful readers, who still find them enjoyable today, and like meeting the same characters, like old friends, in the different books.

It was at this time that he also began lecturing on a regular basis. Like most officers, he had of course been pressed into service as a lecturer in the Army from time to time. A cutting from the local Penrith paper in February 1946 reports a return visit by Lt Tranter to a local Youth Club to discourse on critical reading and the basic requirements for writing a novel (getting the right balance between narrative, action, dialogue and description). After his return to civilian life, his platform performances on behalf of the Clan Albainn Society, the Roads Committees, the Scottish Convention and, eventually, the National Covenant Association gave him experience of a more demanding and critical audience. Later still, the Forth Road Bridge Committee would have him speaking on platforms all up and down the east coast of Scotland. He rose to the challenge and in particular became adept at dealing with questions, and he enjoyed the contact with an audience. The invitations to speak to private organisations, local history associations, writers' groups, librarians, Burns Clubs and so forth, started to pour in. To begin with, he worked from a prepared text, but quite soon, as he became more confident, he left the manuscript behind and worked from the briefest of headings. With his humorous, deprecating style and his head stuffed with facts, he was a guaranteed winner. The only problem was getting him to stop: he had so much to say, and his audiences were so keen to hear him say it, that he had a tendency to over-run. Faithful May kept a diary of private speaking engagements in the 1950s and early 1960s, speaking engagements, that is, other than political engagements and engagements on behalf of the Forth Road Bridge Committee, from which it emerges that he was averaging twenty a year, on the whole for expenses and hotel costs only: it was not until the end of this period that she recorded the occasional fee. Later, speaking engagements arising out of the writing of the historical novels would take him on repeated visits to the United States. The problem was that he was then, and still remains, a genuine enthusiast, whose gut feeling is that as long as people want to listen to him, he is ready to enlighten them. Despite his own experience on the receiving end of education, his instincts are those of the born teacher, and he dearly likes a disciple. It doesn't make good economics, but it keeps the adrenalin flowing. In recent years he has cut down a bit: he has given up Burns Suppers.

While they lived carefully, certain standards were nevertheless maintained, just as they had been in Nigel's own impecunious youth. The annual holiday was sacrosanct. September was dedicated each year to a family holiday, when they would take a house for the whole month, first at their old favourite, Elie, on the Fife coast, and thereafter in the Highlands, at Dalnivert for a couple of years and then, when the farmer moved, at Auchnahatnich on the Rothiemurchus estate in the Cairngorms, where they took over the roomy, white-washed farmhouse while the farmer and his family moved out to one of the cottages.

Rothiemurchus is a magical spot, and quickly came to occupy a special place in their affections. It is the archetype of every romantic concept of the Highlands: high tops on every side, deep forests, glittering lochs, the scent of pines; the shadow of deer flits in the forest and floats on the hills. Remote from what passes for civilisation, it is a place of perfect peace and extraordinary beauty, with the clear, high air that goes with mountain-tops that are seldom wholly clear of snow. It is also a hill-walker's paradise, which of course was a large part of the attraction. Each day they would set out after breakfast on a different walk, covering anything up to twenty miles a day; and they thought nothing of running up and down any peaks they passed on the way. The children were included in these expeditions from an early age and guests staying in the house were expected to go too: only the strongest-minded stayed behind. And there were frequent guests, often people May had never seen before. Some of the women found it more than they had bargained for: one recalls that "Long before we were home, I would lose all sense of where I was: all I could think of was somehow managing to go on putting one foot in front of the other." When they were on their own, all four would go out together during the day, but for their evening walk they would split two ways: Frances May and Philip running up another mountain, while Nigel and May took a more sedate route. May packed packages of sandwiches, a hard-boiled egg, and an apple for everyone: when they got home at night, however tired she might be, she set about cooking a hot meal.

In the early days, it was of course Nigel's phenomenal energy that carried all along in his wake, but later Philip led the way. "His long legs just seemed to go on and on, up and up," his sister remembers. But before he reached that stage, there had been an incident when he was about nine, which was to have far-reaching repercussions. When the little family party emerged one day onto the top of a sheer 2,000ft drop on the Cairngorm, all went forward to look over—except Philip. Frances May accused him of being a scaredy-gowk and he gradually edged forward, but unhappily. Smarting from his sister's taunts, he went home from Rothiemurchus that year determined to conquer his fears. Nigel taught him the rudiments of rock-climbing on the mini-rock-face of Maggie's Loup at Gullane Bay, and once he had shown him in rough and ready fashion—for Nigel himself was never a rock-climber—what to do, he went off on his own and practised and practised until he got the hang of it. Eventually the day came when he went off on his own one evening at Rothiemurchus and climbed the 2,000ft face from bottom to top, only telling his parents where he had been and what he had done when he got back. He was eleven. By April 1958, when Philip was 19, the roles had been reversed, at least on the hill. In his holiday diary for that year, Philip records a climbing expedition undertaken with Nigel on Ben Lui when he blithely left his father, who had omitted to bring an ice-axe, stranded on an icy scree, while he went on himself along the ridge to the summit, enjoying on the way "a delightful climb up a snow and ice gully" before going back to rescue him. It says something for the relationship that, according to Philip, Nigel "did not seem to have taken too unkindly to the experience, the blame for which was entirely mine". Nigel can hardly have envisaged what those early lessons in rock-climbing would lead to, but May remembered and would occasionally upbraid him, as they worried at home in later years when Philip was off on climbing expeditions. But the damage was done. Philip, like his father, seems to have been a man of enduring and single-minded passion—in his case, for the high tops.

Deer stalking was another activity indulged in at Rothiemurchus, and it was here that Nigel initiated Philip into the sport. "Quite fun," he recorded in his holiday diary that year. Nigel himself had discovered stalking on Highland holidays in the 1930s and it forms the background to many of the early novels, including *Trespass*, the first one to be published. Deer stalking is an exacting and challenging sport, now particularly associated with the hunting of the red and roe deer in the Highlands of Scotland, where the deer roam over the bare hillside and there is little if any cover for man or beast. In the 16th century and earlier, in the periods when most of Nigel Tranter's historical novels are set, deer were hunted on horseback and shot with cross-bow or longbow. The country was still heavily forested and there was plentiful cover: the sport called for accuracy of aim and quickness of eye when a beast broke cover. Stalking is very different and calls instead for endless patience: to avoid giving away his presence the stalker must keep downwind of his prey at all times, making as little noise as possible, and, since his only protection from visual discovery is the folds of the earth itself, he must also keep himself below the sky-line at all times. He must be prepared in other words to spend his day crawling as close to the ground as possible, often soaked to the skin, through heather and peat-bog and rough scree, downwind and mute. As like as not, he will no sooner have got within range when something will happen to disturb the beast and he'll have to start all over again. When an opportunity to shoot presents itself, he must take aim with great accuracy so as to kill, not wound, his beast: he may well get only one shot. Having killed his beast, he must be prepared to disembowel it and then, if he has no garron, carry it on his shoulders for miles, warm and bloody, until he gets it back home. The rewards of stalking are the challenge it presents and the chance to come as close to nature as it is possible to get, in one of the most beautiful lonely places of the world. It is no sport for the dilettante. But it is unrivalled in developing the eye for terrain and second-nature sensitivity to sightlines which Tranter constantly demonstrates in the many chases across wild country he describes in his books. Venison is also the one meat he confesses to having a taste for.

Deer stalking is still characteristically a male sport and until Philip was able to join him, Nigel's stalking expeditions were conducted alone, without the other members of his family. A practice was also quite soon established whereby he would go off each spring for a week or two on his own, with May's full approval. He went in May, "apt to be one of the finest months in Scotland, with the cuckoos calling, the larks singing, the gorse and broom blazing . . ." as he writes in *Crusader*, and the first call of the cuckoo was the signal (the cuckoo's haunting call haunts the books as well, and is often a hint that he is thinking of May) but he waited always until after his wife's birthday on the 22nd. These bachelor holidays—"Daddy's week" his children called them— were dedicated on the whole to active, male pursuits designed to contribute actual experience either to the plot or the setting of future books—crewing on a yacht in the Western Isles, for example, which he did on several occasions, and which was put to good use in books like *High Kings and Vikings* and *Lord of the Isles*, or walking in Norway or Denmark. A solitary walking expedition on the Danish island of Bornholm in the southern Baltic at the interface between East and West provided the material for *The Man Behind the Curtain*, and *Cache Down*, and the children's book *Pursuit* grew out of holidays in Andorra, also located conveniently at the interface between two countries and offering opportunities for cross-border mayhem. These holidays were not without financial calculation: travelling alone without his family and with a book at the end to show for them, he could hope to claim them as costs against income in making his tax return. No one ever suggested that May, who kept house, cleaned and washed at Rothiemurchus as much as she did at home, only under more primitive conditions, might have appreciated a reciprocal break. It was the way things were in those days and she had the children to look after. But Quarry House, nestling behind its low stone wall halfway round the Bay, and the beautiful garden James Grieve's grand-daughter created there, was their Camelot.

Quarry House was the somewhat unlikely dower house of nearby Luffness, on whose land it lay: unlikely in the sense that it is later in style and appearance than the corbelled and turreted late 16th-century Luffness House with its ramparts and martial memories, and is instead modest and domestic in character. Luffness itself, earlier the seat of Haldanes and Lindsays, the present tower house put up by a Hepburn, has been home to the Hope family since the early 18th century. Quarry House itself is deceptive however, and is probably older in origin than the present Luffness, since the quarry itself was mediaeval and has been abandoned for centuries. Traces of a much older structure have almost certainly been absorbed into the present building. The earliest date, 1747, which now appears on the pedestal of the sundial, probably relates to the later part, originally the smiddy. In outward appearance the house looks somewhat later than 1747, a sturdy low L-shaped structure of dressed grey stone with corbelled gables. In reality, it is two cottages put together although the "House" of its name suggests something grander. The first was built to house the quarryman who worked the quarry behind the house (and this may be the explanation of why it is such a solid, indeed superior, stone structure) and the other, on the Gullane side, and now a spacious sitting-room, was the smiddy. Tacked on at the back was a wooden extension, put up by a previous tenant whose wife had TB. Interestingly, another previous tenant had been the sculptor Charles d'O Pilkington Jackson, creator of the striking equestrian statue of Robert the Bruce at Bannockburn. Nearly fifty years later, in September 1997, Nigel would unveil the statue of another national hero—Tom Church's "Braveheart" statue of Wallace at Stirling. A generous garden surrounds the house, with a big lawn, herbaceous borders and a little copse by the gate, where daffodils blow in the spring. The fields on either side still bear their ancient names, Cow Park lying on the Aberlady side.

The Tranters found a roomy, rambling house, all on one storey, when they moved in. The two cottages were wholly integrated but the place was in need of some improvement and over the years they opened up windows and doors, sealed off the old pump, improved the plumbing and added an airy upstairs sitting-room from which they could enjoy the view over the Bay in the summer months. Nigel built a little glazed wooden porch at the front door, where a large brass dinner bell was later added, with a note reading Please Ring for Attention. No one ever did: they banged on the door and walked in. They had their own apples and the Hopes let them have as much fruit as they wanted from the walled garden of Luffness House, where Nigel was already a familiar figure, with his folding stool and fistful of notes. They had the run of the little wood to gather firewood and there was always a log fire in the sitting-room grate. It is Nigel's boast that he never bought a bag of coal or a sack of wood in all his years in Quarry House.

Deeper into the wood, where there were majestic mature trees, chestnuts, sycamores and a couple of walnuts, lay the ruins, thought to date from the 13th century, of a Carmelite monastery and chapel, the first such to be built in Scotland, and it was here that May, who was part-Highland and "fey", susceptible to supernatural manifestations, had a ghostly monk cross her path one afternoon and hurry on into the trees without acknowledging her greeting. The chapel walls stand only about a foot above the ground now and the interior is grassed over, but the ground-plan shows it to have been a place of some size and importance. On the left of the high altar, in the place normally reserved for the founder, a barrel-vaulted niche contains the stone coffin of a crusader with an effigy on top, so broken as to be barely recognisable: in a sense David de Lindsay, whose last resting place this is, was indeed the founder, for as he lay dying of a fever in Acre in 1264, cared for by a monk expelled with his brothers from their monastery at Mount Carmel, he gave instructions for his body to be carried home and buried in a new chapel which his brother Sir John would build for the Carmelites on his land at Luffness. It is a notably beautiful place and immaculately kept, green and tranquil, and it has an air perhaps of waiting for the monks to return. It was to become a special place for them all. Nigel and May in particular made a point of visiting it together, sometimes by moonlight, on days that were important to them, taking the big things of their lives, good and bad, to lay before their God. Nigel has the most vivid sense of its holiness despite its long disuse. When he stumbled across a broken stone cross in the undergrowth alongside, it so distressed him that Colonel Hope let him take it home to Quarry House and erect it, decently, in the garden there, where it remains. Close to the chapel lies the mediaeval quarry from which Luffness House, the monastery, the chapel and the original quarryman's cottage were all built: not a quarry hacked out of the side of a hill, but rather dug down, a deep hole, disused for centuries, flooded and choked, dank and obscurely menacing now.

X

THE DAILY ROUND,
THE COMMON TASK

Quarry House, the Easter holidays. 1954 or thereabouts. Philip in the doorway off left, Nigel in the foreground, booted and spurred, field-glasses strapped on, striding out of the frame, impatient to be off. Cross about something, walking away from an argument. Philip, at fifteen, all legs and already towering over his father, hovers in the doorway behind, with a despairing air. The press photographer, anxious for a last picture, has caught the moment like a fly in amber. Nigel's routine has been interfered with and Philip, who has seized his chance at the end of the photography session to importune his father about some concern of his own, has drawn the short straw.

Discipline is essential to the professional writer. If he does not sit down every day at his desk or, in Nigel's case, set off on his daily walk, no book will be written, or at any rate not in time to pay the bills. Nigel Tranter is pre-eminently a man of routine. He rises around seven, makes his porridge, says his prayers, washes and shaves, glances through his mail, collects his notes, has a quick look at what he typed up the previous afternoon and sets off for the Bay. Nothing has ever been allowed to interfere with this routine: he may make an exception for the press—and indeed he is endlessly patient with both journalists and photographers, posing with the ease of long practice—but a son should know better and must wait. There can be little doubt, from the expression on his face, that Philip's plans for the day have been wrecked and that May will have him hanging around the house, moody and thwarted, until some new plan takes shape in his head.

Tranter may be out on the shoreline for anything up to six hours, covering ten or twelve miles in the process, and he has a sandwich or an apple, possibly a bar of chocolate, in his pocket. He will be home late for lunch unless the weather turns too wet and stormy to write. When he gets in, he has a scratch meal and types up his pages quickly, while he can still read them or remember the thread if he can't, then spends the afternoon doing practical chores about the house or in the garden, cutting up logs and sawing wood. After he moved out of Quarry House, he found the afternoon a bit of a desert, with no logs to cut. He has a cup of tea around four, socialises a bit, maybe drops off to sleep for a few minutes in his chair, then tackles his postbag and is ready for a high tea/supper around six. He is exceptionally abstemious as far as food is concerned: in addition to being a lifetime tee-totaller and non-smoker, his preference is for plain food and not much of it. He seldom eats meat. Like most Scotsmen, however, he has a sweet tooth and can usually be tempted with a biscuit or a piece of home-made cake. Tea is his great standby: plain, ordinary, old-fashioned Indian or Ceylon, with sugar and no milk. The evening is devoted to preparation for the next day, research conducted primarily in his own bookshelves, for by now he has built up a comprehensive library of the things he needs for his work. The evening is also the time for *The Scotsman*, which he reads with care, and by 9 o'clock he is ready for the TV news. He tries to keep up religiously with events. After the news he sits quietly in his chair for half an hour or so, saying his prayers, wrestling with his conscience and praying for a catholic collection of family and friends. He is ready for bed soon after ten and sleeps like a log. He begins to re-surface around half-past six, with half an hour to go until alarm-time at seven, and this is when he dreams, and May comes back to him, as he drifts in and out of sleep. He doesn't dream about the characters in his books, otherwise so vivid to him, nor does he work out plots. Sundays apart, when the routine is broken to observe the Sabbath and go to church, this has been the pattern of his working day for over fifty years, and it has produced a total of over 130 books, and still counting. He is quite incredibly fit, and has to be forcibly restrained from climbing up on his garage roof, and leaping five-bar gates.

It goes without saying that, since it was on the free flow of Nigel's pen that their livelihood depended, the requirements of everyone else in the household had to be subordinated to Nigel's needs from the outset. May willingly complied and, while Nigel was grateful, he came to take her compliance as a matter of course. Since he believed that man and woman were equal in the eyes of God, he saw their marriage in terms of a partnership, but perhaps also assumed unthinkingly that he would always be the senior partner. But this was probably May's assumption too: she had grown up in an age which assumed that the man was the driving force. But as long as she lived, May was involved in every aspect of his life, including his work. Every new idea was discussed with her and she read every chapter of every book as it was written, her pencil in her hand, advising and checking assiduously for errors and inconsistencies. It was May who kept the records, did the accounts, kept track of diary engagements, map-read when they drove around the country in pursuit of castles, helped with research, hunted down out-of-print reference books to add to his library, did the preparatory work and took the notes that made possible the gigantic task of *The Queen's Scotland*, compiled the huge library of press cuttings, covering reviews and publicity for books, all the hundreds of letters to editors and the replies, and the press reports of public meetings, and pasted them into albums; noted, when no one else did, exact publication dates, looked after private business correspondence (and incidentally wrote an excellent business letter), and kept him right when his imagination ran away with him in public or he got a date wrong. She was also his shield and buckler against unwelcome intrusions—including designing ladies, of whom there were not a few. Her entire life was devoted to freeing Nigel to write and pursue his public career: it was the most extraordinary labour of love. Her reward was his success, but she had no desire to share the limelight with him, indeed actively disliked that side of his life and his nature: her joys were the private joys of children and grandchildren, home and garden and a few old friends.

XI

THE PHRONTISTERY

A cluttered broom-cupboard, you might say, except that there are no brooms. And there's a window. Otherwise, a table loaded with books and papers, an elderly manual typewriter presiding, the whole arranged with its back to the window. On the desk, an old shoe-box full of laces, broken and ragged with age, most of them apparently from trainers. Bookcases, crammed and teetering, a huge set of folded maps, a steel filing-cupboard. At the table, typing fast but unscientifically, with two fingers, best-selling novelist Nigel Tranter. You would never think it to look at him. But then, he goes back a long way to well before the days of computers. The old Imperial typewriter goes back a long way, too.

Although Tranter does the actual composition walking round the Bay, the typing-up and most of the research for his books is done in what he calls his "phrontistery" or study. It was May that stumbled upon the name somewhere and it stuck: she was good at names. The *Oxford English Dictionary* defines a phrontistery as "a room for writing or thinking in" deriving it from "phrontist", meaning a deep thinker, and used by Aristophanes ironically of Socrates, and adds for good measure a quotation from the *American Journal of Philology* of 1888 to the effect that "the inside of the phrontistery is never seen". Not a think-tank, with its connotations of brainstorming by a group, more a think-shop patronised by a solitary. Like most author's writing-rooms where the writing is actually done, as opposed to the studies in which they pursue their researches, Tranter's phrontistery borders on the austere. In the case of the phrontistery at Quarry House where he tapped out the *Bruce* trilogy, the *Montrose* books and the *Wallace*, almost perversely so. The contents of the old phrontistery have moved from Aberlady to Gullane and although the house is smaller, the room is larger and they are more spaciously disposed. There is still a battered bookcase full of battered books, the *Douglas Peerage, Debrett* and *Burke's Landed Gentry* cheek by jowl with the eleven volumes of *The Register of the Great Seal of Scotland*, Grub's 1861 *Ecclesiastical History of Scotland, Roget's Thesaurus*, the *Oxford English Dictionary, Groome's Ordnance Gazetteer* and a complete set of the inch-to-a-mile maps of the *Ordnance Survey of Scotland*, many of them with their spines held together with sticking plaster, their pages worn and brown with use.

The desk is a work-bench, made once upon a time by May as a surprise, and topped by a sheet of chipboard, pride of place occupied by the old Imperial typewriter. For years he used a machine on which the "b" was broken, and typed in an "o" instead: one of his chores each evening was to add the strokes that would turn them into b's and his children referred to his nightly tussle with the typewriter as "Daddy doing his b's". The carbon paper has gone now and the manuscript pages are photocopied on completion, but the pages are still quarto-sized, not A 4, and the ribbons well-worn. He types fast and confidently, but without science. "I suppose I could run to a word processor if I wanted one," he says, "but my old Imperial serves me well." Some of the array of old typewriters he carefully preserved failed to make the cut to the new house in Gullane, but he has kept the portable that accompanies him everywhere he goes. Even on research trips, he likes to get in his daily stint on the current book so as not to lose the flow: writing is a need for Nigel Tranter, not a penance. He needs the shoe-laces, lovingly salvaged from Jovey's Neuk, for lacing his manuscripts together. When he presented the original manuscript of *Warden of the Queen's March* to the Marquis and Marchioness of Lothian as a token of gratitude for hosting a party at Ferniehurst Castle in celebration of his 80th birthday, Lady Lothian, who envisaged putting the manuscript of the book, which is about Ferniehurst, on display at the Castle, took it, lace and all, to Asprey's in Bond Street and asked them to make a display case for it, matching the colour to the colour of the shoe-lace, which was brown. Another shoe-box holds a filing system of lecture notes, endlessly in demand. A steel cabinet contains more precious papers and a bedroom cupboard holds his capital of completed, but as yet unpublished, manuscripts, currently running around seven. Bookshops are unhappy about hardbacks appearing too fast one upon another, and publishers bow to their foibles, hence the build-up. He sits half turned away from the window, from which there is in any case no view, to aid concentration. No gazing out of the window for inspiration here: he has it all inside his head. Hidden from view in a hanging cupboard is another unlikely item: the black velvet cloak with its green shoulder cross of St Lazarus edged with white to which he is entitled as a Knight Commander of the Order of St Lazarus of Jerusalem.

There is a sense in which Nigel Tranter's life as a writer has been supremely undramatic. He sold his first book to the first publisher he offered it to. The second book, his first novel, admittedly was rejected. But from then on, he wrote the books, they were accepted, they sold, and that was that. From the age of 26 he could describe himself as an author: from the age of 37, he was a professional writer, writing full-time and living on his earnings as a writer. He walked, he composed, he typed up and the typescript was transferred to print. Day after day, book after book, year after year for over sixty years. There are many extraordinary things about Nigel Tranter as a writer, but surely none so extraordinary as the fact that the production of the books really has been as simple as that, for what flows from his fertile imagination also flows straight onto the printed page. After the preliminary planning and research, he simply writes it down: he scraps a passage now and again, but by and large he does not chop and change, does not re-draft, does not re-cast. For Nigel Tranter writing a book is a bit like knitting a scarf: he starts, he goes on, he finishes, in one seamless whole. Of course this is to over-simplify and do a great injustice to the books with their great set-scenes, their carefully-crafted climaxes, the suspense main-tained, the page-turning qualities. But the actual writing is achieved as painlessly as the analogy suggests: there is no agonising over the need to re-write, no black holes when inspiration dries up, no ghastly doubts about the whole project. Editorial intervention is minimal. And there is no rejection. He sees himself as a storyteller, whose job is to keep people impatient to find out what happens next; and he believes that by re-drafting the freshness is lost and the tempo destroyed. He is primarily a visual writer, seeing the scene in his mind's eye in all its totality of detail as he writes: his problem is getting the picture down, finding the words to describe what he sees, not imagining the scene. Of course it is true that re-drafting and doubts are not in his nature, but it is a remarkable record just the same. He is furthermore a compulsive writer, and it is one of his superstitions never to write the final page of one book before he is ready to start the first page of the next the same day. A seamless life of seamless writing.

His career as a novelist nevertheless falls into certain distinct phases, through which, or parallel with which, run a number of important non-fictional works. The over-ambitious unpublished first novel apart, the facility was always there: even in the very earliest published works, the romantic adventures set against Highland hills, he writes easily, with a deft, humorous touch, the characterisation is direct and convincing and he draws from life. His middle-class heroes are distinctively Scottish: they are brave, they are romantic, they are modest, they are thrawn, they have an underlying seriousness, they are at home on the hill or in the burn, but above all, they are capable of kicking over the traces and taking the law into their own hands should the need arise. He also has a keen ear for the pawky wit and irreverence of the common man, the ghillies and the Home Guardsmen, the fishermen and the Glasgow keelies of the modern books and the faithful retainers and esquires of the historical works, who leap from the page. They have become fewer, however, with the passage of time. He has a good eye for the telling detail, and, through it all, the story romps convincingly on.

The modern adventure stories however quickly began to show signs of that nose for the dramatic—and comic—possibilities of contemporary issues, which is so noticeable in the postwar books. *Mammon's Daughter* and *Eagle's Feathers*, published in 1939 and 1942 respectively, both deal with the confrontation between the old way of life in the Highlands and the demands of the modern world. *The Chosen Course*, published in 1949, brings the conflict up to date and is more specific. Its theme is the advent of hydro-electric power and its effect on the glens, but it also spots the potential for private speculation, and describes—just ahead of a real-life case involving a millionaire contractor—the speculative purchase of land likely to be the subject of compulsory purchase, in order to make a quick financial killing. *The Chosen Course* was followed in 1950 by *The Freebooters*, written to highlight the accelerating unviability of the crofting communities and their resultant depopulation, together with Tranter's own ideas for remedying it through the offices of the Clan Albainn Society. *The Freebooters* however falls into a new category, the novel deliberately employed as polemic in an active cause. *Ducks and Drakes*, which pokes fun at the antics of the ornithologists in the wildfowlers' dispute over shooting rights in Aberlady Bay, and *Kettle of Fish*, which turned the spotlight on the iniquities of arrangements for the protection of salmon off the mouth of the Tweed, fulfil the same function.

Although the predominating themes at this time were modern, a marked fascination with the Highland Clearances in the 19th century also early became apparent, not surprising perhaps in one who regularly spent time in the remoter parts of the Highlands, where the ruined and abandoned cottar houses are a constant reminder that the empty places once held families evicted under a harsh, self-seeking regime. *The Gilded Fleece,* published in 1942, was the first to deal specifically with this theme, and *The Flockmasters*, published in 1960, covers the same ground. *Island Twilight*, too, is set in the time of the Clearances. These books about the Clearances are period pieces, dealing with a historical conflict of interests and its tragic consequences, but, except incidentally, they do not deal with historical figures. In this sense, they are essentially fictional: but they perhaps represent a first taste of the heady brew of serious historical fiction.

The young author: an early publicity photograph of Nigel Tranter, aged 26 years

Above left: Gilbert Tranter, Nigel's father (front), with his brothers John (centre) and Godwin

Above right: Nigel's mother Eleanor Tranter, aged 36, with baby Nigel

Left: Nigel the rabbit-farmer, with one of his angoras

Opposite: Nigel and his mother in the late 1920s

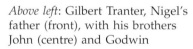

Above: Nigel and May's wedding day at Athelstaneford in 1931, with best man Eric Stevenson (left), and Nigel's sister Phyllis (2nd from left)

Left: Nigel with his first car

Opposite above left: Carefree days at the beach with May and Eleanor

Opposite above right: Special Constable Tranter in 1940

Opposite below: Nigel and May with an angelic-looking Frances May in 1937

Scottish Covenant

WE, the people of Scotland who subscribe this Engagement, declare our belief that reform in the constitution of our country is necessary to secure good government in accordance with our Scottish traditions and to promote the spiritual and economic welfare of our nation.

WE affirm that the desire for such reform is both deep and wide spread throughout the whole community, transcending all political differences and sectional interests, and we undertake to continue united in purpose for its achievement.

WITH that end in view we solemnly enter into this Covenant whereby we pledge ourselves, in all loyalty to the Crown and within the framework of the United Kingdom, to do everything in our power to secure for Scotland a Parliament with adequate legislative authority in Scottish affairs.

Left: More than two million people signed the Scottish Covenant in a bid to secure a Parliament for Scotland within the UK

Opposite: Shooting at Aberlady Bay

Below: The £50 bond, issued to raise funds for the Scottish Covenant

Quarry House in Aberlady on a glorious summer's day in 1966

With the family at Quarry House, 1958

XII

HOME IS THE HUNTER

"With Soutra Moor behind them, and the head of Lauderdale, the travel-stained and battle-scarred group of young men gazed down over the lovely spread of East Lothian, all green pastures barred by the golden rigs of harvest, dotted with demesnes and manors and castles, their villages and hall-touns, to the far blue haze that was the smoke of Haddington, its capital. Out of it all rose the isolated and abrupt humps of the Garmyleton Hills, Traprain and North Berwick Law and the soaring Bass, like leviathans from a verdant sea, whilst beyond stretched the silver-and-blue mirror of the isle-strewn Forth, to the distant cliffs and strands of Fife— surely one of the most fair and fertile prospects in all Southern Scotland, from these Lammermuir Hills." This was the view that opened up to Jamie Douglas and his companions in Lords of Misrule *and it is still the returning traveller's view, the place to pause and take stock, the longed-for spot where the heart suddenly sings, for this is one of the lovely places of the earth and it is home. However weary the journey, from here it will be made on wings.*

East Lothian, which Nigel Tranter has made his home for the past sixty years, might fairly be said to hold all Scotland in miniature: it has hills, it has sea, it has broad acres, it has desolate places, it has ancient houseproud little towns, it has castles, it even has coal.

Lying east of Edinburgh on the east coast of Scotland, it looks north across the Firth of Forth to Fife and stretches south across the high expanse of the Lammermuir Hills to the edge of the Border country. Along the coast lie a string of busy fishing harbours and little ports once lively with trade to Scandinavia and the Netherlands but now home mainly to small pleasure craft, and out in the Firth, with its scatter of rocky islands, the tankers lie off, waiting their turn at the oil terminals, while coastal freighters, the occasional naval ship and the occasional cruise liner pass. Where the bays shelve into the sea, a wilderness of sand and dunes and bent grass and salt-marsh stretches eastward round the little bump of land from Seton past Longniddry, Aberlady, Gullane and Dirleton to North Berwick, where a rash of rocks breaks through and soars, a couple of miles further on, to the massive cliffs at Tantallon. Just offshore is a necklace of little islands, almost all of them with its hermit's cell, from the rocky islets of Fidra, the Lamb, and Craigleith, their names familiar to every school child, to the huge offshore presence of the Bass, gleaming white now with guano, its green cap of grass almost wholly obscured. In the distance, out to sea, guarding the entrance to the Forth, lies the Isle of May, flat as a ship's biscuit with its pimple on the top, where the beacon burned before there were lighthouses. The coast's most kenspeckle landmark is the strange volcanic cone of North Berwick Law with its ruined hermit's cell and pair of rotting whale's jawbones on the top. On land, too, are two great fortresses, both ruined: Dirleton, with its back turned to the sea, couthy now with its little castleton, and rose-red Tantallon, impregnable on its rock. The 20th century has added the Cockenzie power station and the nuclear plant at Torness.

Behind lies the Vale of Peffer, a rolling plain of rich farmland, studded with little castles and watered by the Peffer Burn, a broad highway up which the armadas of geese fly in the winter months, on their way to graze on the lochans to the south-west. Among the little hills lies Athelstaneford, where the Celtic armies fought Athelstane in 832 AD and the white saltire cross of St Andrew appeared in the sky; below them the strange hump-back of Traprain, where Loth held court in the Dark Ages; and beyond them Haddington, the county town. Haddington's walls too have resounded to the clash of arms down the centuries, and the stench of burning has hung heavy on this now peaceful place, for it lies right in the path of Scotland's history, athwart the main route of English invading armies making for Edinburgh and Stirling. Here Edward III took his revenge in 1356 for the seizure of Berwick, here an English garrison stood siege in 1548 at the time of the Rough Wooing. No wonder the castles lie in ruins. It is "here, for better or for worse," as Tranter writes in *Land of the Scots*, "a major part of Scotland's story has been spelt out . . ." Beyond Haddington, to the south, lie the desolate Lammermuirs, where the sheep roam and the curlew calls and the snow lies deep in winter.

Starting from the west, along the coast, Nigel Tranter's personal patch of East Lothian is bounded perhaps by the policy walls of Gosford House, seat of the Earls of Wemyss, with its dense thicket of trees bent and shaped by the wind rampaging off the North Sea. The walls follow the corkscrewing road, and the road follows the sea. Between lie the Bents, a land of dunes and bent grass and buckthorn and darting, swooping dunlins, designated a Site of Special Scientific Interest some years back. Where the walls turn from the sea, the road turns too, cutting off a little triangle of land to make for Aberlady. There are dunes again at Shell Bay and Kilspindie but the road ignores them. Aberlady, once the port of up-country Haddington, is white-walled and straggling, with an old square-towered church. The house where Nigel eventually settled fronts the Bay, in the policies of Luffness House, home of the Hope family, which most would term a castle. East Lothian is full of territorial magnates with ancient names. The Bay itself, flooded at high tide, is vast, with a sand-bar across the entrance, the graveyard of many small craft and, more surprisingly, the last resting-place also of a couple of midget submarines run aground there deliberately once upon a time for target practice. Nigel used them occasionally as a hide in his wildfowling days and fantasised about a conning-tower hatch slamming down on him one day and jamming.

Half a mile further east, the golf courses start, no fewer than five of them at present count ringing the next village of Gullane, where the children are born with a golf club in their hand instead of a silver spoon in their mouth, or sometimes both, for Gullane has more than its fair share of millionaires. It, too has its ancient core of cottages and goose green and smiddy and ruined ivy-covered church, the victim of some long-ago sandstorm. Over the centuries, the villages along this sandy coast, like other North Sea villages from the Moray Firth right round to Danish Jylland, have changed character and contour with the shifting of the sand. The beaches between Aberlady and Gullane, where Nigel walks, are a treasure-trove for beachcombers, of whom he is one, the dunes behind a paradise for golfers. After Gullane comes Dirleton with its pretty village green and ruined castle, and then North Berwick, a sizeable place this, taking the full blast of the sea, off which James VI encountered such a violent storm on his way back from Denmark with his new bride Anne in 1589 that he persuaded himself he had seen a sieveful of witches whipping it up off the Bass and embarked on a vicious witch-hunt—one of the more unattractive episodes of his career. Beyond North Berwick again, with the sands left behind for the moment, lies the great wedge of Tantallon on its cliff, once a stronghold of the Douglas Earls of Angus, and well-nigh impregnable, but now a ruin, and eight miles on again Dunbar, still a busy little fishing port, the entrance to its harbour barred by a castle perched improbably on a series of rocky pillars, where Black Agnes famously dusted the ramparts with a fine linen cloth to annoy a besieging English army.

XIII

SALTIRE

A pretty whitewashed hamlet, straggling along a ridge, spilling down at the end towards the Vale of Peffer. Broad grass verges, widening to the merest hint of a village green, flowers burgeoning under cottage walls. A grey stone church and a little flag-pole flying the Saltire, some seriously old gravestones, a doocot, a commemorative tablet set into the wall. Consider the flag. Pare all else away, for it is extraneous, and listen in the silence for the clash of arms echoing faintly down the centuries. A famous battle was fought here once, right here, right below this peaceful village, more than a thousand years ago. Consider the flag. By rights it should be bigger, on a higher pole. By rights it should be streaming free, high, wide and handsome, far above the pantiled roofs and grey stone steeple. Consider the flag, for this is where it all began, this is where the seed was planted that became Scotland.

The village of course is Athelstaneford, where Nigel and May were married and where the saltire cross of St Andrew appeared in the heavens against a blue sky when the Picts and Scots fought Athelstane in 832 A D. If St Andrew brought them victory, King Angus vowed that from that day forward, and for all time coming, St Andrew would be Scotland's patron saint, and the white saltire cross on blue with which he is associated the Scottish flag, a national rallying-point before Scotland was even a nation. Nigel has told the story of Scotland's emergence as a nation in his novel *Kenneth*. The drama was played out on a wider canvas than this of East Lothian but it was here that the first inklings of nationhood began to be discernible, the direction of march was first sketched out. It is thanks to Nigel Tranter that the blue and white Saltire of Scotland now flies day and night over the village where it was born, for it was he who was instrumental in setting up the Flag Fund in the 1960s and establishing the Flag Heritage centre in the doocot behind the kirk. In the kirkyard stands the Saltire Memorial, with a plaque, designed by his best man Eric Stevenson, depicting the scene. It is a windy spot and they get through two flags a year, selling the tattered remnants to sentimental tourists to take home with them to Canada or the United States.

Like many another of his generation, it was war service that brought Nigel Tranter into unremitting contact with Englishmen for the first time, and gave him a sense of being different. Most of his time was served in regiments with no territorial base and although they contained a substantial number of Scots, the vast majority of officers and men were English. One of the jobs that fell to his lot more than once as an over-age subaltern was that of censoring soldiers' letters. He could tell within a sentence or two whether a letter was written by a Scot—not so much because it contained Scotticisms, but because the Scots had a wider vocabulary, were the product of a different education system. But there was more to it than that. The Scots reacted differently, seemed to be more independent-minded, were less class-ridden. There was a kind of subliminal difference between the two, of which he was made aware for the first time. National difference had never impinged on him before: as an Edinburgh man he was accustomed to make certain unthinking assumptions of superiority, about Scotland and about its capital, which were now challenged by a different assumption of superiority, that of England, to whom

Scotland was a province and her capital a fiction. It was the confrontation with England that turned Nigel Tranter into a fervent Scot.

Politically, he is not, and has never been a Scottish Nationalist: he is a patriot, a nationalist with a small "n". He remains loyal to the Crown, and he believes in Home Rule for Scotland, but not complete independence. Politics do not interest him, except as a means to an end: but like all Scots—and few Englishmen—he does fervently believe that Scotland is a nation and it was, and is, the need for recognition of the worth and dignity and nationhood of Scotland that fuelled his energy in her cause. But although not yet a burning issue for Nigel Tranter, nationalism was already an issue in Scotland right through the 1920s and 1930s. Great wars are by definition social watersheds and none more so than the Great War of 1914-1918. When the Scots came home, they wanted something better than they had left behind: educational grants helped the talented but impecunious to a university education that might otherwise have been denied them, and the universities, Glasgow perhaps most of all, were soon seething with the new ideas. The upheaval in Ireland and the eventual concession of an Irish Free State put ideas into people's heads: if Ireland could break away, why not Scotland? At the same time there was an upsurge of new writing in Scotland, to be known collectively as a modern Scottish Renaissance. Foremost among these new writers was Hugh MacDiarmid (C M Grieve) whose *A Drunk Man Looks at the Thistle*, with its hard look at the state of Scotland, published in 1926, was to prove seminal. Grieve himself was a Communist, and was a heavy drinker himself—always a turn-off as far as the tee-total Tranter was concerned—but he was a founder of the National Party of Scotland, the precursor of the Scottish National Party, in 1928. A number of Home Rule measures were put forward as Private Members' Bills in the House of Commons but never got beyond a First Reading. The Depression, which hit Scotland, with her reliance on heavy industries, particularly hard, gave people other things to think about but inflamed sentiment. When Nigel's war came in 1939, nationalism was already established as a sub-stratum of Scottish politics, not particularly respectable, since it often had a republican tinge to it, and not particularly influential, but undeniably there. In 1945 the Scottish National Party won their first Parliamentary seat in a by-election at Motherwell, though they lost it again in the General Election a few weeks later. Still, from this point on, Scottish representatives of the London parties would have to take national feeling increasingly into account. It was to this fertile field that Nigel Tranter returned in late 1946 with his own new sense of Scottish individuality. India and Pakistan were partitioned and won their independence in 1947, and as the 1950s and 1960s unfolded, the movement to grant independence to virtually all the countries of the old Empire gathered pace and the old question began to be asked again: if Belize and Bangladesh, why not Scotland?

Tranter is a practical man, and he came early to the conclusion that, as a novelist, he must not allow himself to withdraw from the world and become immured in his study: instead, he must keep in active contact with events. Given the flame that burned in him for Scotland following his war experience, it was not difficult. The causes were coming up thick and fast to which he could lend his voice, and he was to prove a natural-born agitator with a gift for publicity. If he was not much interested in politics as such, neither did he have much faith in politicians. His primary purpose was to raise public awareness as a preliminary to getting something done. If political involvement was called for, he would accept it, but only as a means to an end.

One of the first causes to catch his attention was the scandalous state of rural roads, particularly in the Highlands. There had been growing concern among thinking people right through the inter-war period about the depopulation of the Highlands. The process which emptied the glens in favour of sheep in the mid-19th century had now led to a pattern of tiny, scattered, ageing communities which were rapidly becoming unviable. The few who managed to scratch a living from crofting and fishing and beating for absentee masters in the shooting season were not enough to sustain schools and churches and public transport and the process was accelerating. The children were going away to school and not coming back, there was no one to look after the old people while they lived and no one to bury them when they died. The coming of the internal combustion engine had brought the Highlands within every man's reach, Nigel's among them, but it had also revealed the deserted crofts and the heather engulfing once more the tiny hard-won patches of cultivated land. Huge areas of the Highlands and Islands were becoming economically unviable except as a playground for the very rich, and time was short if the process was not to become wholly irreversible.

The urgent need to get something to halt the rot quickly became apparent once the War was at an end and a new Labour government installed. As depopulation continued, the children who were the future of these tiny communities had to go farther and farther afield to get to school, often over roads that were uneconomical for their owners to maintain. The government was providing a free public education but what was that worth in remote places where it entailed travelling forty miles a day over difficult roads, often impassable in winter conditions? Similarly, the government was providing free health care, but hospital facilities were rapidly becoming centralised and doctors' efforts on their patients' behalf were sabotaged by the roads over which ambulances and patients, and, for that matter, the doctors themselves, had to travel, at least the first part of the way.

Tranter was not the only man to come back from war service with a strong determination to get something done, and the letters began to thud down on the desks of MPs and newspaper editors.

Before the War, he had already got to know Wilfred Taylor, a fellow member of the Scottish Arts Club, whose daily column in *The Scotsman*, 'A Scotsman's Log', most people from Edinburgh to Inverness turned to first when they opened their paper in the morning. They were made for each other, for Taylor was a lively personality, always on the look-out for material for his column, and, wearing his other hat as Deputy Editor of the paper, could see to it that any letter Nigel wrote to the Editor would be published: as a columnist, he could ensure that it also got read. Alastair Dunnett, the editor of *The Scotsman*, whose wife Dorothy was destined to become the other best-selling Scots historical novelist of her generation, was also sympathetic. And then, as now, Tranter wrote letters with the greatest facility. He was familiar with the depopulation question from his own experience in the Highlands: the highly-charged history of the Highland Clearances in the previous century was one that exercised a particular fascination for him, and the present crisis was traceable, at least in part, to the Clearances. In tackling the matter, his role would be twofold: to wake people up to the urgency of the situation in the hope that public pressure would galvanise the authorities into action, and to promote what practical measures he could to alleviate matters.

In those early years, he was to run two inter-related causes in tandem: fixing the roads and resettling the empty crofts. The Clan Albainn Society, founded in 1948, which was barely a society at all, and, during Tranter's chairmanship at least, just Tranter under another guise, sought to tackle the problem of resettlement directly. Many men had come home from the war vastly different from the way they had left. The jobs to which they were expected to return were in many cases now wholly inappropriate for the matured, toughened, resourceful men they had become. In addition to being unwilling to accept the wage-slave existence some of them had left behind in 1939, the idea of being cooped up in an office from nine to five each day had become in many cases anathema. At the same time what little cultivated land there had been in the remoter parts of the Highlands and Islands was rapidly reverting to the wild, and this at a time when food was still in short supply. The situation was further exacerbated by government schemes encouraging young men to settle in other under-populated corners of the globe such as Canada and Australia. The landlords themselves in many cases had neither the will nor the means to stop the rot, and shooting-tenants, often their main source of income, had little interest in agricultural produce. The Government, for its part, was more interested in exploiting Highland rivers for hydro-electric power. If men willing to embark on a pioneering life in the Highlands in exchange for the freedom of being their own masters could be matched with landlords who saw advantage to themselves and were prepared to take a risk, perhaps a start could be made. The plight of Highland crofters is vividly described in *The Freebooters,* where the problem is tackled in the more unorthodox style fictional treatment permits, in this case, freelance unsanctioned and covert action on the Robin Hood principle by the Gregorach, a splendid band of free-spirited riveters and Glasgow keelies led by Roddie Roy Macgregor, physically a rumbustious ringer for Tranter's later portrayal of Rob Roy himself. In the novel, the proposal for a more formal arrangement comes from the landlord, who offers some derelict crofts rent-free, to be worked in connection with the home-farm on a sort of communal basis.

As Tranter himself admits, putting the scheme into effect was no easy task. *The Freebooters* was probably the most powerful weapon in his arsenal, but not everyone read books. He started publicising the idea at public meetings and in articles and letters to the press, with great success as far as would-be settlers were concerned but a signal lack of interest among landlords. Eventually Sir Michael Peto, the proprietor of the Scoraig peninsula in Wester Ross, came forward, and the first pioneers were installed. All went well to begin with and the settlers set about clearing the land with enthusiasm. The first spring and summer they lived in tents, but when the question arose of constructing more permanent housing, it emerged that under the Crofters Act landlords would be liable to pay compensation for any improvements effected should a tenant of crofting land vacate his holding after only a few years: not surprisingly, the landlords took fright. No amount of lobbying on compassionate, nationalistic or even rational grounds could persuade the Government to amend the legislation, and eventually the Clan Albainn Society had to admit defeat. The affair ended in general recrimination as a result of which Tranter resigned, but not before some home truths had been exchanged, Tranter, for his part, loudly critical of "ill-advised and raucous publicity at too early a stage", and allegations from the opposite camp of high-handedness on the part of the Society's governing Council. He concedes it was not the most successful of his ventures. A handful of families made the transition to the Highland way of life, however, and although most have now left the area, mainly because the next generation in its turn was looking for what seemed a better way of life, this time in the towns, the experiment is still remembered locally. *The Freebooters* was written to dramatise the affair—not the last of his books to be written for such a purpose.

The road problem was handled somewhat differently. Between them, Tranter and Taylor worked out a technique whereby they would set up pressure groups in the form of three-man road committees, one for each road. (Tranter would quickly become addicted to committees. Show him a problem, and he sets up a committee. But he was to develop a talent for filling them with some very distinguished names.) Tranter and Taylor provided the clout through the columns of *The Scotsman* and the third member represented the local community. Both had regular daily stints to perform at their desks if they were to earn a living, but they managed nevertheless to get in a remarkable amount of campaigning on the ground.

One road in particular sticks in Tranter's mind, for it was to prove lucky for him personally. It was the road running from Inversnaid on the east side of Loch Lomond over wild hill country to Loch Katrine and the Trossachs. It was the responsibility of the City of Glasgow, which drew its water from Loch Katrine and nearby Loch Arklet, and it had been allowed to get into a grievous state of disrepair—ostensibly, to help protect the water against pollution by keeping casual visitors out. Whatever the effect on Glasgow's water, the effect on the little community of Inversnaid, whose only other access to essential services lay across the waters of Loch Lomond, was dire. The nearest school was eleven or twelve miles away in Aberfoyle at the eastern end of Loch Ard. When the road deteriorated to a point at which it became impassable, the children had to go by boat to Luss on the other side of Loch Lomond: in winter conditions, when a storm blew up, they were cut off, sometimes on the one side, sometimes on the other. This was MacGregor country and Tranter's attention had been drawn to the bad state of the road when doing field research in the area for *MacGregor's Gathering*, the first volume of the *MacGregor* trilogy. At the Loch Lomond end, farming Garrison, near Inversnaid, on land acquired by Rob Roy in the early years of the 18th century, where the farm buildings incorporate barracks put up in 1713 to house government troops detailed to pacify this wild country, lived George Buchan, whose young children were affected, their schooling suffering as a result. Buchan was to be the local representative on the Glen Arklet Road Committee.

The Glen Arklet road was a particularly sensitive case, involving two conflicting public interests, but eventually they succeeded in arousing public opinion and the City of Glasgow set about repairing the road: in gratitude, Buchan, who had the stalking of a huge tract of land behind Inversnaid, offered Tranter a day's stalking whenever he wanted. He accepted with alacrity: from his house in Aberlady he could reach the Trossachs by car in little more than three hours, enjoy a good day's sport and be home in time for bed. When the time came to launch *MacGregor's Gathering*, his publishers marked the event with a cruise up Loch Lomond: when the royalties began to flood in, he treated himself to a kilt of MacGregor tartan—Tranter, which means, variously, a pedlar, a porter or a man who retrieves game, denotes a trade, not a clan.

Involvement in the Glen Arklet Road Committee produced more than just stalking—and Tranter's stalking experience can be traced directly and indirectly in virtually all his books, to the extent that he sometimes gives the impression of having crawled over every inch of Scotland—it also fuelled a deeper interest in Rob Roy MacGregor, the architect of countless adventures and a folk hero who had the additional attraction of being a controversial figure, often operating on the wrong side of the law. The country over which he roamed was at Garrison's back door, and Tranter now had the chance to get to know it intimately. Rob Roy's story was an intriguing one, familiar to Scots for the most part from the writings of Sir Walter Scott, whose version Tranter believed to be a travesty of the truth and deeply unjust. His interest eventually matured into the three novels of the *MacGregor* trilogy and a shorter non-fiction book called *Outlaw of the Highlands: Rob Roy MacGregor*, a bit of a hybrid with novelistic features, in which he sets out to refute Scott and defend his own reading of MacGregor's character and history. The involvement in the Glen Arklet Road Committee had yet another, even more far-reaching result, for *MacGregor's Gathering*, although a bit of a romp, not in the classical mould of the later historical novels, was nevertheless a firm step in the direction of the *Bruce* trilogy, the *Montrose* omnibus, and *The Wallace*.

XIV

THE COVENANTER

1950, Waverley Station, Edinburgh, an early evening train to Glasgow. Hurrying along the platform, peering through the windows, looking for the familiar faces, with only a minute or two to spare: Jo Grimond, Liberal chief whip, Johnny Bannerman, broadcaster and Gaelic enthusiast, Andrew Haddon, solicitor and Secretary and Treasurer of the Scottish Liberal Party, or Nigel Tranter, popular novelist and Scottish patriot. All four are members of the executive of the Scottish Covenant Association and they are bound for an evening meeting, a regular engagement. They will travel back again together on the last train. As always, wherever he goes, Tranter has a notebook in his pocket in which to scribble down instalments of his current novel if conversation flags.

Parallel with the long rise of the Scottish National Party to become a serious force in United Kingdom politics, an equally dramatic change had taken place in moderate opinion, which demanded a focus. One of the problems after the War for moderates supporting a measure of home rule for Scotland short of full independence was that they had nowhere to go. Although his position was frequently misunderstood and he had at one time or another close contacts within the Scottish National Party, Nigel Tranter was essentially a moderate, and loyal to the Crown, whereas the

Scottish National Party wanted full independence for Scotland, and always contained elements that were lukewarm about the monarchy or rejected it entirely. Those who, like Tranter, thought full separation misguided, but recognised that a measure of self-government would not come of its own accord but would call for concerted political action backed by broad popular support, found themselves in a quandary. John MacCormick, a young Glasgow lawyer, originally a member of the Scottish National Party, now a Liberal, and widely regarded as a saint by those who knew him, provided the answer. In 1928, while still a student at Glasgow University, then a hotbed of nationalism, MacCormick had been instrumental in founding the National Party of Scotland, which merged with the Scottish Party in 1932 to form the Scottish National Party, of which he became National Secretary. He resigned from the party in 1942 over policy regarding the conduct of the War, and instead formed the Scottish Convention as a cross-party pressure group: Convention was the old Scots name for a national assembly. A number of National Assemblies held in the postwar years provided a forum for Scottish debate, in which the General Assembly of the Church of Scotland and its Church and Nation Committee took a benevolent interest by permitting the use of their own Assembly Hall, later to be the first home of a new Scottish Parliament in 1999. Given his now passionate interest in a measure of self-government for Scotland, Tranter joined the Convention in 1946, the moment he got out of the Army. By the following year he was playing an active role in the Edinburgh branch, taking part in public meetings, explaining the Convention's aims. He was a good public speaker, an excellent chairman and he soon became convener of the Edinburgh branch. He was also possessed of boundless energy.

In 1932, in his Nationalist days, MacCormick had launched a Scottish Covenant or bond which aimed to restore Scotland's status as a nation: in 1949, Scottish Convention launched a similar

Covenant which was to have a run-away success. The choice of name—Covenant—was deliberate. Like the National Covenant of 1638, it was to be, quite simply, a contract: in this case a pledge to work for a Scottish Parliament. It was couched in simple, dignified, straightforward language and Tranter had a hand in drafting it. It ran, with a fine turn of phrase recalling the Constitution of the United States, the benchmark for many later, democratic constitutions:

> "We, the people of Scotland who subscribe this Engagement, declare our belief that reform in the constitution of our country is necessary to secure good government in accordance with our Scottish traditions and to promote the spiritual and economic welfare of our nation.
>
> "We affirm that the desire for such reform is both deep and widespread throughout the whole community, transcending all political differences and sectional interests, and we undertake to continue united in purpose for its achievement.
>
> "With that end in view we solemnly enter into this Covenant whereby we pledge ourselves, in all loyalty to the Crown and within the framework of the United Kingdom, to do everything in our power to secure for Scotland a Parliament with adequate legislative authority in Scottish affairs."

The underlying philosophy was spelt out by John MacCormick in an address to a meeting of the University Societies of Edinburgh in March 1950, when he said that it was right that nations should govern themselves, and Scotland was a nation. He told his audience that Scottish Convention, now re-formed as the Covenant Association, would be approaching the two main political parties, Conservatives and Labour, with a reasonable request that they pledge themselves to act either in the present Parliament or the next; but if persuasion failed, the Covenant Association would challenge the politicians on their own ground and put up their own candidates in future elections. Tranter told a public meeting in Kirkcaldy on 2 December 1950 that the Association could put up 70 candidates "tomorrow".

The Covenant itself was backed by a Blueprint setting out in some detail their proposals for self-government and a Scottish Parliament, the scope and functions of such a Parliament, and how it should be elected. To finance their activities, they issued £50 Bonds which it was hoped the Government of Scotland would redeem "when it comes into being": they also hoped it would be deemed "proper for the first Scottish Government to regard repayment at face value [plus $4^1/_2$% interest to run from the date of the proclamation of the first Scottish Parliament] as a charge upon the National Revenue."

As chairman of the Edinburgh branch of Scottish Convention, it fell to Tranter to launch the Covenant in Edinburgh. The Covenant was intended to be cross-party in its appeal and Scottish Convention's role initially was to hold the ring and provide a common platform. In November 1949, Tranter was to be found vehemently denying, in a letter to the *Edinburgh Evening Dispatch*, any connection whatsoever between either the National Covenant Committee, the Committee of the National Assembly or Scottish Convention and "any political party or sectarian interest". At the Fourth Scottish National Assembly in April 1950, there was virtually universal support for a six-point resolution aimed at securing devolution, and later the same month a 12-man Commission was appointed, whose honorary presidents included the Duke of Montrose and Lord Boyd-Orr, and whose members included John MacCormick, John Cameron KC, Councillor Robert Gray, businessman John Rollo and Tranter himself, to act as a kind of shadow cabinet and handle approaches to Government and Opposition leaders concerning the Covenant's proposals. Initially, their aim was the setting up of a Royal Commission to consider the reform of government in Scotland and the holding of a national plebiscite. In the meantime, Scottish Convention re-formed itself, via the National Covenant Committee, as the Scottish Covenant Association and Tranter emerged as Vice-Convener for the East of Scotland. From now on, he was to be heavily engaged in promoting the Covenant, travelling the country explaining its terms, writing letters to the press, conducting an acrimonious debate with the extremer elements about whether they should be permitted to sell their own material at public meetings, and engaging in serious criticism of the editorial policy of *The Haddingtonshire Courier*, which disapproved. Although there was massive support for the aims of the Covenant, it was by no means universal, and one of Tranter's regular chores was responding to allegations of Anglophobia from the more conservative element. But above all, at this stage, he was engaged, like everyone else, in the collection of signatures. There were lists all over the place: lists in the baker's, lists in the butcher's, lists in offices, lists on clipboards with pencils on strings, lists in wire-baskets, lists in cardboard boxes, lists by the lorry-load. The original target was one million signatures, but the response was phenomenal and, in the two years of the campaign, over two million people signed, more than half the population over the age of eighteen, and well above the highest number of votes ever registered for any political party in Scotland in a general election. It was far more than they had anticipated, even in their wildest dreams. Not much wonder one or two of the lists silted up among Tranter's papers.

The Covenant text had been brief, as befitted a document designed to attract broad support. In due course it was presented to the Government, and the Scottish Covenant Association dedicated itself to keeping the flame alight and turning the Covenant pledges into reality when a Scottish Parliament was granted. But in the event the Covenant which had seemed to offer such hope proved to have been much too gentlemanly in its approach to be effective, and it disappeared into Whitehall's maw:

to be effective, it should have embraced sanctions. There were general elections in 1950 and 1951 and if the Covenant had included a pledge not to vote for any parliamentary candidate not committed to devolution, matters might have been different, and Tranter, who had helped draft the Covenant, afterwards blamed himself bitterly for its omission. The Covenant Association continued to function but the heart went out of it for good when John MacCormick died in 1961. In any case, its activities had been eclipsed long since by a much more dramatic freelance enterprise.

XV

THE CONSPIRATOR

Edinburgh, 7 April 1951, a polite drawing-room in Regent Terrace. Disposed about it, in close consultation about what to do about a piece of stolen property, the Countess of Erroll, Hereditary High Constable of Scotland and her husband, Sir Ian Moncreiffe of that Ilk, Dr Charles Warr, Dean of the Thistle and minister of the High Kirk of St Giles, John Cameron, Dean of the Faculty of Advocates, and Nigel Tranter, Vice-Convener of the Scottish Covenant Association and chairman of the Edinburgh branch. They are discussing what to do with the lump of Old Red Sandstone retrieved a couple of months ago by Ian Hamilton from under the Coronation Chair in Westminster Abbey, current whereabouts unknown. Outside, the police are lurking, the hour is late and the heat is on.

The failure of the Covenant to achieve any practical results was a grievous disappointment and the movement was withering on the vine, when out of the blue, a Glasgow University law student named Ian Hamilton decided in December 1950 to take matters into his own hands. With great aplomb, minimal finance and total success, Hamilton, with Kay Matheson, Gavin Vernon and Alan Stuart, succeeded on Christmas night 1950 in extracting the Coronation Stone from under the Coronation Chair in Westminster

Abbey and spiriting it away. Hamilton, now transmogrified into a Queen's Counsel, has told the story with suitably dramatic effect in *The Taking of the Stone of Destiny*. It is impossible adequately to describe the reaction. Scotland of course was cock-a-hoop: at last something had happened, it was one in the eye for the English, the old insult had been wiped out, the Stone was on its way back. There were few who worried about sacrilege: Scots in general tend to be less exercised about the sanctity of church furniture. But there were not a few Englishmen who were amused by this flouting of the Establishment. One of the curiosities of the whole story is that it gave an extra fillip to Christmas celebrations in England as well as Scotland, the Dean of Westminster, the Home Secretary and King George VI always excepted. It was widely known that the King, who was already ill and worried that his daughter's coming coronation should be valid, was deeply distressed about the whole affair.

The plans to retrieve the Stone had been kept, necessarily, a deep secret, to which Tranter, for one, was not party. But MacCormick was in the know, and so was Councillor Robert Gray of Glasgow, who was Tranter's opposite number as Vice-Convener of the Covenant Association for the West, and, incidentally, a monumental stonemason. In an inspired move, Hamilton and his associates had secreted the Stone south of London, not north, and it had disappeared from view. In fact it had broken in two on removal from the chair and the two parts thereafter for a time pursued an independent existence. But with the passage of time, the need to produce it began to be paramount. Somehow the Stone had to be brought back to Scotland and be seen to be brought back. Thereafter it had to be disposed of decently, even if this meant ultimate return to London: there is no point in snatching a powerful national symbol from the grasp of an oppressor and then allowing it to moulder in a ditch. The police hunt was hotting up and had moved from random checks on car boots to serious detective work—pursued, however, with qualified urgency north of the Border. There was a further pressing reason to act: both pieces of the Stone had in fact been back in Scotland since early in the New Year, the smaller piece lodged in an old HP Sauce carton in the knee-hole of a desk in James Scott's garage in Scone, while the main part was being shuttled round central Scotland in deepest secrecy just a couple of jumps ahead of its pursuers. Eventually, it spent some time in Bertie Gray's stonemason's yard, where he bolted together the two component parts, and it nestled for a time thereafter under John Rollo's factory floor in Bonnybridge. The Scottish Nationalists were believed to have their own plans for it. According to information received, Scottish Nationalist activists had a boat standing by to take the Stone out into the Firth of Clyde when it turned up and sink it, thus putting paid once and for all to its connection with kingship, of which they disapproved. If Hamilton and the Stone, in their several ways, were only two jumps ahead of the Police, they were only one jump ahead of the Nationalists. The whole point of removing the Stone had been to make a gesture, to draw attention to a legitimate and strongly-felt desire on the part of the Scottish people to take control of their own destiny. The Stone had been removed from Scotland by Edward I in 1296 in order deliberately to humiliate the Scots and as far as Scots were concerned it was a symbol not of kingship, in its location in Westminster Abbey, but of oppression under the English yoke, and its removal had wiped out the stain. The problem was what to do with it.

Tranter of course does not believe that the stone lodged under the Coronation Chair in Westminster Abbey for the past seven hundred years is the true Stone of Destiny. He believes, with Dr James S Richardson, a former H M Inspector of Ancient Monuments for Scotland, who wrote a seminal monograph on the subject almost fifty years ago, basing himself on early seals and documentary evidence, that the true Stone was made of basalt or marble, elaborately carved with Celtic patterns and having volutes on either side to carry it by, and was probably originally an ancient altar, possibly a Roman altar later embellished with Celtic lacework. Possibly it was Columba's portable altar which he brought with him from Ireland. Tranter further believes that this Stone was successfully hidden from Edward Longshanks by the Abbot of Scone, in whose care it was kept, and the present block of sandstone substituted for it. Common sense suggests that the present Stone, now back in Scotland, is exactly what it most resembles, a roughly-dressed builder's block of the local Scone sandstone, "the great skelb of stone cut out of the quarry" the Abbot of Scone describes in *The Path of the Hero King*, possibly rejected on account of the flaw which caused it to break in two when it was removed from the Coronation Chair at Christmas 1950. The belief that the stone which reposed under the Coronation Chair was a fake was shared by Bertie Gray at least. Gray, the man who repaired it in 1950, inserted at the same time a note which read, according to Pat Gerber, author of *Stone of Destiny*, "This Stone was stolen by Edward I in 1296 and it should be returned to Scotland", and, according to Tranter, "This is a block of Old Red Sandstone of no value to anyone". But Bertie Gray had made a couple of replicas of the Stone in his monumental sculptor's yard in Glasgow as early as the 1930s when there were other abortive plans to remove it, which confused the issue still further, and doubts developed about which was the Stone retrieved from under the Coronation Chair in Westminster Abbey: was it the Stone later returned by Ian Hamilton to Arbroath Abbey and now back in Scotland, a Stone now in the keeping of the Knights Templar, or a third Stone whose whereabouts are unknown? The puzzle is not made any easier by the fact that Bertie Gray, who seems to have been a bit of a joker, said a decade later "Oh, I can't really remember which Stone I sent back to London—there were so many copies lying about". Whatever it was that Hamilton removed and Gray repaired, Tranter has a few crumbs of it, porous and friable, presented to him after the event by Bertie Gray.

As to the true Stone of Destiny, the ancient and hallowed coronation stone of the Kings of Scots, the chronicles which pre-date its removal to England in 1296 describe a "marble" stone, carved and decorated, with a hollowed out upper surface and elaborate volutes or scrolls, which could act as handles when it was moved. It is "a block of stone that gleamed black and polished in the lamplight . . . about twenty-four inches high and twenty-eight long by twenty wide . . . its top dipped slightly in a hollow, the whole curiously wrought and carved with Celtic designs" that Tranter has chosen to describe in *The Steps to the Empty Throne*. Various conflicting traditions exist to account for what happened to it next. According to one, the Stone was secreted in a cave in the vicinity of Scone. According to another, Bruce later entrusted it to Angus Og Macdonald, Lord of the Isles, for safekeeping, and in one of the closing scenes of the last book of the *Bruce* trilogy, *The Price of the King's Peace*, Tranter has Bruce say to Angus Og "The true Stone of Destiny, at Scone . . . Take it, Angus, take it. After my son's coronation. Take it to your Isles, where none shall be able to follow it. And keep it safe, on some fair island. Until one of my line, or whoever is true King of Scots, requires it again for coronation. Will you do this for me, old friend?" Tranter's own view is that the Stone is probably somewhere on Islay, and that Edward probably realised he had been duped, but was disinclined to publicise the fact.

The actual provenance of the Stone kept under the Coronation Chair for seven hundred years is of course in a sense immaterial, for it has in any case been hallowed by use throughout that time in the solemn ceremonial surrounding the coronation of, first, the Kings and Queens of England, and, subsequently, the Kings and Queens of the United Kingdom. But there is one important difference in its significance for Scots and English: it was carried off by Edward precisely for the purpose of humiliating the Scots, and, even if it was a fake, it continued to bear this connotation, while the true Stone is for all practical purposes lost.

It is at this point that Tranter comes into the story. Hamilton was in contact with MacCormick and Gray, the identities of the perpetrators were known to the Police, arrests were believed to be in prospect, and the heat was on. In particular, the heat was on as far as the Glasgow headquarters of the Covenant Association was concerned. It was decided that any moves about returning the Stone would have to be handled at the Edinburgh end, which meant Tranter. With his inventive genius and love of intrigue, nothing could have been more to his taste.

A diary fragment, the only one in his papers, here somewhat condensed, and headed 'Part of a Much Longer Story', records Tranter's role thereafter. At the end of March, the *Express* newspaper took a hand in the affair and announced that the paper was willing to pay to have the Stone restored, and on 29 March, John MacCormick revealed to Tranter at a Saltire Society meeting in Inverness that he had been acting as mediator between the people who now had the Stone—which he assured Tranter was safe—and authority. MacCormick also revealed that he had been retained as legal representative by "the boys" (who in fact included a girl) and was anxious in the first instance to try and arrange immunity for them, out of consideration for their parents and their own future careers. Arrests were believed to be imminent, the perpetrators' names having been traced through library slips at the Mitchell Library in Glasgow where Hamilton had done his research on the Westminster Stone. Tranter counselled caution: if MacCormick's name were to be linked with the plot, it might do the Covenant Association irreparable harm. Tranter was evidently aware at this stage of Hamilton's identity, but refers to him consistently throughout as "X".

Over the next few days, the press was full of the Stone story, its

interest sparked by a front-page splash in the *Sunday Express* for
1 April claiming that a plan to return the Stone had failed. *The
Scotsman* and other Scottish papers felt they had been scooped and
suspected the *Express* of having access to inside information, and
Tranter agreed to meet Wilfred Taylor on 4 April to try and placate
his editor. (They were right about access to inside information: "X"
was reported to be holed up in Abingdon writing a 40,000-word
piece for the *Express*, proceeds to be paid into Covenant funds,
according to Tranter.) At this meeting, Taylor revealed that two
letters would appear in *The Scotsman* the following morning: one
from the Countess of Erroll, Hereditary High Constable of Scotland,
expressing fears that the Covenant Association was allowing itself
to be used as a cloak for disloyal elements and wondering whether
she and her husband, Sir Ian Moncrieffe of that Ilk, might have
to withdraw their support, and another, from Lord Belhaven,
suggesting that Lady Erroll, as Hereditary High Constable, should
take custody of the Stone. Tranter immediately contacted Lady
Erroll to reassure her concerning the Covenant Association's
loyalty to the Crown, and urge her to withdraw her letter, since it
was likely to have serious repercussions. He also told her about
Lord Belhaven's suggestion, at which she quailed. She eventually
offered to withdraw her letter but by this time it was too late in the
day: *The Scotsman* had gone to press. They agreed instead that
Tranter would write a letter for the following day's *Scotsman*
couched in reassuring terms and Lady Erroll would follow up
with a second letter expressing satisfaction. Tranter duly composed
his letter which he offered to show her before sending it to the
paper. They went through the letter over lunch, when Tranter
explained the Covenant's position and the general situation, from
which it emerged that Lady Erroll personally deplored the whole
Stone affair, but that her husband was rather more favourably
inclined. Tranter then took his letter to *The Scotsman* where he
handed it over to the editor in person.

The following day, 6 April 1951, the letter appeared in *The Scotsman*, which however also printed a letter the same day from John MacCormick (who had been unaware of Tranter's negotiations) supporting Lord Belhaven's suggestion that Lady Erroll take custody of the Stone. Tranter immediately realised that quick action would be necessary to forestall a statement from Lady Erroll washing her hands of the entire affair. He therefore called her, urged her to make no precipitate statement, and asked whether he might call. She invited him to lunch again. With May's assistance he then concocted two alternative lines for Lady Erroll to adopt. Over lunch, they argued it out at length and Tranter eventually convinced Lady Erroll that it was her duty to make a moderate and helpful statement, proposing that the Stone be either handed over to the Earl of Mansfield, as successor to the Abbot of Scone, or deposited in one of the Royal properties in Scotland. A careful statement was drawn up, and Tranter then travelled to Glasgow to put it before John MacCormick. MacCormick approved and urged him to go ahead. Taylor met Tranter's train that evening at Waverley Station, Edinburgh and together they went back to the Errolls' house which had been besieged by the press all day. Independently, the Errolls had been in touch with Dr Charles Warr, Dean of the Thistle and Minister of the High Kirk of St Giles in Edinburgh, who was helpful. They had failed to get in touch with the Earl of Mansfield who was out of the country. But Lady Erroll had now backed off from the Royal property idea, as involving the King in possible opprobrium. Partly as a result of Warr's input, opinion in the little group now moved in favour of depositing the Stone on Church property instead and Warr agreed to meet Tranter and the Errolls on the evening of Saturday 7 April to discuss this alternative. Taylor would also attend and, in the event, John Cameron, Dean of the Faculty of Advocates, was there as well. A final statement was composed for publication in *The Scotsman* the following day. It is this final, crucial meeting at the Errolls' house on the evening of Saturday 7 April that is sketched in the vignette at the head of this chapter.

By the time the group reconvened at the Errolls' house that evening, their statement had appeared in *The Scotsman*, John MacCormick had telephoned his approval and had issued his own statement urging moderation, and Wilfred Taylor had been in contact with Jock Cameron, Dean of the Faculty of Advocates. Opinion in the group and among the few others in the know had crystallised in favour of Church property. Charles Warr had however made clear at an early stage that he would not welcome the Stone at St Giles since he would be compelled to inform the Police and feared the resultant opprobrium attaching to any suggestion that he had been responsible for "giving the Stone back". Without exception, all the men of the cloth approached were unwilling to be seen to be responsible for giving the Stone back. They were probably not alone in this sentiment: the Principals of the Scottish universities, who had also been mentioned as possible recipients, and other public figures might well have reacted in the same way, but it was the Church that was in the firing line. As alternative solutions Cameron now suggested, first, the Assembly Hall of the Church of Scotland (where the Covenant Association held its National Assemblies) and second, Arbroath Abbey. With its associations with the 1320 Declaration of Arbroath, one of the key documents of Scottish history, which contains the great declaration of Scottish independence that "It is not for glory nor for riches, neither is it for honours that we fight, but for freedom alone, which no true man gives up but with his life", Arbroath was an inspired suggestion which was instantly adopted. It also had the added advantage of being (a) a ruin and (b) in the custody of the Ministry of Works. Any obloquy would fall, Tranter noted, not on the King but on the Ministry of Works, which no one felt under any obligation to protect. Dr Warr agreed to issue a statement after the Stone was returned, urging moderation towards those who had removed it. Discussion then turned to the likely reaction of authority and they decided to ask Jock Cameron to join them, which he did. He came up with the idea that the Stone formed part of the Scots Regalia, the Honours of Scotland, in which case it was arguable that, however deplorable the manner of its taking, the motives of those who took it from Westminster were precisely those of Sir Walter Scott, who was instrumental in having the rest of the Regalia restored to their proper place in 1818. Because of the risk of telephones being tapped, it was decided that Tranter should go at once in person to report to John MacCormick, still one of only two or three men who knew the actual whereabouts of the Stone. Taylor drove him.

Once in Glasgow, where they arrived around 2am, a scenario developed that fully lived up to their cloak and dagger aspirations. MacCormick was expecting a visit at any moment from Trotter, editor of the *Express*, whom Taylor had no wish to meet, and it was thought politic, for the sake of the Covenant Association, to keep Tranter out of the eye of the press as well. As a result, there was much dodging about in back passages until the coast was clear. MacCormick immediately saw the advantages of the Arbroath Abbey scheme but thought "the boys" would be unwilling to agree to anything which would result in the Stone being whisked back to London. Like everyone else, he had heard the rumour that arrests would be made that night. He pointed out that the people now holding the Stone were not the same people who had taken it and that if the students were arrested, it was extremely unlikely the Stone would ever come to light. Trotter had reported that Hector McNeil, the Scottish Secretary, with whom he was in close contact, was hardening against the Stone-takers, but the general consensus in the Edinburgh group was that if the Stone turned up, the authorities would not be so foolish as to make arrests. MacCormick was doubtful on this point but the need for urgent action remained. Tuesday would be Budget Day and Wednesday's papers would be full of Budget news, the press with other things on their minds: it was decided that Wednesday would be D Day. The main points of a Second Declaration of Arbroath were agreed, to be couched in dignified terms as close as possible to the wording of the original document, and Taylor and Tranter set off again for home, passing "X" and "Miss M" on their way up to MacCormick's house in Park Quadrant.

Tranter's role was now at an end and the diary goes no further. Hamilton and Bill Craig retrieved the Stone from John Rollo at Bonnybridge, took it to Arbroath and left it at the High Altar around mid-day on Wednesday 11 April. Commenting in his book *The Taking of the Stone of Destiny* Hamilton says, "It was a crucifixion. . . . Unfortunately for everyone, Scots as well as English," he observes, "the authorities . . . were incapable of the grand gesture." In a very dubious move and in open despite of assurances from Hector McNeil that there would be a "cooling-off period" before the Stone was returned to Westminster, it was taken from Arbroath to Forfar Police Station, whence it was removed and returned to Westminster forthwith by representatives of the Metropolitan Police who had no status or jurisdiction in Scotland, acting under orders from McNeil's Cabinet colleague, James Chuter Ede, the Home Secretary, who had no jurisdiction in Scotland either.

Four decades later, in a gesture that left everyone gasping, John Major returned the Westminster Stone—whatever it was—in 1996. It crossed the Border under close guard.

Tranter followed up his real-life involvement with the story of the Stone with a novel of the same name, published in 1958. It is an exciting tale of a dastardly attempt by an Oxford research team to find and remove the real Stone from land once held by the fictional Kincaids of Kincaid, to whom Bruce is supposed to have entrusted it. Their impoverished descendant teams up with the "Gregorach" gang under Roddie Roy MacGregor, familiar from

The Freebooters and other earlier novels, and, between them, they foil both archaeologists and the Police. After a wild pursuit across the moors, they eventually lose the Stone when it slips into a bog, never to be seen again, thus neatly resolving by fictional means the problem of where it is now.

There had been minimal publicity concerning Tranter's involvement in the return of the Stone to Arbroath Abbey, but its story and provenance continued to excite people´s curiosity and imagination, and publication of the novel generated a steady flow of correspondence as people wrote in to ask Tranter where he got his historical facts from. Up and down the country, it seemed, people were beavering away at research on the Stone for school essays, undergraduate scripts, postgraduate degrees. People also wrote in claiming personal knowledge of the whereabouts of the true Stone. Some of them had interesting stories to tell and with these, correspondences developed which proved of mutual benefit, but in many cases, internal evidence suggested the writers were fantasising. One series of letters was of unusual interest, however. The writer, who signed himself C. Iain Alasdair Macdonald, and wrote from an address in Brighton, claimed that the Stone was in the safekeeping of his line, the Macdonalds of Sleat (there was a tradition that when the Macdonalds established themselves in Sleat in the seventeenth century, they took the Stone with them). He further claimed that he himself had been initiated into its whereabouts as a boy and was now its custodian: the Stone itself was concealed at a secret location on the Isle of Skye. Tranter exchanged a number of letters with him but some of the information contained in the letters that could be checked, in particular genealogical information, turned out to be inaccurate and he was not convinced that he had got to the bottom of the mystery. In working on her book, *Stone of Destiny*, Pat Gerber noted that Lord Macdonald disclaimed all knowledge, for which he might have had good reason even supposing the story to be correct, but she also decided the evidence was inconclusive.

With the Covenant ignored and the Stone back in London, the time had come to acknowledge that direct action had not worked. The sleeping giant of moderate opinion had been stirred into action only to find that its efforts had been unavailing. There could be no question of a repeat run at any rate in the foreseeable future. The Covenant Association had lost its meaning and the spark had gone out of it. There seemed to be only one solution: to act through the established political parties. The Covenant Association had been apolitical, and had sought to provide a forum in which people of different political creeds could work together to achieve self-government. Once the Covenant had failed, its constituent parts began to fall apart. Some went to the Scottish National Party. But the Scottish National Party was no option for moderates like Tranter who remained loyal to the Crown and the Union; the Conservatives were still opposed to any measure of self-rule, however anodyne; and the Labour Party ditched its original commitment to home rule in the 1950s. There remained the Liberals, the only party to have consistently favoured home rule over time. Tranter, although not a natural politician, decided to throw in his lot with the Liberal Party. Still a force on the so-called Celtic fringe in rural Wales and Scotland, where the Labour Party, with its industrial bias, had never caught on, the Liberals, who had been the long-term champions of Home Rule for Ireland at the end of the previous century, were the only political party to support autonomy for Scotland in all matters short of foreign and security policy and economic policy while still remaining within the United Kingdom, on roughly the same terms as had been granted in Northern Ireland, where the Stormont system had not yet collapsed in chaos. The policy of limited self-rule furthermore sat well with Liberal policies in general, and Tranter was to find many kindred souls in the Liberal Party, in particular John Bannerman, the popular broadcaster and Gaelic enthusiast, Jo

Grimond, at that time Liberal Chief Whip, and Andrew Haddon, Secretary and Treasurer of the Party, all of whom he knew as fellow-members of the Covenant Association executive. Haddon, who farmed at Honeyburn, outside Denholm, as well as running a solicitor's practice in Hawick, came of an old Borders family and had a keen legal brain, and his sound advice can be intuited behind many of Tranter's later campaigns. Over the years, he was one of Tranter's closest friends and allies. Tranter has no recollection now of exactly how and when they met but it seems possible they already knew each other before the War, because David Scott, the farming solicitor hero of *Trespass* and *Delayed Action* appears to be modelled on Haddon. Writing in *Delayed Action* in 1942 of the fictional David Scott, he says—and it seems likely that it was Andrew Haddon he was describing—". . . whatever else he was, David Scott was a farmer. Always the Scotts had been farmers, as should any man be that owns his own land, great or small; reivers they may have been, warriors, lawyers, merchants, priests, like any other Scots lairds with land not rich enough for easy wealth, but always they were farmers at heart, with flocks and herds and crops as the touchstone of their success, their content . . ." Tranter was to write several more books about the fictional David and Margaret Scott. Margaret was however modelled on May, not Dorothy Haddon. Andrew Haddon was by all accounts an exceptionally nice man and the ultimate source of Tranter's love affair with the Borders, documented again and again in the novels. Only very infrequently do any of the books include a dedication, but *The Price of the King's Peace*, Book III of the *Bruce* trilogy, is dedicated to Andrew Haddon.

There was a problem, however, as far as the Liberals were concerned. The Scottish Nationalists, with their more extreme ideas, were getting the headlines, and this was putting moderates off the broader issue; if anything was to be achieved, the Liberals would have to raise their profile. It was decided to put up candidates nationwide in forthcoming parliamentary elections and to work hard on building up the party organisation. Because he was by now a seasoned campaigner and a good speaker, a familiar figure on platforms up and down the country, the approaches began to come in from constituency associations: would Tranter consider standing for parliament? But the answer was always No: he was a writer, not a politician. He was however active on behalf of others: as chairman for many years of the East Lothian and Berwickshire Liberal Association he played an energetic supporting role in the campaigns waged in 1964 and 1965 in the Roxburgh, Selkirk and Peebles division by a promising young man named David Steel, who would pop up again in 1999 as Presiding Officer or Speaker of the newly reconvened Scottish Parliament.

XVI

THE HONORARY BORDERER

Summer, the Redeswire Stone, high on the Border with England. A group of men are enjoying the spectacle of the mounted cavalcade streaming up to the summit on their annual ride-out. It is a sight to stir the heart. But not, it seems, the heart of the man standing on Nigel's right. An English doctor on a visit to friends, the triumphalism inherent in the display has got under his skin. "Just you Scots blowing your own trumpet," he says. And adds for good measure, "Pure xenophobia, if you know what that means." If he had sat around and thought about it for a week, he could hardly have come up with anything more calculated to get Nigel Tranter's dander up.

It was Andrew Haddon that turned Tranter into a kind of honorary Borderer. In 1951, he arranged for him to attend the Hawick Common Riding as an honoured guest, participating in the Provost's Breakfast and standing for the singing of the Hawick anthem "Teri Odin", so ancient that no one is sure any longer exactly what it means, and the seed was sown for the first of many books. By the following year, he was at Hawick as a speaker. Haddon rightly calculated that Tranter would find the spectacle of the horsemen riding flat out as they beat the bounds of the common land and streamed for the Redeswire Stone at the heart of the old debatable land irresistible. Although Hawick was the most impressive, all the Border towns had common ridings in the summer months and from then on, he was in constant demand to "sash" a Callant or deliver a speech, at Flodden, Redeswire, Langholm, Jedburgh, Duns and Lauder as well as Hawick. He never actually rode out with the horsemen, preferring to attend instead by car, but the romance of the Border country, the independence of the little towns, the proximity to the Border with England and the ancient licensed lawlessness captured his imagination and found expression in books from *Cheviot Chase* in 1952 to *Sword of State* in 1999.

The chance remark of the English doctor sowed a seed too. Despite the intense rivalry between the various towns, there were always fraternal delegations present at Ridings from the neighbouring communities. But there were no fraternal delegations from the English side, with whom they shared a common heritage and with whose people they probably had more in common than with the people of the rest of Scotland. Why, he wondered, did the English Border towns have nothing of the kind? Was there anything he could do about it? He set out with a couple of friends to find out. (One interesting difficulty emerged: while the Scottish Border towns were all burghs, it appeared that most of the communities on the English side were not self-governing towns but rural district councils answerable to a County Council, and thus not always free to decide for themselves how they spent their money.) But Morpeth was a burgh, and Tranter recalls that the mayor of Morpeth was a bookseller, with whom he had had dealings in connection with the publicity for *Cheviot Chase*. He would start there. Anxious to spread interest in these delightful events and pacify any residual enmity of the kind evinced by the doctor, Tranter suggested that if an invitation was forthcoming, Morpeth might like to attend the next Hawick Common Riding and see how it was done. Not unsurprisingly, the response was distinctly wary: Morpeth would think about it—as long as it was clearly understood there would be no question of attending on a horse. The Scottish Border burghs made their approaches, delegations from Hexham and Morpeth, at least, crossed over into Scotland to participate or observe, and some of the English Border towns devised celebrations of their own, but the Common Ridings as such remained in essence a Scottish phenomenon. It is difficult to see how it could ever be otherwise. Cross-Border co-operation is all very well but expecting English towns to participate very heartily in what was in essence a celebration of defiance directed against themselves was asking a lot.

The first books set in the Borders are modern adventure stories, an extension of the hard-riding buccaneering exploits of the old Border reivers into modern times. *Cheviot Chase* is a re-run in modern times of the Hornshole Raid of 1514, subsequently described in its proper context in *Balefire*. *The Night Riders,* also a modern adventure story, describes another exciting but improbable campaign to whip up the interest of the English towns in the Common Riding tradition by reviving the spirit of the Border reivers and stealing their cattle. All the Border books consist in large measure of marathon rides across trackless wastes. While the Highland books give the impression that Tranter has crawled over every inch, and rightly so, the Border books suggest that he has criss-crossed the entire area on horseback. In fact, he has not: the impression created in these early books written in the 1950s and in later historical novels like *The Marchman* was achieved on the basis of walking with the Haddons, observation, and a stupendous capacity for translating into concrete reality the information contained in maps. From time to time, others have questioned whether it was possible to cover these huge distances in the times he gives; but this, too, he researched carefully and Doubting Thomases who set out to prove him wrong have usually found that these fictional feats of endurance are all feasible, if punishing, when carried out under extreme pressure.

It might fairly be said that it was this confrontation with the vivid reality of Border traditions and the sturdy independence of these communities, isolated, with their southern neighbours, from both the Scottish and English heartlands, that first whetted Tranter's appetite for serious historical writing. *Cheviot Chase*, published in 1952, offered a dreamlike sequence in which the Hornshole Raid, the glorious act of defiance staged against the English by the youths of Hawick in the aftermath of Flodden, is played out in the imagination of the hero as he ponders the modern re-enactment: Mark Douglas, the hero, "saw it all, as clearly as if he had taken part in it himself. He saw it all, every face, bearded and callow, and alight with passion, he saw the foaming horses and the streaming wild-eyed cattle, he saw the flaming homesteads, the laden dule-trees and the wailing women . . ." It was a first window into the past, a first visualisation of a real historic event and a first indication of the way in which Tranter would later work. *Balefire*, published in 1958, goes a step further in describing the Hornshole Raid direct, as part of the story of its fictional hero Sim Armstrong, a survivor of Flodden, in which virtually the whole of Scotland's fighting strength perished. Armstrong, who is gravely wounded, is cared for by an English Borderer and his daughters and survives to cross back and forth across the Border on some of these epic rides that Tranter describes so well. But while the events in which he takes part are historical, Armstrong himself, the hero of the novel, is not. While the descriptions of Flodden and the Raid, together with several of the characters prominent on both sides, are described with the verisimilitude that would later characterise Tranter's serious historical fiction, *Balefire* is nevertheless a kind of halfway house—good on action, splendid in its portrayal of the Hawick callants and Cessford, the Baillie who stayed home from Flodden, but limited in scope and essentially, perhaps, a romance dealing with a fictional, rather than an historic, hero. But Hawick must have loved it.

XVII

THE BATTLE OF ABERLADY BAY

Quarry House, 12 August 1953, evening. Cars in the drive and more littered about the grass verge outside. A little crowd of men standing about, duffled and flannelled and tweed-jacketed, some with cameras. Waiting for something to happen. The gentlemen of the press are here. In their midst, three men in waders, shotguns over their arms. At the epicentre, Nigel Tranter, silent and grim; at an upper window, Philip, armed with Nigel's old binoculars, spying out the land; on the edges, May, counting up cups in her head and wondering whether she should start making scones. Frances May, who has seen the press before, has retired to the back regions and is getting on with her own affairs. The village has got wind of something up and, having had its tea, is drifting, happenchance, down the road along the Bay in the hope of seeing some fun. Dusk is falling and the men with the guns are about to go into battle. This is serious.

Shortly after he acquired a wife, a house and a daughter, Nigel Tranter also acquired a shotgun and started shooting wildfowl over the mud-flats at Aberlady Bay. Wildfowling turned out to be an absorbing interest, producing the occasional goose or, more often, duck for the pot. But apart from the challenge, its main attraction was that it brought him into the closest possible touch with nature, crouching in a hide waiting at low water for the dawn flight in fair weather and foul, sharing the company of the democratic assortment of local tradesmen and other enthusiasts who also enjoyed the sport. As the pattern established itself, Nigel's passion for wildfowling was less than popular with May, who complained that she never saw him: he worked all week and disappeared to Aberlady Bay at the weekends, while she was stuck at home with the baby. It was one of the reasons they settled in Aberlady: at least the travelling time would now be spent at home.

Wildfowling was not a rich man's sport: once you had the gun and the dog, it was free, apart from the cartridges, and Tranter and his friends were exercising an age-old and hitherto unquestioned right. He had been introduced to the sport sometime in the 1930s by a family friend, Harry Brydon, who had a holiday house in Aberlady and had been shooting over Aberlady Bay since the 1880s. But the election of a reforming Labour government after the war brought that right into question with the introduction of a new National Parks and Access to the Countryside Act in 1949. This Act made possible the establishment of Local Nature Reserves to protect areas of special natural interest on account of their flora or fauna. Aberlady Bay and the stretch of coast immediately adjoining it were of special interest on both counts, but perhaps particularly so as the habitat or resting-place of a wide variety of seabirds and wildfowl and, in response to pressure, in particular from the local ornithological interest in Edinburgh, it was decided that Aberlady Bay would be constituted Scotland's first Local Nature Reserve. In August 1952, the usual notices were posted in the local press and on public notice-boards inviting a response, but none of the wildfowlers was contacted personally, they missed the notices and continued to shoot, under the impression that the whole idea was still no more than a gleam in the ornithologists' eye. They were wrong, and by the time they realised it, the

1500-acre Aberlady Bay Nature Reserve was a *fait accompli*, by-laws were in place, a Local Management Committee—on which they were not represented, not being at that stage an organised body—had been set up to manage the Bay, and, under the new by-laws, they were required to apply for permits to shoot which they believed were unlikely to be granted, or if granted, would be granted only on conditions that were unacceptable to them.

The general ban on shooting came into force in November 1952. If the ornithologists, of whose heightened activity in the Bay Tranter was already aware, were congratulating themselves on their victory, they mistook their man, for he already had a novel on the stocks, *Ducks and Drakes,* which described a similar dispute prudently, if improbably, set in Kintyre, and scheduled for seriali-sation, as it happened, in a widely-read family newspaper called *The Bulletin,* now defunct. In this novel the ornithologists were depicted as alternately figures of fun and menace.

When the seriousness of the threat to their interests finally dawned, Tranter the practised campaigner took prompt action. Overnight, he set up the East Lothian Wildfowlers Association, with 85 angry members and himself as President, and demanded a hearing. With his ready pen and flair for publicity, he was to prove a formidable opponent. He also had a useful pipeline to *The Scotsman* newspaper in the person of Wilfred Taylor, who knew a good story when he saw one. But the birdwatchers also had a ready pen in the person of the Revd. George Carse, an Edinburgh minister and dedicated ornithologist, who had been the driving force behind the establishment of the Aberlady Bay Local Nature Reserve. Between them the two men generated a white heat of passion seldom experienced in the staid pages of *The Scotsman*: in due course the affair proved a gift to the tabloids. In December 1952, the Reverend Mr Carse may be found writing in response to a letter from Tranter that "The establishment of a nature reserve is for the greater good of the community, which is infinitely more important than the alleged liberty of a few individuals to monopolise this area in pursuit of their own sectional interests." And in January 1953 Tranter hits back, "The impression to be gained of Aberlady Bay from the letters of certain of your correspondents is surely laughable in the extreme—something of a combination of Wild West show, abattoir and battlefield, with the cries of dying and distracted wildfowl drowned in the crash of discharging firearms and the shrill screams of frustrated bird-watchers . . . I could have wished that the wealth of material now available for my fantasy had been forthcoming before [when he was writing *Ducks and Drakes*]."

In the Aberlady Bay affair, the wildfowlers' opening shot was to demand a hearing before the East Lothian County Council and a place on the Management Committee, which would control the Nature Reserve and issue the permits to shoot. The ornithologists meanwhile were contending that the issue of permits to shoot was contrary to the meaning and purpose of the Act, which was to protect flora and fauna against molestation: there had been instances of indiscriminate shooting—strenuously denied by Tranter in respect of Aberlady Bay—and bird populations were at risk. Initially, Carse had the upper hand, since—although not a local resident, another vexed point—he had been appointed a member of the Management Committee. The Management Committee was dilatory in issuing permits and refused applications from outwith the County. Tranter immediately took up cudgels on behalf of shore-shooters from outside East Lothian as well, and widened the scope of the dispute by drawing attention to a potential threat to shooting elsewhere along the coast and on the Solway.

Initially, of course, few outside those immediately concerned were moved by the dispute, which looked to most ordinary citizens like a tussle between representatives of two vested interests, both out to defend privilege: the shore-shooters, who were identified—incorrectly, as it happened—with the landed gentry, and the ornithologists, whose activities were by and large incomprehensible and in any case irremediably identified—also incorrectly—with the middle class. It was only as the affair progressed from the wildfowlers' demand for a hearing before the County Council to identification of the legal point at issue that the affair began to assume a wider importance.

In Tranter's mind, it had begun as a simple issue of public rights, which were being denied. In publicity and political terms it was not an easy point to put across: nature reserves were new and fashionable and appeared at first glance to accord wider, not narrower, rights to the citizen. The moment lawyers were consulted, however, an altogether larger issue emerged. The denial of rights hinged on a difference between Scots Law and English Law. In drafting the United Kingdom Parliament Bill on National Parks and Access to the Countryside, the law-makers had failed to take account of a difference between Scots and English law with regard to ancient rights along the foreshore, and a difference, furthermore, in the definition of the foreshore. The Bill had become law and, in the first flush of enthusiasm for a new idea, was now being implemented in respect of Aberlady Bay without a cheep of protest being heard from anyone in Parliament, the Scottish Office or East Lothian County Council. The issue of disregard for or ignorance of Scots Law at Westminster was not new: in the early 1920s no less a figure than John Buchan MP was taking Parliament to task over the iniquitous practice of "tacking Scotland onto English measures in one or two interpretation clauses, which are usually obscure and sometimes quite impossible to construe."

Scots Law afforded citizens an inalienable right of recreation over the foreshore, which included the right to shoot wildfowl for recreational purposes: the foreshore was public property held in trust for the public by the Crown and these rights vested in the Crown could not be set aside by the new legislation. It appeared that Scots law furthermore defined the foreshore as the area between the low and high-water marks, unlike English Law which apparently used a median high-water mark definition, potentially an important difference in the case of the mud-flats and long shelving bays frequented by wildfowl. Tranter contacted Andrew Haddon, who obtained counsel's opinion on behalf of the wild-fowlers. Counsel's view was that the action of the East Lothian County Council in prohibiting shooting at Aberlady Bay was invalid and illegal, and their by-laws, insofar as they related to shooting and other recreation below the high-water mark, unenforceable. When this was put to the Council, the County Clerk, in his turn, sought counsel's opinion on behalf of the County, who opined that the Council had not exceeded its powers. The County Council therefore decided to make no change either in its policy or practice.

In summer 1953, Tranter might be found pontificating in the press against the "increasing wildness of [Carse's] averments and charges" and wondering "how anyone who does not claim to keep a 24-hour watch on my doings and who lives 17 miles away could have the effrontery [to suggest that when he claimed to be shooting in Aberlady Bay he was in fact shooting elsewhere]". The argument raged on all summer long without making any material progress, and as the new season approached with the matter still unresolved and no permits issued or applied for, Haddon advised that the best option open to the wildfowlers might be to provoke a test-case and so obtain a definitive ruling, and this they proceeded to do. That evening of 12 August 1953 Tranter and his two col-leagues were out to get themselves arrested, having duly alerted the Police and the press. Local bobby PC George Richardson was there with a colleague to represent the long arm of the law. The press, with its duffles and cameras and unsuitable footgear, was there to record the event. As light faded, they set off for the Bay. It fell to Alexander Barclay, an animal handler from Penicuik, to fire the first shot and he was duly charged with "molesting or wilfully disturbing birds in the Nature Reserve at Aberlady Bay, by firing a shot from a double-barrelled twelve-bore shotgun". Tranter himself went out again the following night, this time with a very reluctant Constable Richardson in attendance, to make doubly certain by getting himself arrested as well. But the charges were dropped after a fortnight. The wildfowlers continued to shoot. Somewhere along the line Tranter, who always had friends in high places and was not afraid to use them, obtained an informal view from the Secretary of State for Scotland which suggested that the ban on shooting was inoperable.

The matter could not however be left in limbo indefinitely and the Secretary of State ordered an official Inquiry, which opened in the Sheriff Court in Haddington on 8 November 1953 before Sir James Gilchrist QC, Sheriff-Principal of the Lothians and Peebles. Tranter and other wildfowlers were among those to give evidence, along with legal experts and representatives for the County Council and the ornithologists. Commenting on Carse's statement to the official Inquiry, Tranter came up with "Wildfowlers are also humane, it is not the preserve of the ornithologists, who consider it right to seek to take from others their lawful rights and liberties if they do not coincide with their own conception of what is proper. The protests . . . are slick propaganda. Hitler used almost identical arguments." In practical terms, the upshot of the inquiry was that the Secretary of State confirmed the by-laws made by the County Council and all references in the by-laws to the Crown's rights and trusteeship on behalf of the public were deleted.

When the new season opened, Barclay got himself arrested again and this time the case went to court. Haddon, who was still acting for the wildfowlers, obtained Counsel's opinion again, which suggested this time that costly litigation could be avoided by filing an "irrelevancy" plea, on grounds that the charge was invalid, as being wrong in law. The local Sheriff Substitute in Haddington dismissed the charge but cannily sought confirmation of his ruling by referring the whole matter to the High Court of Justiciary in Edinburgh as a Stated Case. When the High Court in due course pronounced, they delivered a majority judgement which over-ruled the Sheriff Substitute, ruling instead that the right to use foreshores for recreational purposes could be restricted or withdrawn under by-laws creating nature reserves. The wildfowlers had obtained their definitive ruling and it had gone against them. From now on, they would have to shoot within the restrictions imposed by the by-laws or not at all. Most of them continued to shoot. For Tranter's part, the battle with Carse was not however at an end. In 1956, with the Aberlady dispute long since over and done with, they were still at it hammer and tongs in connection with a similar dispute at Tyninghame, when Carse opened the batting with "It was too much to hope that Nigel Tranter would not intervene in the debate. . . . He certainly seems unable to keep to the point and his power of guessing seems to be little better than his sense of logic." The dialogue might have continued indefinitely if news-paper editors had not finally decided they had had enough and closed the correspondence.

By this time, the press had learned that Tranter could be relied upon to make waves. As the story of the Aberlady Bay dispute proves, one of the distinguishing features of the many campaigns he waged in the columns of the press was that sooner or later he could be guaranteed to use intemperate language, provide a sound-bite, come up with some remark that made headline material. He had of course many weapons in his verbal arsenal, and might start in "concerned citizen" mode, working his way up through "more in sorrow than in anger" and "yours indignantly" to a full-blown slanging match. For such a mild-mannered man, he has a remark-able capacity for invective. When challenged on this point, he says "I could see something needed to be done, and I got angry".

It all took up an unconscionable amount of time, however. At one time or another, in addition to writing letters for publication in the press, and often concurrently, Tranter was corresponding with the Scottish Office, the County Council, the Royal Society for the Protection of Birds, the Wildfowlers' Association of Great Britain and Ireland (surprisingly acrimonious, this, for the East Lothian Wildfowlers Association operated on a shoestring and did not think initially that affiliation was worth the candle: the WAGBI, for their part, thought the East Lothian Wildfowlers were parochial and free-loading, and said so), the Scottish Rights of Way Society, the Scottish Wildlife Trust, the Nature Conservancy, various landowners facing actual or threatened intrusions of a similar nature, representatives of other nature reserves and wildfowlers' associations, countless individual wildfowlers from all over the country (in particular, one from Cramond, to whom the supposedly skinflint East Lothian Wildfowlers lent financial assistance in fighting a court case, and others from Tyninghame and the Solway Firth), various solicitors (Haddon was acting for the Association, but there were other solicitors involved in other, parallel, cases), legal counsel, various interested organisations up and down the country looking for a speaker, and Gullane Golf Club, which complained that campers denied the right to camp in the Nature Reserve were now camping on their ground instead and claimed that "Nigel Tranter had told them it was all right ". When it was all over, he became an active member of the Management Committee and its Biological Sub-Committee, which met, for reasons unrecorded, in Edinburgh, interviewing applicants for the post of part-time warden in 1960 and being appointed a Voluntary Warden himself in 1970, with licence to kill carrion crows. He also found time for recreational shooting: after the permits were introduced, he regularly applied for, and received, permits to shoot mallard and widgeon, duly making the required returns showing the number of occasions on which he visited the Reserve to shoot, and the size of his bag. Philip featured for a couple of years in the returns made by permit-holders after he was old enough, but not as frequently as his father.

In 1952, 1953 and 1954, while all this was going on, Tranter managed to produce three Westerns, three modern adventure stories (one of which was *Ducks and Drakes*) and *The Queen's Grace*. *The Queen's Grace* is perhaps the first true historical novel and is worth a second look, not for that reason alone, but because it is a rare exploration by Tranter of the otherwise much-written-about Mary Queen of Scots. He has chosen, on the whole, to avoid her precisely because so much has been written by others and because there are so many preconceived ideas about her. *The Queen's Grace* deals with a period when Mary was virtually the prisoner of her half-brother James, Earl of Morton, and describes her visit to Aberdeen in 1562, where she gets caught up in the rivalry between Morton and the Gordon Earl of Huntly for domination of the kingdom. The hero is a junior scion of the house of Gordon, employed as a go-between (a typical Tranter device) who attracts the attention of the Queen and her tirewoman, Mary Mackintosh. Neither Patrick Gordon nor Mary Mackintosh are historical figures, but the book gives a vivid account of conflicting political and religious loyalties among the Aberdeen burgesses as well as the noble families, with an exciting escape from Aberdeen and a convincing account of Mary herself as beautiful, susceptible to male charms and more intelligent, with more potential as a ruler, than she is often given credit for. The plot describes an unfamiliar episode in Mary's life but its historicity is convincing, the plot dramatic and exciting, with the usual marathon cross-country rides, and the book successfully combines dramatic action, exploration of character, brutal reminders of a brutal age, including the grisly trial of Huntly's corpse in Edinburgh, and a convincing play of emotions in the love story between Patrick Gordon and Mary Mackintosh, without leaning too heavily on any of these elements.

XVIII

THE QUEEN'S FERRY

1953. The Queen's Ferry, established by Malcolm Canmore in the 11th century to carry his Queen, Margaret of Scotland, across to Fife to visit her fine new abbey at Dunfermline. Down the Hawes Brae and under the Bridge snakes the queue at the Edinburgh end: past the breaker's yard and down the hill snakes the queue at the Fife end. Twenty minutes, half an hour, an hour, an hour-and-a-half, the minutes tick slowly by as the cars inch painfully forward, drivers fuming at the delay. Under the great iron railway bridge the ferries ply busily back and forth, crammed to the gunwales. In the queue on the Fife side, Nigel and May, tired and hungry, with another hour's drive on the other side before they get home. With a woman's touching faith May turns to him and says "Nigel, you'll have to get something done about this." Or at least that's the way he remembers it.

Of course the story of the Forth Road Bridge was older than that. The first serious plan for a bridge had been put forward in 1817 by James Anderson, an Edinburgh engineer, who called it a project "of the greatest utility, indeed of the first national and commercial advantage". Nothing came of it. Before work started on the railway bridge in the 1880s there was talk of a combined road and rail bridge. But nothing came of that, either. It was the coming of the motor car into general use that began to bring matters to a head, and the Government ordered the first official survey in the 1920s. The matter progressed by slow degrees, and some wrangling over who would pay, to the point at which general agreement had been reached in 1935 on the site, and an application was made to the Government for funding. But by 1936, when the matter came up for final decision, government money was being committed to defence, not bridges, and the scheme fell into abeyance. A new road bridge was built upriver at Kincardine in 1935 to complement the ancient crossing at Stirling and this shortened somewhat the routes between Edinburgh and the North. But the return of private motoring after the War was accompanied by a huge increase in the car-owning classes and the effect was explosive, nowhere more so than at the Queensferry crossing. The 30-mile detour by Kincardine was not an attractive alternative, served as it was by narrow winding roads, and most people took a chance on the overcrowded ferries and lived to regret it. A new road bridge at the Queensferry crossing would shorten the distance between Edinburgh and the North very considerably and relieve the pressure on Fife, islanded in the new motoring age between two wide and unbridged estuaries, Forth and Tay. If it had been true in 1817 that a road bridge over the Firth of Forth was a matter of national importance, it was doubly so now. Bridging the Forth however called for major public investment, for Forth was wide and deep and the approach roads would have to be built high, over rocky terrain. The bridge would furthermore have to be high enough to allow the passage of big ships going up and down to the naval base at Rosyth and the oil refinery at Grangemouth. The bulk of the money would have to come out of public funds but the Government was being dilatory. In fact, however, the legislation was already in place. The Forth Road Bridge Act had passed into law in 1946, immediately after the War. The estimated cost at that time was £4.5m. The Forth Road Bridge Joint Board had been set up in 1947 to administer the bridge, and preparatory work, which had begun in 1948, had progressed to the point at which the Board was ready to award contracts when, out of the blue, the Minister of Transport announced in 1953 that he could not approve the £200,000 needed to finance ongoing preparatory work, and the entire project ground to a halt.

In the absence of any official lead in what was now a matter of some urgency, popular frustration was palpable. As Vice-Convener of the Scottish Covenant Association, Tranter had the means at hand to act, and in July 1953, at the height of the holiday season, he hosted a crowded protest meeting in the Central Hall at Tollcross in Edinburgh. Letters went out to the Scottish MPs inviting them to attend: only one did, but there were messages of support from several others. The platform speakers however included representatives of a wide variety of interests and Dr Nina McLardy, a Pumpherston GP and a member of the West Lothian County Council, enjoyed a brief moment of fame with her story of an ambulance with a seriously ill miner stuck for a couple of hours in the ferry queue. The campaign followed a now familiar pattern: the Covenant Association acted as facilitator by providing the venue and offering an opportunity to mobilise cross party opinion on a burning issue not being sympathetically addressed at Westminster. The Provost of South Queensferry, one of the two local authorities immediately affected, chaired the meeting. As a matter of policy, Tranter did not himself speak, but his energy and his reputation as a seasoned campaigner impressed and when the inevitable *ad hoc* committee was set up he emerged as chairman. There was a general feeling that if anyone could stir things up and get something done, it was Tranter. The National Forth Road Bridge Committee was formally constituted in December 1953 with Tranter as chairman and Sir Andrew Murray, a former Lord Provost of Edinburgh, and Provost J A Lawson of the little burgh of South Queensferry as a pair of very active deputies. Between them they represented the big guns and the little men. The position of the various Edinburgh Provosts was to prove anomalous: as Lord Provost each of them in turn was an *ex officio* member of the Joint Board, a statutory body with a strictly limited remit, which was much misunderstood but tended to hamstring any Lord Provost currently in office. In addition, the office changed hands a couple of times and the politics changed with it. The appointment of a former Lord Provost to the National Committee was thus the best option open in the circumstances to represent Edinburgh opinion and Sir Andrew Murray, after campaigning on behalf of the bridge for the past thirty years, was an energetic, vocal and committed deputy as was Provost Lawson.

Whitehall's contribution continued to be insensitive, to say the least. There was at this time no block vote for the Scottish Office from Parliament and priorities were set in London. In October 1953, the Minister of Transport announced the appointment of a board of civil engineers to consider proposals for a road bridge superimposed over the present railway bridge, an option long since rejected, and in November the Minister told Sir Will Y Darling, a local Edinburgh MP, in a written reply to a parliamentary question, that various other roadworks in Scotland such as the Whiteinch tunnel under the Clyde and the widening of the Glasgow-Stirling road would have priority over a bridge over the Forth. The fact that the Minister's reply was wrapped up in references to lack of materials and lack of labour as well as lack of money did nothing to ameliorate matters. But when it was announced in December that work would go ahead on the Severn Bridge, it was the last straw, and the mood in the queues turned angry. It was clear that the money was there, but the Government had chosen to put it into the Severn Bridge instead of fulfilling the earlier commitment to a bridge over the Forth. In February 1954, the Minister added insult to injury by telling a Scottish delegation that the less noise Scottish campaigners made about the Forth

Road Bridge the sooner they would get it. (Reading between the lines, it seems likely that Tranter was among those present.)

With hindsight, the need for a road bridge seems self-evident, of obvious benefit to the entire community right up and down the eastern half of Scotland. But in fact it did not have universal support at the time, and this of course did not help. Local authorities on the north side of Forth close to the Bridge worried about the effect on trade, as shoppers defected to Edinburgh. Others worried about being swallowed up by approach roads. Landowners were unwilling to see their estates bisected: those who owned chunks of local communities north of Forth saw rent income falling. Chambers of Commerce were enthusiastic in direct ratio to their distance from the Bridge. The motoring public of course were all for it, provided they were not opposed as shop-keepers or householders who feared the approach roads would pass right over their houses or swamp their villages: as might have been expected, although the term had not yet been invented, there was an element of "Not in My Backyard" at work.

As far as Nigel Tranter was concerned it was to be far and away his most demanding challenge. In the first place, there was the cost: originally projected at £4.5m, it had escalated to an estimated £14.3m by the time work started and by the time it was finished the price-tag read £20m. The cost of the campaign was higher too, and fund-raising rapidly became a top priority: an office had to be staffed, printing costs had to be met for pamphlets and posters, halls had to be hired, the two ex-servicemen hired to thrust leaflets through car windows in the ferry queues had to be paid. The cost to Tranter himself in time was to be immeasurable. And this time he was tangling with Whitehall, not isolated MPs. The first step was to get a fighting fund established on a sound basis, and an approach was made to local authorities, with mixed success. At one stage, Glasgow, which had got the go-ahead for its tunnel and its roadworks, had contributed money, with various small communities and odd members of the public, but the City of Edinburgh had not. But one of Tranter's qualities as a campaigner is never to give up, and he meant to get everyone involved. The collecting-boxes went out in the Edinburgh shops so that, as he put it, "people can put in a sixpence or a shilling and feel they have a greater stake in the Bridge". And he set out once more on the campaign trail, eating up the miles to speak at public meetings all over the East Coast. He even made sorties to London in search of support from the British Roads Federation, whom he startled with some impassioned advice: "Don't be overawed by these wretched politicians . . . they don't like trouble so give them trouble. . . . The way to get things done is to badger and bombard, harry, harangue and harass . . ." His own technique, exactly.

But the Government still had no intention of giving way. In November 1954, Sir Will Y Darling put up a proposal for financing the Bridge out of private capital—a proposal to which Tranter was in principle opposed—and the Government, which had hitherto pleaded poverty as its primary excuse for doing nothing, turned wary but indicated it might consider it. Tranter's comment to the press was that if this was the only way to get the bridge it was better to have it this way than not at all, but hammered home yet again the point that it had already been approved. The refusal to vote funds was the Treasury going against the express will of Parliament.

In early 1955, the Ministry of Transport announced that a start would be made on a crossing within the next four years but took the gilt off the gingerbread with the news that it would be conducting an inquiry into the possibility of laying a "tube" or tunnel along the sea-bed: the comparative price-tags were now understood to be £5.5 m for the "tube" and £15 m for the bridge. Tranter was not convinced and told the press, "The Committee have grave doubts whether one or other form of crossing is indeed assured within the next four years. The Committee intend to maintain pressure for an early decision on bridge or tube and an immediate start thereafter." A few weeks later he was telling a meeting in Kirkcaldy "It is quite unrealistic that Scotland should have to wait four years for a start on the Forth crossing. . . . We are not paupers in Scotland. We pay our full share of taxation and are entitled to the facilities of 20th-century transport." The "tube" idea was widely regarded as yet another delaying tactic, and was dropped the following year, following advice from yet another panel of experts. In November, the Government announced concrete plans for funding: £4.65m from public funds, £500,000 from the local authorities and the balance to be paid for out of revenue from tolls. In 1957, the Secretary of State for Scotland at last announced a firm date: work would start in the summer of 1958. It had taken, in Tranter's own words, "four years to gain the day, years of meetings, rallies, letters to editors, agitations, with not a few dignified toes trampled upon". By rights, the campaign should have been at an end. But he continued to fight a running battle on the toll charges which he believed to be inequitable. The Bridge formed part of the national road network and if there were no tolls on motorways, there should be no tolls on the Bridge. But this part of the campaign he lost: motors crossing the Bridge are still, theoretically at least, making their contribution to the capital costs a generation on.

As a self-employed person, the huge amount of time he sacrificed to the Forth Road Bridge campaign was taken directly from his livelihood. As his friend Wilfred Taylor pointed out in his 'Log' on 25 November 1958, he had devoted an enormous amount of energy to the publicity campaign on behalf of the Bridge, all done "at the expense of time which otherwise he would happily have devoted to earning his living". Taylor went on, "We have no doubt whatsoever that the fact that work on the bridge has now started was partly due to the vigorous action taken by him and his committee." Why did he do it? The grudging would have said self-aggrandisement or an inability to say No. But the truth was much simpler: in his own words, he saw something needed to be done. Why was Taylor writing about him in November 1958? Because the Secretary of State for Scotland had just opened the steam valve that drove the first pile and Tranter was not among the distinguished guests present for the event: official bodies, as Taylor pointed out, regard people like Nigel Tranter as infernal nuisances and tend to treat them accordingly.

XIX

PERMANENT LINK

A slender spider's web structure, two towering piers linked to land and to each other by wire cables spun on site. No carriageway yet, only a workmen's walkway that follows the cables, swinging and swaying in the wind, 512 ft above the Firth at the highest point. Struggling up it, hanging on like grim death, two distinguished visitors are conducting their own, private inauguration of the Bridge. Willie Merrilees, Chief Constable of Edinburgh and Lothian, and Nigel Tranter, chairman of the National Forth Road Bridge Committee. Far below in the car park waits May, trying not to think about it.

There are many structures scattered across Scotland, mainly little castles rescued and brought back to life, that owe something to Nigel Tranter, but surely none grander than the Forth Road Bridge. Not that he built it, or designed it, or in the last resort, got it built. But he did perhaps get it built a little earlier than might otherwise have been the case, and his name was associated with it in the public mind. And he took a justifiable pride and personal interest in it, so that when Willie Merrilees, Chief Constable of Edinburgh and Lothian, and a fellow Knight of St Lazarus, offered to arrange for him to make an early crossing on the walkway used by the workmen, before the carriageway was constructed, he accepted with the liveliest anticipation. It was fortunate that neither of them suffered from vertigo, for it was not for the foolhardy, and neither of them was a young man any more. However, they struggled on and were rewarded with an experience few, apart from professional construction workers, have shared. As for Nigel, with all his experience of hill walking and his extraordinary gift for translating maps into a bird's-eye view, he was closer here to the experience of the bird than perhaps on any other occasion in his entire life. May was right to try and think of something else down there in the car park for it was a dangerous crossing: the Bridge claimed six lives before it was finished.

It took six years to complete and throughout that time Tranter continued to hammer away at the vexed issue of tolls, but without winning the day. It kept his name in the columns of the public press, however, and memories were long. In the event, it was fortuitous that Merrilees had arranged his own private inauguration, for when the time came for the official opening by Her Majesty the Queen in September 1964, the invitations went out in the name of the Lords Lieutenant of the neighbouring counties and there was no invitation for Nigel Tranter. If it was an oversight, it was disgraceful: if it was deliberate, even more so. Presumably it was the price paid for harrying, haranguing and harassing authority. But it did not go unnoticed, for when the press rang up to ask the favour of an interview at the opening and he said he wasn't going, the cat was out of the bag and one journalist had the bright idea of interviewing him as he sat alone at home, watching the event on TV. It made an unforgettable picture.

With all the calls on his time, there had been little opportunity to settle down to more serious writing, and although the books continued to pour out, the works he published in the mid 1950s tell their own tale. In 1954, *Rum Week,* a skit on Skye Week, *The Night Riders,* a less convincing follow-up to *Cheviot Chase,* with its cattle raids and stampedes, and described by himself as "a kind of home-grown Western", and a regular Western called *Cloven Hooves*; in 1955, a Western called *Dynamite Trail*, and *Rio d'Oro* and *There are Worse Jungles*, two books inspired by the exploits of the explorer Col P H Fawcett, who disappeared on an expedition up the Amazon in 1925 and whose fate much exercised his contemporaries; in 1956, *The Long Coffin*, another book inspired by the Fawcett story, and a Western called *Rancher Renegade*; at the beginning of 1957, another Western called *Trailing Trouble*. Only then do we find a more serious work, *MacGregor's Gathering*, the first book of the *MacGregor* trilogy, which he had had at the back of his mind for some years. He had managed to keep the flow of writing going through the early, more demanding period of the Road Bridge campaign, but at the expense, at times, of quality.

If *The Night Riders* was a kind of home-grown Western, the *MacGregor* trilogy also made good use of experience derived from the Westerns, for the MacGregors' business was cattle and the tribute in cattle they collected in return for the protection provided by the Highland Watch, and they well knew how to deploy a stampede to advantage against Government troops. In *MacGregor's Gathering* he describes one of the most memorable, that which takes place at the Town Cross in Crieff, when a Redcoat sergeant sees "coming charging and careering down the hill . . . a great mass of cattle, filling every inch of the street. . . . Tight-packed, heads down and tails up, bellowing their alarm, horns clashing, hooves thundering, they came in a crazy stampede under a cloud of steam . . ." The main theme of the trilogy is of course MacGregor support for the Jacobite cause from the aborted Rising of 1708 on, but the basis of their influence exerted through the Watch is never lost sight of, and their skills with cattle and horseflesh constantly reiterated. We first see Glengyle himself, Rob Roy's nephew and co-hero of the books, on duty collecting tribute on his uncle's behalf at the cattle-market in Drymen, and he gains his spurs in an epic—and comic—tussle with the White Bull of Gallangad. The trilogy, which probably wasn't envisaged as a trilogy when the first book was written, follows the fortunes of the MacGregors, uncle and nephew, landless and outlawed from 1715 on for their support for the Jacobite cause, right through to the final stages of Charles Edward's flight in 1746, when the promised French gold arrives too late, and sets out to present them in a more heroic mould than that popularised by Walter Scott, who also wrote memorably about Rob Roy. In his foreword to *MacGregor's Gathering* Tranter writes of the problems involved in portraying a character of whom so many legends have been told, and says, "I have sought to cull, from the mass of lore and legend and history, such incidents as seem to me to present a recognisable and fairly consistent picture . . . not hesitating to invent wholly imaginary incidents and individuals. . . . Much herein, therefore, is no more than a product of my fancy—but I have sought to keep the background of the times as accurate as I know how, and not to traduce any historical character unduly." Although the mix of fact and fiction would alter, this was to be his policy in dealing with historical characters henceforward: to present portraits that were recognisable and consistent and not to traduce unduly.

As far as Rob Roy himself was concerned, Tranter was convinced that he had been much maligned by Scott, who allows him few heroic qualities either in the introduction to *Rob Roy* or in *Tales of a Grandfather*. The difference between Scott's version and Tranter's touches on the role of the Watch in keeping the peace, which is difficult to prove, and on the subsequent fate of Prince Charlie's gold, also difficult to prove, but hinges mainly on the reasons for Rob Roy's late arrival with his force at the Battle of Sheriffmuir and subsequent refusal to fight. In 1965, three years after completion of the trilogy, he published a short polemic, *Outlaw of the Highlands: Rob Roy MacGregor* in which he set out his case. This little book, in effect a mixture of argument and historical fact, with a novelistic opening, produces evidence in support of the view that Rob Roy and his force had been delayed on a secret mission to guide a Highland force across the Fords of Frew, one of their areas of expertise, and that by the time they arrived on the field, the outcome of the battle had been decided and commitment of the MacGregors would have been suicidal. He has some good points to make about this and other incidents in Rob Roy's career, but is perhaps tempted too often to make the kind of sweeping statements he so objects to in Scott.

Taking on Sir Walter Scott on Rob Roy was not to be done lightly, for Scott is widely acknowledged farther afield than Scotland to be the father of the historical novel. While admiring Scott as a writer and propagandist for Scotland, Tranter does not greatly admire him as a storyteller. This is because he is too easily distracted, in Tranter's view, by intellectual argument and development of minor invented figures, which get in the way of the action: he is, in a word, too wordy. This is of course to miss the point about Scott, for it is in the movement back and forth between causes and characters, the one illuminating the other, the vivid insights we are given into co-existing worlds, the uncertainty we experience about the outcome, about which side, which philosophy, will prevail, that the interest lies. The minor characters are the ones we remember, and it is through the interplay of different ideas that we get the flavour of the age. But Scott and Tranter see history differently and are setting out to do two different things: Tranter is primarily concerned to record events, produce the necessary links between them and bring to life the characters involved, whereas Scott is more interested in looking at and recording social change and using his characters mainly towards that end.

Like the *MacGregor* trilogy, the *Master of Gray* trilogy, published 1961–1965, is firmly labelled "mere fiction" by its author in his foreword. The great bulk of the characters, including the Master of

Gray himself, the Duke of Lennox, Morton, Esmé Stuart and of course King James VI & I are all nevertheless historical characters. An aura of mystery however surrounds all Patrick Gray's doings and this allows the novelist plentiful scope for his imagination. In the foreword, Tranter asks the question "Was he the devil incarnate?" and it is his art not to give us an answer. Clever, cunning, slipping in and out of countries and courts, exulting in his talents, not to be trusted with women or money, the Master of Gray is something between a secret negotiator and a spy, taking to himself wide powers to make deals. Devilishly clever, and devilishly attractive, we are left with a vivid sense that the Master's machinations and comings and goings were an unsolved mystery to his contemporaries and remain so to us: he is ultimately less glamorous and much more untrustworthy than many similar heroes—a Bond, perhaps, or a Francis Crawford, but perhaps more realistic, as is only appropriate.

The historical events apart, the *Master of Gray* books are yet another stepping-stone on the way to the *Bruce*, still more of a romance than a history. But here we have for the first time the classic Tranter "reporter" in the person of the Master's illegitimate half-brother David, the two brought up together and yet of different station, the Master assuming a natural superiority, and riding roughshod over his half-brother when it suits him, David Gray remaining nevertheless his own man, the more admirable, if less dazzling, of the two. David is not however the only noble by-blow to play a central role in the story for the Master's own daughter Mary is also destined to spend a lifetime tucked away in the closet as the enduring love, but not the wife, of Ludovick, Duke of Lennox. These relationships between half-brothers—illegitimate offspring brought up in the vicinity of noble houses but not of them, centrally placed but without status until it is conferred by their own talents—and the recognised but not legitimised long-term partnerships between men and women, which were the by-product of the need to make dynastic marriages, clearly fascinate Tranter who had half-siblings of his own, and who had tales in his own family of noble blood inherited on the wrong side of the blanket: they appear again and again throughout the books. Many other historical novelists get round the problem of providing insights into historic events by using the first person, telling their central character's story from the inside, often in old age, but Tranter found the mode of reporter served him well and stuck to it.

XX

BRIDAL PATH

Easdale, Argyll, September 1958. Cameras, caravans, camera-tracks, a chuck-wagon, make-up vans, canvas director's chairs rocking crazily on the tussocky grass. Never before has the village postmistress handled so many trunk-calls. But the sun shines on and a picnic mood prevails, with none of the usual flashes of hysteria. Having got themselves here, the London contingent intend to enjoy themselves. Frank Launder's Bentley has been blocking the road for hours but no one has felt the need to get by. The star is stretched out reading Time *magazine, there is some kind of not very urgent flap on about Mrs MacAllister and her goat, the child actors are running riot all over the place and the tiniest one is feeding fried sausages to her pony. The author is a little way off, conferring with the female lead about the script—or so he says. Tonight they will be reconvening in the village hall, where the usual hard core of card-players will find themselves buffeted alarmingly by unruly attempts at an eightsome whenever the scratched record can be persuaded into action. Clearly, the soft Highland air has got to them all.*

There was a welcome diversion in 1958, when British Lion decided to make the ten-year-old *Bridal Path* into a film. Following the great success of *Geordie* some three years earlier, there was pressure to make more films on location in Scotland, particularly from the Films of Scotland Committee, which came up with the idea that *Bridal Path*, a lighthearted romance about an islander who sets out to find himself a wife on the mainland, and ends up marrying the girl back home after all, might prove a worthy successor, particularly if Bill Travers, who had had such a success as Geordie, could be persuaded to play the lead. The part called for good looks and a fine hand with light comedy, both of which Travers possessed in good measure, and he was easily recruited. A strong cast of character actors who were later to make names for themselves as the stars of long-running TV series and a fine array of pretty girls made up the rest of the company, with local talent providing the extras. It was, furthermore, a Launder and Gilliat film, which guaranteed quality. The film was made on location in and around Oban, Easdale and Appin, and Nigel entered thoroughly into the spirit of the thing, even emulating Hitchcock and, closer to home perhaps, Compton Mackenzie, in trying to infiltrate himself into the finished result in a walk-on part. Fortunately for his fans, a budding film career came to an abrupt end on the cutting-room floor: much to his relief, for he had seen the rushes.

His family came up for a couple of days to join in the fun and enjoyed themselves greatly, although Nigel drew the line at allowing them to queue up for their money as extras, decreeing that this was beneath his dignity as author. And Wilfred Taylor came too, treating the readers of 'A Scotsman's Log' to a blow-by-blow account for three days in a row, from which one of the more unexpected details to emerge was the fact that the weather was so fine they had the Paisley Fire Brigade standing by with their hoses to provide rain. The making of such a film in Scotland attracted enormous publicity, as *Geordie* had done before it, and Nigel managed to insist that the world premiere be held in Edinburgh, so that Scotland got maximum mileage out of it all over again. It was a charity premiere with a prestigious guest-list of sponsors and celebrities. Nigel and May of course attended but, mysteriously, found they had to pay for their own tickets; otherwise they enjoyed their evening. The script was well done, and the finished film funny, innocent and idyllic, set against stunning scenery.

Naturally, they hoped that in course of time another book would catch a film-maker's attention. But time was running out for lighthearted romances set against Highland hills, and the Swinging Sixties, Bond and the Caribbean lay ahead. When Tranter turned to historical novels, although options were taken on the *Bruce* trilogy and *The Wallace* and treatments for films and stage plays were done of *Bruce* and *The Stone* and *The Wisest Fool*, nothing ever materialised. It's difficult to prove rights in history. And when *Braveheart* was eventually made, it was light years away from anything he would have approved. He did however agree to unveil the Stirling Wallace statue modelled on Mel Gibson, the *Braveheart* star.

In the meantime there had been developments on the matrimonial front at home. Philip was the only consistent diarist in the family and it is in Philip's diary for June 1956, when Frances May was just 20, that Robert Baker, the young naval officer she was to marry, first makes an appearance in the Tranter family annals. It was the usual strenuous family outing, a camping weekend on Loch Rannoch, but, perhaps as a concession to the newcomer, an unusual amount seems to have been done by car. Not, of course, over easy, tarmacadamed roads; and Philip records in his diary struggling up what was "little more than a hill path" in a pretty little glen until Robert's little car gave up. It was not the standard way of spending time together with the family of the girl you hope to marry, but perhaps as good a try-out as any. At any rate he seems to have persevered and forty years, four children and eight grandchildren later, he's still there. In any case, Rob Baker, who came of farming stock, reverted happily to being a countryman too after he came ashore for good.

They were married in August 1959 and after a preliminary

hiccup when Rob was posted temporarily to Devonport and then Elgin pending a sea-going assignment with a new squadron (he was an air engineer officer), and Frances May came back home to stay with her parents for a few months, they spent the next ten years in Cheriton in Hampshire, and it was here that their four children were born and the older ones started school. She chose to have her babies at home, and May went down for the births, accompanied on at least a couple of occasions by Nigel. Curiously, Nigel, who does not blench at the facts of life and death in his books, turned queasy, and said "Never again": his own babies had been born in nursing-homes decently out of sight and sound. He relented however and the older children remember him reading to an inattentive audience behind a firmly-closed dining-room door as they listened for the new baby's first cry. In due course, threatened in 1977 with a desk job, Rob opted for early retirement and they moved back to Scotland, eventually settling in the old manse in Athelstaneford, which greatly pleased Frances May's parents. In the event, it proved fortuitous, for when May became ill, Frances May was close enough to keep the household turning over, and after she died, keep an eye on Nigel. When Rob retired from a second career in business, they moved to the Borders as they had always planned.

XXI

THE SALMON WAR

Eyemouth, Berwickshire, 31 August 1961. A crowded and angry meeting, hurriedly called, 200 attending. On the platform, holding forth, Nigel Tranter, hero of Aberlady Bay, author of Kettle of Fish, *and chairman of the East Lothian and Berwickshire Liberal Association. In the hall, the massed fishing communities of Berwickshire and East Lothian, the press, an assortment of local politicians, the local MP and a representative from England. The air is heavy with the "strong and virile aroma of fish, tarred rope and black twist tobacco" he describes in* Kettle of Fish. *The meeting has been called to see justice done in the inflamed dispute over the drift-netting of salmon off the mouth of the Tweed, and Tranter is discoursing on the differences between Scots law and English law, the Law of the Sea, the injustices of the Tweed Act of 1857 (here at least they are right there with him), the value of test cases and Clause Twelve of the 1707 Treaty of Union. Their minds are on the risk of nets, catches and even boats being confiscated. As might have been anticipated, they are going to a) call for a public inquiry, b) set up a Fighting Fund and c) elect a Committee. As might have been anticipated, Tranter will be on the Committee.*

Berwick-upon-Tweed is an anomaly, an English burgh whose county lies in Scotland. The port through which most of the lucrative Lammermuir wool trade passed on its way to the Low Countries, it first acquired political prominence in the 13th century when the border between England and Scotland was fixed along the line of the Tweed, on whose north bank it lies. From then on, it changed hands regularly for over a century, sacked by Edward I in 1296, besieged by Wallace in 1297, taken by Bruce in 1318, retaken by Edward III in 1333, and resettled from England. It ceased to be a Scottish royal burgh in 1338, and it was finally ceded to England in 1482. Since that date, it has been essentially an English frontier town. Edward VI and Mary Queen of Scots agreed in 1551 that it should thenceforth be *sui generis*, independent of both states, and for some centuries it did indeed feature independently in treaties between the two and in treaties with third countries. Remote from other population centres on both sides of the Border, it still retains the air of an independent outpost. In the 20th century, under the influence of growing nationalism in Scotland, there were occasional flurries of interest in having it returned to Scotland and in these Tranter of course took an interest. In 1963 there was trouble when it set about having its armorial bearings properly registered and approved. Garter King of Arms, the competent authority in England, would not grant arms featuring Berwick's traditional witch-elm and bear badge. They therefore applied to Lyon King of Arms in Edinburgh, who had been responsible for approving arms for Berwick as a Scottish burgh centuries before. Lyon King of Arms approved a grant of arms, with bear supporters, whereupon Garter King complained that the 1707 Treaty of Union had laid down that the two courts would have exclusive jurisdiction, each within its own country, and Lyon King of Arms was out of order. Berwick nevertheless had the grant of arms it was after and proceeded to use its Scottish armorial bearings.

Hot on the heels of this somewhat abstruse quarrel an altogether more serious dispute blew up over salmon-fishing rights off the mouth of the River Tweed, which were regulated under an arcane piece of legislation known as the Tweed Act of 1857. River, estuary and inshore fishermen on both sides of Tweed were affected, and Tranter could see a potential plot for a novel as well as a thorny problem that needed unravelling. As the Covenant Association dwindled and died, Tranter had thrown in his lot with the Liberal party, the only one of the Scottish parties to support wholeheartedly a measure of self-government for Scotland within the Union, and he served from 1960–1970 as chairman of the East Lothian and Berwickshire Liberal Association. As this area included the fishing ports of Dunbar, Eyemouth and Burnmouth, he had a certain tenuous status in the drift-netting affair.

The trouble had been escalating for the past eighteen months or so, and had several causes, the most important of which were the long-term decline in the herring fishing, the increased commercialisation of the fishing industry in general, and the shortage of white fish. Herring had been the staple of the Scottish fishing industry in the 19th century and fishing communities were still dimensioned accordingly, with harbours designed to accommodate the huge fleets that followed the shoals round the coast. By the time the shoals dwindled and moved away, time was also beginning to run out for the little three- and four-man drifters for other reasons: boats were getting bigger and after the War the competition from the big deep-sea boats with their refrigerated holds began to threaten the existence of the small inshore operators. At the same time, a simpler technical development was working to their advantage, for the coming of nylon ropes altered the weight ratio of nets and tackle relative to their capacity. These various factors meant that skippers of smaller, usually family-owned, boats were looking around for new fishing grounds and had the capacity to contemplate potential new catches.

Salmon is a game fish in which the Crown takes an interest and the fishing of salmon round Britain's coasts has been regulated for centuries. When this dispute blew up, salmon could be fished relatively freely under Scots law to within one mile of the low-water mark: inside that limit fishing rights were firmly vested in the Crown and a licence was required. Under English law, salmon could be fished freely to within three miles of the low-water mark. The limit of territorial waters was set at three miles, applicable in both countries.

The situation was complicated in the vicinity of Berwick by special legislation which regulated the fishing of salmon round the mouth of the Tweed, Scotland's salmon river above all others, ostensibly to protect salmon stocks. The Tweed Act of 1857, drawn up under totally different conditions from those which now prevailed, defined the mouth of the Tweed as extending five miles up and down the coast from the point at which it exited to the sea, and another ten miles out to sea, and was designed to protect river fishing: fishing for salmon within the mouth of the Tweed, as defined in the Act, was prohibited. The Act also classified the Tweed as a Scots river for the purposes of the law. When the fishermen at Seahouses on the Northumbrian coast cast around for a means of increasing their takings by netting salmon—at that time, before the farming of salmon, a most valuable catch—they were confronted with an anomaly. The Tweed Act debarred them from fishing, save by permission of the Tweed Commissioners, inside a ten-mile limit off the mouth of the Tweed whereas, under the legislation defining the territorial limit, foreign boats could fish up to a three-mile limit. When they challenged this in a practical way by shooting their nets inside the ten-mile limit, they faced prosecution and confiscation of their gear. The Scottish boats had been slower to adapt to the new conditions, but when they did, they faced a similar problem in respect of fishing off the mouth of the Tweed, but with the added difficulty that whereas the Northumbrian fisherman had a possible defence against confiscation or arrest other than on the high seas, since Scots law could not be applied on English soil, the Scottish fishermen were at risk whether they were at sea or in port. In fact, token boats were placed under arrest in the harbours of Burnmouth on the Scottish side and Seahouses on the English side of Tweed in January 1961, but later released. The fishermen reacted angrily on both sides of the border, took legal advice, and set up committees and fighting funds A debate was provoked in the House of Lords which, not unexpectedly, favoured the landowners' case and was described by Tranter in a letter to *The Scotsman* as "disgraceful". He also pledged the East Lothian and Berwickshire Liberals—without consulting them—to support for the Eyemouth fishermen, thus provoking one or two resignations. In committing them, he accused the Secretary of State for Scotland of "bowing to vested interests" in introducing a Bill to make all drift-netting for salmon at sea illegal.

It is relevant to the whole story to know that the Tweed Commissioners charged with the administration of the regime were all owners of salmon fishing beats upriver valued at £400 or more and that the Tweed Commissioners owned and operated a thriving river netting business of their own at Berwick, inside the area defined by the Tweed Act. Claims that the special legislation regarding fishing limits was designed to protect salmon stocks therefore met with little sympathy, but were nevertheless jealously pursued. To enable them better to police implementation of the legislation, the Tweed Commissioners had furthermore recently purchased a fast launch, formerly the property of Adolf Hitler and now surplus to requirements. It was difficult to know whether to laugh or to cry. But arrest of fishing boats on the high seas and confiscation of catches and gear were no laughing matter. The Seahouses fishermen organised a Petition to Parliament without effect.

With his usual sharp nose for an upcoming story with a potential for drama and skulduggery, Tranter took an interest in the affair from the outset. He was in contact with the fishermen's representatives in Seahouses from an early stage and from the moment he joined the Eyemouth committee he was actively engaged in laying up tactics and publicising their case through the columns of the daily press. Remembering the Aberlady Bay affair, which had also hinged on neglect by Westminster of differences between Scots and English law, he could see that there was an opportunity here to employ a similar approach in the case of the salmon fishing. Forcing a test case had produced clarification at Aberlady Bay, and might do so in the Salmon War. He also saw the potential for publicising what he regarded as a major scandal through the medium of a novel. Keeping a close eye on the development of events, he therefore set about writing a book, which he called *Kettle of Fish*. To his regret, the news about the purchase of Hitler's cast-off launch came too late to go in. In *Kettle of Fish*, the fishermen of a fictitious community just inside the English border north of Berwick—an ingenious idea which enabled him to emphasise that they were in fact Scots but living under English law—shoot their nets for salmon openly and consistently inside the ten-mile limit and charges are brought.

As in the Aberlady Bay case, one of the points of interest to Tranter was that the legislation concerned, in this case the Tweed Act of 1857, had to be applied under Scots law. The Scottish legal system was guaranteed "for all time coming" under Clause Twelve of the 1707 Treaty of Union, and Scots law holds that certain ancient rights, including the right to fish salmon up to the legal limit, cannot be abrogated by Westminster statute. These basic rules had been set aside by a superior (Scots) court in the Aberlady Bay dispute, but *Kettle of Fish* was fiction and might be resolved differently. Transfer of the Aberlady tactics of forcing a test case in the real-life Salmon War was however an altogether more serious and potentially dangerous affair, with all action liable to be transferred to the high seas and the Fishery Protection vessels of the Royal Navy involved. Some of Tranter's verbal interventions were furthermore downright inflammatory, for he is not always circumspect, and some snippets were a gift to the press and endlessly recycled: in a letter to *The Scotsman* on 30 May 1960, for example, he described the Tweed Act as "very one-sided and pro-landlord" and in another on 4 August 1961, he again accused the Secretary of State for Scotland of "bowing to the clamour of vested interests in one of the most one-sided and trumped-up agitations of recent times" in upholding the Act. The choice of language immediately suggested extremist politics.

In the meantime, all tactical considerations forgotten, a Scottish skipper from Eyemouth jumped the gun and was caught drift-netting for salmon three weeks ahead of the opening of the season. *Kettle of Fish* was written, but not published, just before matters came to a head and the case came to court, which should have been an adequate defence against any charge of incitement. But Tranter had been an interested and active adviser on tactics, a prolific writer of letters to the press, and his fine Italian hand was suspected behind the bombardment of letters issuing from the fishermen themselves. Since it had seemed like a telling point, he had furthermore introduced the spectre of Iceland, with whom Britain had been waging a cod war: what if the Iceland skippers decided to come and fish inside the Tweed Commissioners' precious ten-mile limit? It would have been strange indeed if none of the members of the Tweed Commission or their representatives had seen his involvement as gratuitous interference in an arrangement which had worked well for over a century and had never been questioned before. It appeared, furthermore, that one of the landowners involved was the Earl of Home, to whom it must have been a particular irritant, all personal considerations apart, supposing he had time to focus on it at all, for he was now Her Majesty's Principal Secretary of State for Foreign and Commonwealth Affairs, responsible *inter alia* for relations with

Iceland, and one of the fattest dossiers currently on his desk concerned the ongoing 2nd UN International Conference on the Law of the Sea, which it was hoped, in vain as it turned out, would settle once and for all the vexed question of international territorial limits.

Ward Lock & Co, Tranter's publishers at the time, were sufficiently alarmed to consider delaying publication of *Kettle of Fish* in order to guard against a *sub judice* prosecution but eventually decided to go ahead; however the *Daily Mail*, which had planned serialisation, got cold feet and withdrew from the deal. It was the closest he came to real trouble over the content of a book. But it was not the only book that could have been construed as inflammatory, for *The Chosen Course*, which appeared to condone blowing up hydro-electric plants, also sailed close to the wind in this respect. At the time, and for some time thereafter, the politics of the affair obscured the merits of *Kettle of Fish* as a novel: a pity, for the story swings along at a fine lick, with a sensitive picture of a little fishing community, some splendid set-pieces and a real smell of the sea. The dispute itself however came to no very satisfactory conclusion, Tranter's book came out and provided some amusement, he made some enemies in lairdly circles and life moved on. Illicit drift-netting continued to take place under cover of darkness, poaching of river salmon also continued where feasible and Tranter moved on to bigger things: he was already half-way through the *MacGregor* trilogy and the next book published after *Kettle of Fish* was *The Master of Gray*. The era of modern novels as propaganda was coming to an end. But of all his lost causes, the salmon drift-netting off the mouth of the River Tweed is the one he most regrets.

The Salmon War and its accompanying novel *Kettle of Fish* in a sense also marked the end of the era of Tranter's modern novels in general. He had moved to Hodder & Stoughton in 1957, the first two books of the *MacGregor* trilogy had been published and the first book of the *Master of Gray* trilogy came out in 1961, the same year as *Kettle of Fish,* and the transition to historical writing was well under way. The historical works required much more research than the modern novels and he was also about to embark, with May's assistance, on the major enterprise of *The Fortified House.* Perhaps fortuitously, the Salmon War was to be the last of his high profile campaigns. At any rate, he turned now to less overtly political causes, closer to home.

But why did he do it? Why did he involve himself in all these causes, at times to the detriment of his writing? Partly, of course, because he believed that a novelist needs some way of keeping in touch with people—although that could have been done with less expenditure of time. But mainly, he says himself, "because causes just kept cropping up. And I suspect that I am in any case a sort of interfering, know-all character, with a tendency to put my oar in. . . ."

As a professional writer, Tranter was of course a member of the writers' professional associations, PEN and the Society of Authors, and with his phenomenal energy and gift for attracting publicity he quickly rose to the top of both. Throughout the 1960s and into the early 1970s he was successively President of Scottish PEN and chairman of the Society of Authors' Scottish branch: he was an official of PEN for sixteen years in all. He was also chairman of the Scottish branch of the National Book League, a somewhat different kind of organisation geared to promoting the reading of books in a more general way, from 1971–73. PEN and the Society of Authors have somewhat different functions: PEN—it stands for Poets, Essayists and Novelists and has been in existence since the 1920s—is more internationally orientated and concerned with matters of high policy, the protection of free speech, the operation of the Berne Convention on Copyright and such matters. When Tranter was Scottish president its main function was fostering international contacts, mainly in the Western world, and one of his duties was to attend international conferences, which he greatly enjoyed whether they were just across the Irish Sea in Belfast or on the other side of the Atlantic in Brazil. The Society of Authors is the writers' trade union, very necessary for members of a solitary profession, concerning itself with the day-to-day terms and conditions which affect the way writers earn their living, scrutinising contracts, advising on tax matters, offering access to information, providing a forum to meet and discuss concrete issues.

It was during his time at the head of the Society of Authors that Tranter became heavily involved in one of the great practical issues to affect writers' conditions in the 1960s and 1970s, the question of public lending rights. Writing is not a lucrative profession and few make much money out of it: the rewards are instead the opportunity to lead a free life, doing what you want. But by and large, the financial compensation is totally inadequate compared with the labour involved and in the recent past it was predicated exclusively on the purchase, not the borrowing of books. The coming of free public libraries, which bought a single hardback copy of a book and no more, and thus contributed only a single royalty payment to an author's income, regardless of how many people the book gave pleasure to, had long been a source of grievance. In the days of subscription libraries, there had at least been a kind of economic limit to the number of loans. Although it is nowadays regarded as self-evident that a writer should be compensated in relation to the number of people who read his books, whether they purchase them or borrow them from a public library, it was not a popular issue. The main battle for a public lending right was of course fought in London where there were opportunities for lobbying and high-profile demonstrations, but Tranter discovered that among the principal opponents of such a scheme were the librarians themselves, who foresaw endless bookkeeping, a penny a time, if the idea was put into practice. He therefore set out to convert librarians locally and toured the country talking to local branches of the Librarians' Association, eventually winning them over to the extent that they made him an honorary Librarian. But when the Public Lending Right was eventually incorporated in law in 1984, he found that as a Scottish writer writing mainly for a Scottish audience, with large sales in Scotland and very much smaller sales in the south, he was discriminated against: the sampling system was not weighted to take account of regional differences. He nevertheless accounts the campaign a major success, in particular for popular novelists and the authors of children's books, whose works are recycled endlessly through the public libraries, even if the Government, which provides the money, keeps rates down.

XXII

THE FORTIFIED HOUSE

A mouldering shell lost among the nettles, just recognisable as walls, a roofless ruin on the point of collapse, home only to pigeons, an ancient core obscured by neo-classical "improvements", a shelter for farm machinery or feed-sacks, a heap of stones. A little castle: a sixteenth century fortified house. Falling down fast, not of sufficient importance for authority to step in, except to order demolition if it becomes a public danger. To the expert eye, just redeemable, but at huge cost: to the romantic, irresistible.

Publication of the first volume of *The Fortified House in Scotland* in 1962 marked a major change in the public perception of Nigel Tranter. Hitherto known as a successful author of light fiction, with a wicked ability to poke fun at authority and stuffiness in general while drawing attention at the same time to legal anomalies and injustices, he was admired for his professionalism and enormous output. At the same time, he was feared by authority for his gadfly presence on the political scene. But he was not seen as a serious author, other than in his determination to make a living by his pen. *The Fortified House in Scotland* changed that, and brought him to the attention of a different public. By comparison, his early book on *The Fortalices and Early Mansions of Southern*

Scotland 1400-1650 was unambitious and pedestrian. The cut-off dates were roughly the same. In 1400 the advent of cannon was bringing about a revolution in castle design: the only defence against a cannon outside your walls was a new kind of structure which sent walls up, and living accommodation with them, producing the tower houses so familiar to us in Scotland. And 1650 was, roughly speaking, the point at which the gun-loop disappeared from Scottish domestic architecture. But *The Fortified House*, with a different publisher, although dealing in basically the same material, was recognised instantly as something new, serious but manageable, intellectually satisfying but accessible to non-experts. He was furthermore producing a catalogue of the Scottish hallmark *par excellence*, the little castle, instantly recognisable as the distinguishing symbol of Scotland, more distinctive than tartan, which had become debased by too much imitation, more distinctive than the shortbread tins with the Nasmyth portrait of Burns. The little castle was the essential adjunct of the Scottish landscape, the stuff of the calendars so treasured by Scots abroad, the very stuff of romance.

In the first instance, the work proposed, from the start, to cover virtually every fortified house in Scotland of which anything worthwhile was left standing and to do so at double the length of *The Fortalices*. (It did not set out to cover fortresses, a point which was consistently missed by readers and many reviewers from the first volume on: the fortified house, which we are often accustomed to call a "castle" is exactly what the name suggests— a dwelling-house which can be defended, not a military stronghold.) By the time they were finished, the five volumes covered a grand total of 663 in the revised edition: as late as the 1960s, when Tranter was writing the books, there were in all something like one to every five thousand of the population. The drawings, whose great charm was immensely important to the success of the books, and which have been relentlessly copied by castle-owners ever since, all too frequently without reference to the owner of the copyright, were enlarged and given greater prominence, the architectural descriptions were subtly altered to make them more accessible to a lay public, and the whole was enhanced by historical sketches which were more ambitious than the earlier rehearsal of ownership: in general, an interpretive approach was adopted which breathed life into old bones. It was a winning formula, the ideal quick reference book, as complete as he could make it, and it quickly found a place on the shelves of people who had never read the novels. From Tranter's own point of view, there was a difficulty, however. Oliver & Boyd, his publisher, imposed a strict format: each piece should be roughly 800 words in length, with only about 200 words devoted to history, which meant that he was seriously constrained when dealing with the history of the more important and interesting houses. Sales were disappointing, however: the books enjoyed a *succé d'estime* but it was not reflected in the sales.

In researching the books, it had been necessary to go over all the ground again—a ruin can after all deteriorate considerably in the twenty-five years which separated *The Fortified House* from *The Fortalices*—and in the process of visiting every castle that made its way into the books and many that did not make the grade—some 6,000 sites in all—Nigel and May, who went with him on all the research trips, had also talked to virtually every owner or occupier. Some were wary at first, but once convinced that this was a serious approach and not unjustified intrusion, they poured out their stories: all the detailed family history and traditions that seldom find their way into the history books, either because they cannot be proved or because their interest is deemed to be too narrowly academic. Tranter quickly realised that he was becoming a repository of information seldom confided to others and seldom found in one person's possession. Its volume far exceeded anything that could be included in *The Fortified House* but it was all carefully noted down and it was to prove of inestimable value when he later turned to historical themes in the novels. In return, castle-owners themselves benefited: his expert knowledge and wide experience, combined with his novelist's gift of imagination, enabled Tranter to interpret their castles to them, explain features whose significance had been forgotten over the centuries, give them the vocabulary to describe what they had, advise and counsel, and generally put their own historic houses into context.

Almost as soon as the first volume was published, the letters started coming in: if these little castles were lying around, neglected, and in danger of disappearing completely into the nettles, perhaps Tranter might know of one that might be available for restoration. This unforeseen result was to give him untold pleasure over the years, for he responded in virtually every case with energy and enthusiasm, counselling, assisting, guiding, and, when there was no obvious suggestion to make, filing away the appeal for help at the back of his mind to go back to when something came up. Since his primary interest in writing the castles books had been to record them for posterity before they collapsed into hopeless ruin, it followed that he took the keenest interest in the possibility of restoration. It goes without saying that he and May would have liked to embark on something of the sort themselves, and fantasised about Auld Hame Castle on its rugged clifftop; but by the time he might have had the means to do it, May was dead. He settled happily for doing it vicariously. Here was an area in which he was an acknowledged expert and all who sought out his advice benefited enormously. Castle restoration is not for the faint-hearted: at a rough estimate it is likely to cost five times what you bargained for and take five times as long. It is a process fraught with frustration because with buildings of such venerable age, forming part of the national heritage, the relevant government authority, in this case Historic Scotland, takes the closest possible interest in even the tiniest detail. Would-be restorers have to hunt the length and breadth of the country to find the right materials: no builder's merchant is going to hold in stock exactly what is required. As the bills pile up, not all take kindly to the discovery that where buildings of this calibre are concerned, there are no shortcuts or easy options. One owner, not a rich man, confided "Without Nigel's help, we would have ended up, twenty years on, where we began, the owners of a ruin. He interpreted our ruin to us, disinterred the 17th-century castle from the 18th-century 'improvements', helped us find our way through the red tape, eased our path by making introductions, buoyed us up when we were despondent, rejoiced with us when things went well. All the time, he could see in his mind's eye the bones of the structure beneath the rubble, all the time he could see our ultimate destination. Without him, we could never have done it. We may now be ruined ourselves, but thanks to Nigel, we've got a castle." He has had a hand in bringing back to life something like 61 castles by now.

Another by-product of the work done on *The Fortified House* was the charming little book entitled *Scottish Castles: Tales and Traditions*, another collection of bite-sized pieces that nestles in the glove-pocket of many a car.

With such a long list of titles to his credit, Tranter has had a number of different publishers, among whom some have had a decisive influence, sometimes inadvertently, on his writing career. The Edinburgh-based Moray Press took *The Fortalices*, his first book, and their imprint is also on his first published novel, *Trespass*, but they went into liquidation shortly thereafter and he was never paid for it. He offered his next book to Ward Lock & Co, who had a long list of popular fiction, and they published his modern novels from then on: they also put out the Westerns. After a couple of false starts with Collins and Thomas Nelson, he eventually settled down with Brockhampton, now a division of Hodder Headline, for his children's books. Towards the end of the

1950s, when he was seriously worried about whether he could sustain the flow of modern adventure stories and casting around for some new vein to exploit, Ward Lock, which had been very much a family company, also wound up their business in conjunction with a generation change and he transferred to Hodder & Stoughton, a major move which had important repercussions.

The move coincided with the appearance of the first historical novels. Hodder published the modern adventure stories and the historical novels in parallel for a few years but decided fairly quickly that his potential now lay with the historical books. Publishing is not conducted in a vacuum and books are subject to fashion trends as much as other consumer products. Tranter's first historical novels happened to coincide with two important trends: a surge of interest in historical novels in general and a marked surge in nationalist feeling and consequent interest in Scottish themes north of the Border. At the end of the 1960s, Hodder told him that his name was now firmly established as a writer of historical novels and that was what they wanted from him from now on. They did not however object to his continuing to publish the occasional modern novel elsewhere. The change-over to historical novels chimed well with his own interest and, as quickly emerged, inclination. The school fees were all paid by now but had been overtaken by another financial pre-occupation: how to provide for their own old age. There are no pension schemes for writers. It furthermore solved the problem of flagging inspiration, since he rightly perceived that Scottish history contained enough material to see him out. The historical novels, particularly the earlier ones, nevertheless called for a formidable amount of research and from his own point of view he would have welcomed the opportunity to interleave them with something less demanding: he solved this problem eventually by interspersing the meatier works, running in many cases into trilogies, with one-off books on more minor themes. He also found that books about heroes like

Bruce and Montrose took more writing, and were in fact less fun to write, than books about rogues. His old favourite James VI, the wisest fool in Christendom, is still a preferred indulgence when casting around for something to provide a respite.

Towards the end of the 1960s another important development was taking place in the publishing world—the apparently unstoppable rise of the paperback. Unlike continental publishers, who used mainly softbacks, British publishers had stuck heretofore to hardback publication, even for novels. Penguin had made an instant hit when they introduced paperbacks in 1935, but Penguin, whose huge success was almost certainly influenced by the demand for easily portable, inexpensively-produced books in wartime conditions, had no hardback titles. By the late 1960s all the traditional publishers were setting up their own paperback divisions to take advantage of this lucrative new market, which would eventually far outgrow the market for hardbacks, and Hodder was no exception. Tranter was naturally anxious to break in. Since he has never employed an agent, pointing out that he has never had any need of one, he conducted the negotiations himself direct. His own recollection is that it was Hodder who urged him around this time to spice up his love-scenes a bit, in conformity with the sexual revolution currently sweeping the country, and since his mainstream editors disclaim all responsibility, it seems at least possible that this suggestion came from the paperback division. At any rate, this was the impression he came away with, and he acted accordingly, despite his own strong sense that sex is best kept behind the bedroom door. His sex scenes are not, however, by and large, the best things in the books. But from now on virtually all his books were eventually paperbacked, and B&W Publishing of Edinburgh started paperbacking some of the earlier out-of-print Ward Lock books in the 1990s.

Alongside the fictional works, Tranter was also publishing a number of non-fiction books. These fall roughly into three categories: factual, although this is a far from adequate description of *The Fortified House*, arguably his most important work; polemics of various kinds; and coffee-table books. The monumental but uncompleted *The Queen's Scotland* was a Hodder title: the non-fiction in general went to Neil Wilson and other Scottish publishers and the coffee-table books went to a variety of different publishers. The hugely popular country notebook *Footbridge to Enchantment* eventually wound up with B&W.

XXIII

THE HISTORICAL NOVELIST

The Phrontistery, any time from the 1960s to the present day. Open upon the desk, Douglas's Peerage *and one of the huge volumes of* The Register of the Great Seal of Scotland. *Working back and forth between the two, making notes on his customary little slips of paper, Nigel Tranter is preparing a new historical novel. Back and forth he goes, seeking out the names and relationships, the transfers of property through inheritance, marriage, and royal gift that will enable him to weave the dense web of fact against which he will bring his characters to life.*

There are as many different kinds of historical novel as there are historical novelists and, perhaps for this reason, they tend to attract controversy. Tranter himself distinguishes between three kinds: costume drama, in which a romance is set in some remote period simply in order to dress up a banal plot, with no reference to the mores or thinking of the period in which it is set; period pieces, which are more firmly fixed in their historic period but deal essentially with fictional characters, who may or may not be shown against a background of real events; and serious historical novels like his own which fictionalise real people and expand our understanding of them through the informed, imaginative, in-depth interpretation of the writer. Some may contain no fictionalised characters at all, although this is difficult to sustain. It is in the mix of fact and fiction that they differ: the fewer the fictional elements, the more difficult it is to do. A list of *dramatis personae* distinguishing between historical and invented characters was a standard feature of his earlier books but was dropped some years ago—not because, as might be supposed, he was using more fictional figures, but because he was using fewer. Is it important to know which characters are invented? Not very: the central characters who shape events may have some invented traits, some invented personal history, but are never themselves invented. Heavy reliance on historical figures and historical facts however carries penalties in that people expect the stories to be true to the "facts". But the "facts" are often ambiguous and are in any case only as good as the man who wrote them down, who may be biased, ill-informed, writing under duress or setting down an oral tradition centuries after the event. Just as the academic historian is constantly confronted by choices about which to believe of two mutually contradictory accounts, so the novelist, too, must make up his mind which is the more credible of two different versions. Each must use his own expertise to decide which version accords best with the other evidence available to him: in the case of the serious historical novelist, he will look at the choices in the context of his novelist's imaginative interpretation of character, looking to see which version agrees best with what is otherwise known of the personality.

It is a commonplace of reviewers to say that Nigel Tranter has taught most Scots all the history they know. If this is true, and it is probably as true as any general statement ever can be, and if he is doing it deliberately, we are entitled to ask various questions: what exactly is his purpose, how is he doing it, how successful is he, and how good is his history?

One of the implications of the statement that he has taught us all the history we know is that we didn't learn it at school. In a sense, it has been Scotland's misfortune to go, as a nation, straight from over-emphasis on post-Union, British history, shaped in Westminster and English-dominated, into an age in which history itself was being increasingly neglected. But this is to over-simplify: to outsiders Scots seem unusually knowledgeable about their own history, even obsessed by it. It is a trait shared with other small nations in danger of being dominated by larger neighbours: a fear that without constant reiteration the story will be lost, swallowed up in a larger whole. As with the little castles, it has been Nigel Tranter's concern to try and stop the rot before all remembrance crumbles away and Scotland's national identity is lost. Scotland is perhaps unusual in having such a wealth of tangible monuments on which to hang its past. But, whatever the reason, Tranter was satisfying a hunger with his historical novels, not addressing a famine. And he was singularly well-equipped for the task, because he already had at his back the treasure-house of information built up over decades of work on *The Fortified House* and *The Queen's Scotland* which he could bring into play to enrich his books.

Nigel Tranter's own experience of history-teaching in school was that it was dry as dust, "all Henry VIII's wives and nothing about Scotland." On the other hand, he emerged with a clear sense that history was important, "the memory of the race" as he constantly reiterates. A nation that doesn't know its own history, has lost its memory, doesn't understand where it came from, doesn't know itself and doesn't know where it is going. It was partly because he feared that Scots were, as a people, in danger of losing this precious folk memory, that he started writing the first historical novels and why he went on.

When he turned exclusively to the writing of historical fiction thirty-odd years ago, he did so with many years' experience of novel-writing behind him and wide experience therefore of the creation of a believable but imaginary world, the creation of that willing suspension of disbelief that novel-writing entails. As a novelist, he was in a sense a master of the art of deception. He had turned to historical writing as a solution to a problem, that of finding new topics to write about: he once told an interviewer, his real interest in life was the study of the fortified houses, and the novels were written to pay the rent. Nevertheless he quickly discovered that in making the events and characters of his historical novels believable, he was taking on a new level of responsibility. His cause was now revealed as Scotland, not the various subordinate causes to which he had devoted so much time in the past, and Scotland as revealed by her history. But this meant that the characters and events with which he was dealing in his historical novels were not his property to do what he liked with as the invented characters and events of his modern novels had been: they were the common property of the nation and he had a responsibility not to traduce them. He had always regarded himself as a storyteller, a page-turner, and since history to have meaning must be made to come to life, he set about putting the story back into history. But this meant that whatever he wrote would have to have a solid grounding in accepted fact. In the foreword to an early historical novel, *The Queen's Grace*, he tells us that liberties have been taken with historical characters "but not wantonly, nor in a fashion designed to show them in a role markedly other than that accepted by respectable historians", and in the foreword to *MacGregor's Gathering* he writes that he will cull from the material available to him such incidents as present a "recognisable and fairly consistent picture", keeping the historical background as accurate as he can make it. He has continued to apply these ground-rules ever since. From a very early stage he saw his purpose as instilling, not so much a deep knowledge, as a gut understanding of Scottish history.

In the early years he wrote of the great figures of history whose lives and actions shaped the future course of our story, Bruce, Wallace, Montrose, and this was of course a top priority, but as time went on the whole sequence of his work began to take on an epic cast: he would seek eventually to cover the whole sweep of Scottish history in novel form. It was a huge undertaking. Most practitioners of the historical novel tend to concentrate on a particular period: ancient Rome, the 17th century, the Napoleonic wars etc; and this Tranter was denying himself. In taking on Scottish history in its totality, Tranter was taking on a task which, since he took the responsible view, called for a staggering amount of research.

Historical fiction is a contradiction in terms: the purist would say that either it is history or it is fiction, and any combination of the two is likely to be mendacious. This is not of course the way the non-academic book-buying public sees it: for them, history must be pre-digested, reworked by the novelist if it is to be palatable at all. When academic historians complain that the novelists are unhistorical, they forget that the novelists are supplying a need they cannot themselves supply because their approach so often renders what they write inaccessible to the non-academic reader. In any case the allegation of mendacity is too simplistic: fiction can be used to throw light on history, as the novelist's insights into human behaviour and the working of human society open up the character of the past. But this is not what Tranter was setting out to do: he was setting out to recount the events of history by fictional means. He was setting out to fictionalise history—in some cases fictionalise biography—in order to make it easier to understand. He would explore character insofar as it was necessary to make action comprehensible—he would not neglect the whys of history—but his main purpose was to set down what happened and to do so in a proper historical context, generally speaking telling us all we need to know, what kind of weapons were in use at the time of a battle, for example, and how they could be deployed, to understand what was going on and fill in the interstices.

Plot, in the sense of invented plot, is an irrelevancy and Tranter seldom uses the word: he prefers to say theme. In looking at a historical theme, he looks at what happened, what was important and how it affected subsequent developments, the known facts about the principal characters, so that he can create a believable interplay between them. When confronted with two conflicting historical accounts, he goes for the most probable, the action that is in character. Generally speaking, he follows the line of history, but selectively. He has no plan as such: he knows how things start, he knows how they end, he knows all about his characters. But he doesn't know what will happen in between until it comes into his head on his solitary walks around the Bay, and the book takes on a life of its own.

In the circumstances, his manuscripts are extraordinary, spelling mistakes and typing errors corrected and the occasional date altered but in all essential respects untouched from the first same-day type-up to the printed page. He invents characters and events where they are necessary to bring the story to life or bring it into perspective, but keeps them within the logic, as he sees it, of the known facts. Dialogue is of course by its very nature invented and this is one of the things the purists object to, asking for example, "How do you know that was what Bruce said?" To which his standard reply is, "How do *you* know it isn't what he said?" But dialogue is a necessary invention if you are in the business of bringing history to life through the medium of the novel: few novels succeed without dialogue.

Finally, he looks for drama: his novels are action novels, and where the action fails or is inadequate, generally speaking, the novel fails too. One of the few criticisms he acts on with alacrity is any suggestion that he has so overloaded his text with technical information, for example, that it is holding up the action. The action-driven plot however has its disadvantages. We are shown the central characters in terms of action, Bruce, for example, primarily as a soldier and a tactician, particularly in the earlier books, rather than as a king. It is striking how very few glimpses we get in the books of a governor actually governing or a bishop running his diocese. We are shown the trappings of wealth and power and the lust that drives men to seek them without their content. In rather the same way we are shown physical desire in the love stories without very much of the tenderness of love or the obsession with the loved one that normally accompanies it. The importance of the love stories in the books is striking: put in no doubt to give a more human dimension to the characters but surprising nevertheless given the male bias of so much of his historical writing. He was of course writing romances before he was writing historical novels, but some of the love stories sit oddly with the portrayal of men of action, and the intimate glimpses we are afforded of his characters' lives sometimes suggest that it was lust rather than tenderness that motivated them.

By and large, he takes a simplistic view of history. He is not interested in theories of history, nor is he particularly interested in social or economic history. Given the huge part it plays in Scottish history, he is not even particularly interested in the theological differences that underlay the religious wars: he discourses repeatedly and at length on the differences between the Celtic and Roman churches but deals mainly with differences of practice without making particularly clear what these differences reflected in terms of belief. In discussing relations with the Papacy—the dispute over authority, whether exercised by Rome or Trondheim or St Andrews—it is the power play and its effects on historical events that interest him, not the theology. The kind of in-depth exploration of the beliefs and practices of the Covenanters that Scott gives in *Old Mortality*, for example, is not for him. For Tranter, men may be driven by ideas, in particular political or religious ideas, but the interplay or exposition of ideas is not in itself an event and it gets in the way of the action. He is interested in what happened, and why, but there is a limit to how deep he is prepared to go into the why. He believes that this is one of the areas in which the novelist can make a contribution, writing to a correspondent in 1971, "Historians just say what was done. Novelists like myself try to ask why . . ." But on the whole, he subscribes to the view of fiction-writing once pithily summed up by Frederick Forsyth, another best-selling novelist: all you need to know is who did what and to whom. This is not to suggest that he takes a superficial view: not at all, he takes the most serious view of what he is doing. But perhaps because it is image-driven, it is mainly the surface that we see.

Tranter's ideas about historical fiction did not spring fully-fledged into his mind when he turned definitively to historical writing in the 1960s: they matured when he was casting around for new sources of inspiration and his own interest in history, sparked by his interest in the castles, had already produced the occasional book on a historical theme. It was May who put into his head the idea of making more consistent use of his historical material. Once the seed was sown, it seemed blindingly obvious: Scottish history contained more than enough material to see his time out. And no one knew the setting, natural as well as historical, as well as he did. The early historical novels do not of course strike the same sonorous tones as the books of the 1970s and 1980s. By and large, their themes were chosen more for the opportunities they offered of telling the same kind of adventure story he had been telling in the modern books than for their historical significance. *MacGregor's Gathering*, one of the first books of the new dispensation, is a romp about a folk hero, whose epic cattle stampede recalls the humble Westerns, and *The Master of Gray* is the tale of a rogue. The *MacGregor* books in particular have nothing like the close texture of the *Bruce*, say, or the *Montrose* books. But it was with these books that his sales suddenly started to rise exponentially. Whereas the modern adventure stories had sold 12-15,000 copies, the *MacGregor* and *Master of Gray* trilogies sold 150,000 copies of each book. And as he got into his stride and gained confidence, the great national heroes inevitably demanded their due: he developed the command of material that enabled him to fill vast canvases and yet maintain the momentum of vivid, dramatic action. At the height of his powers, in the early 1970s, in an astonishing sequence, he dealt in turn with the central figures of Bruce, Wallace, and Montrose and produced a *tour de force* rehabilitation of the singular James VI & I. Looking back now, he sometimes wonders whether it might not have been better to deal with Scotland's story chronologically: but that would have been to postpone the books on Wallace and Bruce by perhaps five or six years and the books on Montrose and Jamie Saxt by twenty, almost certainly producing lesser works. The switch to historical fiction however produced one side-effect: the amount of research required for the major works of the 1970s was such that time-consuming extra-curricular activities had to be dropped. There could be no question now of taking on any more major campaigns like the Forth Road Bridge project. He did not of course retreat into his chamber; but his priorities necessarily altered.

In order to get inside history and provide an alibi for some of his own commentary on events, Tranter employs a number of devices, one of the commonest of which is the invention of a reporter who serves as intermediary between our own experience and the historical experience. An invented character, often a junior member of a minor house, often an illegitimate half-brother of a more conventional hero, is pitchforked by unexpected circumstances into the midst of great events on which he then "reports" to the reader through his own reactions. By this means it becomes possible to describe and comment upon, credibly and at length, scenes which would be too familiar to warrant comment by the central characters. By making the reporter a young man whose experience of the world is still limited, the opportunities for comment and, in some cases, rationalisation of events are enhanced. And as the reporter matures, the reader also matures in his understanding of what is going on. This approach also enables the writer to communicate information of a more technical nature and one of the great attractions of Tranter's writing for many men, in particular, is that he purveys information about a wide range of technical matters incidental to the main story. Just as the reader of a modern technological novel like *The Hunt for Red October*, say, puts down the book feeling that he is now something of an expert on nuclear submarines, so the reader of one of Tranter's historical novels lays aside the book with a satisfying sense that he now knows a great deal more about castle architecture or the elevation of a mid-15th century cannon than he did before. If Tranter himself is teaching all the time, his readers are anxious to learn. In respect of language, he is scrupulous in avoiding the use of inappropriate modernisms but errs occasionally in the other direction, with too much use, not so much of "antiqued" language as of "antiqued" idiom as in the frequent use of staccato speech in some of the books.

As far as the willing suspension of disbelief is concerned, it is also worth noting the role played by the detailed descriptions of terrain. He says himself, "I like to relate my work very closely and authentically to the actual scene where I locate them so that readers can follow . . . on an ordinary inch or half-inch to the mile map." Anyone who has picked up a book about events set in surroundings that are familiar to him will know the peculiar pleasure recognition affords and is likely to assume, subconsciously, that since Tranter is one hundred percent accurate in his description of the terrain he will also be one hundred percent accurate, that is, factual, in his description of events. The authenticity of the one implies the authenticity of the other.

The role played by close knowledge of local terrain, or, in some cases, inspired interpretation of maps, however goes farther than that. An important part of Tranter's love of country is his love of country in concrete terms, the sense in which Scotland's mountains and moors and islands and lochs are bred into his bones. It is at least arguable that if Scotland is his theme, working right through all the books, the actual topography of Scotland is an important sub-theme. There are problems connected however with writing a long series of novels all of which contribute to a single epic theme, when each novel must be at the same time complete in itself: he is bound to repeat himself. How many times, for example, have we had explained to us the underwater causeways running through the Flanders Moss and known only to the Gregorach? But Constant Reader, who may be irked by reading yet again a story he already knows off by heart, forgets that but for Tranter he would not know it at all, and forgets that for the newcomer it is essential information. Sometimes there is reiteration within the books, but this is only when there is a point that needs to be hammered home: when we are told yet again that the Master of Gray was the handsomest man in Europe, it is because his good looks partly explain why he was able to gain the *entrée* wherever he went.

So how good is he at recreating the past, at bringing the story back to life? No one who has read the books can be in any doubt about the answer: from first to last we believe absolutely in the picture he presents. Even when we can see that some of the ceremonies—the weddings and coronations, for example—are influenced by his knowledge of 20th-century ceremonial, we still accept the world he creates for us, encouraged into acceptance by the wealth of detail he provides, the completeness of the picture. Partly, this is because he is first and foremost a visual artist. He has described the process at the beginning of *Lord in Waiting* when he spells out what is going on in John Douglas's busy mind while he is outwardly at ease, fishing: "He was summoning up pictures, faces, emotions, actions, words, and seeking for due words of his own to describe these adequately; and more than adequately, vividly, dramatically, resoundingly. For John Douglas was a storyteller . . ." Tranter sees pictures, rather than hears words, in his head. His problem is getting the picture down, finding the words to convey the impression made by the picture. Sometimes his picture demands elaboration of technicalities: the ins and outs of siege warfare or the new, improved design of an arrow, for example. In explaining these matters, necessary so that we can understand the action, he is teaching and we in our turn are expanding our experience by a process of osmosis. There is more to it than that, however. He may not hear words, but he certainly hears sounds: the clash of arms, the thud of hooves, the groans of the dying, the wailing of the women, the calling of the cuckoo. And he smells smells: the stench of burning, the sweat of men and horses, the rotting corpses and the scent of bog-myrtle. It is the tight weave of all these things that conveys the sense of immediacy, of being present, and it adds up to a winning formula.

How accurate is the detail, how factual the history that we so readily accept? The answer is as good as he can make it. Underlying all is a strong sense of the responsibility he has taken on in recreating Scotland's history for a wider public. He does no original research: but he carefully compares the accounts given by historians, not confining his researches to the historians of our own century but delving back into much older works, which are often strong on detail. He makes constant use of genealogical works to sort out relationships, marriage alliances and so forth as a means to unravel the hidden links, the ulterior motives that drive his characters: and he makes constant use also of works like *The Register of the Great Seal of Scotland* which provide information about ownership of property and transfers of ownership. And he makes much use of Grub's 1861 *Ecclesiastical History of Scotland*. Part of a typical note carried in his pocket when he was engaged in writing *Lords of Misrule* reads "4th Earl of Douglas & 1st Duke of Touraine. Archibald, Master of Douglas b. 1372, s. of Joanna Moray of Bothwell m. Princess Margaret e.d.Robert 3 accession of Robert 3 1390. 1400 June keeper of Edinburgh Castle for life. Was in command, with D of Rothesay when Henry 4 besieged Aug. 1400. Succeeded 1400 (24th December). Took possession of Castle of Dunbar when Dunbar went in anger to Engl. over marriage. Also got extensive Dunbar lands in Annandale do. Battle with Hotspur at Dunbar Candlemas 1400. In Haddington and Traprain area (see Red Book (i) p 363). Made Chief Warden of Marches just before father's death. Appointed Keeper of Edinburgh Castle for life 4/6/1400. At marriage was given Lordship of Douglasdale, Forest of Ettrick, Lauderdale and Romanno by father. Lost one of his eyes at Homildon & captured. Also captured Moray, Angus, M of Douglas (James). . . ." This was half of one day's note, the whole written in minuscule writing and covering about half a page of a pocket diary: double it for the whole day's note and then multiply by thirty years and you will have some idea of the research that has gone into the historical novels. The reference books are well used: no wonder their backs are broken and the boards battered.

There is another question we are entitled to ask: how good are the historical novels as novels? At their best, they are very good indeed, with all the necessary balance between narrative, action, dialogue, and description he spoke about all those years ago at the Youth Club in Penrith. The characters are real, rounded, with light and dark. Bruce misses his wife and accepts solace in the arms of Christina MacRuarie, Wallace grieves for his dead wife, Montrose unwittingly destroys his marriage in service to the King, Thomas the Rhymer has doubts about taking a new lover after Bethoc dies. The *Bruce* books in particular are full of vivid action and memorable scenes, but, as in so many of the books it is the telling detail that works the magic. Who could forget for example the spark that Edward Longshanks' horse strikes from the stone flags of the chancel at Stracathro in the opening scene of the *The Steps to the Empty Throne*? Who could forget the foxy Argyll watching on the balcony as Montrose is carried up the High Street to his execution? Who could forget the complex Jamie Saxt, rescued by Tranter from the obscurity of eccentricity, sitting up in bed with his hat on? Who could forget his "Ooh, ayes"? Who could forget the beautiful, nubile, red-headed Mary Queen of Scots trifling with Patrick Gordon's affections in *The Queen's Grace*? Who could forget the image of the dying Thorfinn Raven-Feeder being hauled up the hill in his sledge, Gruach at his side? Who could forget the young James Douglas wrestling the bull? Who could forget, however much they might want to, the ghastly image of rapine and pillage with which *Margaret the Queen* opens? Who could forget the Black Douglas thundering down the hill and crashing into the Percys or his sudden revulsion at the ferocity of the men who "killed and killed, apparently for blood"? Who could forget the young Archie Douglas, suddenly sick at the carnage of Otterburn? All of these images are fictional, the product of Nigel Tranter's imagination, but these are the images that stay with us when the historical detail has faded: these are the devices by which the novelist brings his history to vivid, sentient life.

Nevertheless, with so many great things written, there is no denying what he knows himself: that his compulsion to write has sometimes led him to write too much. In part, it is the eternal problem of the writer: if you write for a living, you have to keep the words flowing, and if you keep your day job, how do you find the time to concentrate on writing? And if you aim to cover the whole of Scotland's story from start to finish, even Scotland's tangled tale will produce some longueurs. But with so many books, there are continual discoveries to be made: how good most of the early modern novels are, for example, and how funny; one of the drawbacks of writing about national heroes is that they impose a certain solemnity. One perceptive critic wondered whether Bruce's comparative wooden-ness derived perhaps from the fact that Tranter respected him too much: a perceptive editor noted a difference in style between the books about the great heroes and the rest, noted that in *The Wisest Fool*, for example, he let himself go a bit more, gave himself a bit more elbow-room, with more comic scenes but also much more dialogue. There is some truth in it: one of the great attractions of James VI & I for Tranter is the wealth of comic opportunities he offers. But more than that, James VI offers great variety, rich opportunities, after he went to London, to contrast his homespun ways with the sophistication of the court he inherited, and above all, great naturalness. Tranter could put more or less anything into his mouth, because he depicts Jamie Saxt so successfully that surprise is what you expect. It is a pity the comic scenes have so largely disappeared from the later books, some of which are really just love stories in a historic setting. But there are plentiful opportunities for botanising profitably outside the doorstop trilogies in which so many of the books are nowadays marketed: because *Black Douglas* and *The Patriot*, for example, are both singletons in the publisher's lists now, they sometimes get missed. It is the richness of choice he offers and the unbroken flow of the imagination that is unique to Tranter, and the completeness of the world on which he has opened a window that will not readily be shut. Like all worlds with any claim to completeness it contains some dull patches, but there is always a feeling that lurking just out of sight, there is still something new and exciting to be discovered. As in life, you never know what lies around the next corner.

Tranter thinks of himself as a storyteller, at times a sennachie, which the OED defines as "One professionally employed in the study and transmission of traditional history, genealogy and legend, now chiefly Sc a Gaelic teller of legendary romances." Some have seen him as a mediaeval bard, whose function was to imprint a tale on men's minds by constant repetition, honing the pattern of story and language to a fine level of perfection. Since his theme, ultimately, is Scotland, with a wide cast of characters, others have seen him in terms of epic. There are objections to most of these alternatives: bard too poetic, and epic too grand—the epic sweep is there but, spread over so many books, there is none of the necessary coherence. Sennachie is good and, the bias towards legend apart, pretty close to his own idea of the storyteller: as he always intended, he draws the stories out of history, using his storyteller's technique to make them run on, treating them as new discoveries, unfolding his stories as history was once handed down, a tale full of drama and colour and unexpected adventure, told round the fire in a hall-house on a winter's evening.

The Story of Scotland, published in 1987, is Tranter's own history book—a description strenuously denied of course by himself, since the very word history book suggests to him something dry as dust, which is not what he intends. Perhaps anti-history book would be a better description for it is indeed like no other. Although it is in a sense solid history, with no pictures or conversations, in Alice's words, it is at the same time a very personal book, the mode of writing all the way through part of his comment on what is wrong with the usual presentation of history, or perhaps, to modify once again, his recollection of the presentation of history when he was young. And it is remarkably successful for he writes in his usual page-turning style to make it into a good story, running on, an almost conversational relation of events, sprinkled with his own comments. It is an interesting experiment: in effect, a form of polemic. For the reader with an interest in, but not much solid knowledge of Scotland—the American Scot, for example, several generations removed from his roots, or the tourist who is a regular visitor and wants to know more about the background of the historical monuments he sees, or wonders why the Scots are so resolutely different from the English—it is ideal: told as a story, it contains everything he wants to know.

The foreword also contains an interesting reflection on his own attitude to history-writing. Generation after generation of academic historians, he says, have managed to make history dull by producing "catalogues of dates, births, deaths and marriages, wars, treaties, alliances, movements and so on". These, he says, are but the skeleton of history, while "the flesh consists of the stories of men and women like you and me, their trials, temptations, triumphs, treacheries, even tendernesses."

Tranter's place in Scottish literature and the literary influences on his writing have to be looked at in the context of two separate careers as a novelist: as a writer of modern adventure stories and as a writer of serious historical fiction. The very early influences are difficult to identify after so many years. He read Scott at school and found him heavy going, as most young people do: when he returned to him as an adult, he found much to esteem and admire and he now of course appreciates Scott's key role in the restoration of a sense of Scottish identity. It was Scott who first created the universal modern image of Scotland and the climate in which he would write, but Scott himself was writing for a more leisured age and Tranter found little to imitate: he knew instinctively that Scott was too slow for his purposes, "never using one word where twenty will do". As a man and as a writer, Tranter's dominating characteristic is impatience: he always wants to get on with things and has no time for the slow exposition, as a glance at any of the opening scenes of his most important books will show—*The Wallace*, for example, where in a single page, dramatically told, he establishes Wallace's great size, his emotion, the horror of the scene that caused it, his thoughtful nature, his physical dexterity, the trademark two-handed sword at his back, and "the fearsome, fatal vow".

In his out-of-school reading his preference was for a rattling good yarn in the Percy Westerman style, and classics like Ballantyne's *Coral Island* and Stevenson's *Kidnapped*, but he remembers little now of the detail of this early reading. Quite soon, he graduated to Buchan, who published a string of novels in the 1920s and 1930s which were to become perhaps the strongest influence on Tranter's early, modern, work, with their Scottish settings, middle-class heroes and exciting plots, the action frequently ranging over hills and moors and lonely places. Neil Gunn was another Scottish author whom he greatly admired. Gunn's first novel was published in 1926 to immediate acclaim and he was producing a novel a year right through the 1930s. *The Silver Darlings*, perhaps the finest of Gunn's books, published in 1941, deals with the aftermath of the Highland Clearances, the dependence of a marginal community on the herring shoals (the silver darlings of the title), their vulnerability to poverty and disease and their awakening political consciousness, with a strong mystic element running right through the book. Maurice Walsh, another writer whose work Tranter admired, was also publishing regularly in the 1930s: *The Quiet Man*, published in 1935, dealt with Irish nationalism, the love of Erin and its destructiveness. Gunn and Walsh were both stylish writers and dealt with themes which would later emerge in Tranter's own work, and Gunn in particular was a fine master of a plot. Buchan however was his hero among contemporary novelists. From the first, what he required of a book was a fast-moving plot with plenty of action. The 1930s also saw the rise of the detective story, but while he read them occasion-ally—and still does—he was never remotely tempted to try his hand at detective fiction.

From the mid-1930s on, and particularly after 1942, when he found himself trying to keep a wife and family on a private's pay, he was himself writing obsessively, scribbling away in every spare moment. When he got home again, he was writing for a living and already heavily involved in his various public causes. When he turned to historical novels, he was busy with research whenever he wasn't actually writing. There has been little time in his life as a writer for recreational reading. By and large, he belongs to the Disraeli school of writing: when he wants to read a novel, he writes one. In recent years he has sampled some of the new Scottish writers but is not greatly in sympathy with them: apart from anything else, most of them are writing in an urban environment and in an idiom that is alien to him. George Blake and A.J. Cronin did not greatly appeal, possibly for the same reason.

Though not as much of a stylist, he is firmly in the Buchan mould as a writer of light fiction, but with a distinctive humorous touch of his own. It is also worth noting that he shared with Buchan his extraordinary industry, pouring out novels while at the same time pursuing an active alternative career in the public arena. Like Buchan, as a modern novelist he has been undeservedly forgotten, mainly perhaps because the society he depicts exudes a kind of innocence that vanished forever in the 1960s. The coming of Bond, and later Smiley, altered things irrevocably, and by then Tranter had no desire to make the transition, for historical themes already beckoned.

Among writers of historical fiction he is unique, because when he turned to serious historical fiction he was trying to do something few had ever attempted do before: tell history itself—not a character, or a society, or an incident, or a crisis, but the whole sweep—as fiction. He was done for ever with invented plots: from that moment on, he would re-people the past, breathe life into old bones and put words into old mouths, but he would not tamper with their stories. There had of course been children's books which told history in story form, but Tranter was writing for adults. There are two important differences between his work and that of most other historical novelists: the wide range of periods tackled and the fact that whereas other serious practitioners tend to interpret an age selectively through the imagined eyes of a single key character, using events to throw light on character, or character to comment on events, Tranter fictionalises a full sequence of events and uses a full cast. Of the various mixes between fact and fiction available to him he has chosen the most difficult, that which has the highest factual content and densest concentration of historical figures. To win our trust and make his narrative convincing he is furthermore backing it up with the widest possible deployment of historical detail compatible with maintaining the impetus of the action. He is of course a novelist and it is novels he is writing. But his own preferred definition of himself as a storyteller is a more accurate description: he is telling a story in the first instance, it is a story that already exists, the story is a precious one for it is Scotland's history, and it is history told in a new way. It is by his storytelling skills he should be judged, his ability to revitalise without injuring our national heritage, and at the same time to keep his readers on the *qui vive* and eager for more.

From Scott on, Scotland has produced a remarkable number of historical novelists, no doubt reflecting the hunger for information noted earlier, and the appetite for their work appears insatiable. For a time, women led the field with a more romantic—but not necessarily sentimental—approach: in the 1930s, Margaret Irwin, and from the 1960s on, more or less in parallel with Tranter's own historical novels, Dorothy Dunnett, whose brilliant, romantic Francis Crawford of Lymond owed something to Bond and something to Lord Peter Wimsey and burst on the novel-reading public with an impact comparable with that of Baroness Orczy's Percy Blakeney nearly sixty years before. Both Irwin and Dunnett write in a modern idiom, without anachronisms, but without attempting to replicate an older mode of speech, Dunnett with a high fictional content to her plots but matched with an impeccable historical background. In the work of both, the material is selected perhaps primarily for its romantic potential. In more recent years, two important male exponents, both serious in their approach, have emerged in the persons of Alan Massie and Ross Leckie: both have chosen so far mainly classical subjects, following the lead of Robert

Graves, and write about their heroes from the inside, often in the first person, and typically, perhaps, reflecting on their careers in old age. Tranter in no way fits into either category and seems so far to have had no successful imitator.

It is perhaps inevitable that Scottish writers with an interest in history should be drawn at times to the same subjects, and Scott and Irwin both wrote novels about Montrose, while Buchan wrote a splendid short life. Scott's little book, *A Legend of Montrose,* falls into two halves, the first dominated by the imagined character of Captain Dugald Dalgetty, the battle-scarred mercenary who has fought his way over Europe with the armies of Gustavus Adolphus and cannot forget it, with Montrose only coming into his own— and palely by comparison—in the second half. Irwin's book, *The Proud Servant,* is pure romance, but it is well-written and deals with real people and events: it gives a clear impression of Montrose's nobility of character, with a good portrait of Charles I and some charming images—shooting the arrow over St Mary's by moonlight, for example—but there is little sense of tragic progress in his career. Buchan's book, *The Marquis of Montrose,* is history, not fiction, and yet succeeds in bringing Montrose vividly before our eyes, because of its deep understanding of the subject and the compassion with which it is infused, but also perhaps because Buchan was also a novelist with the novelist's knack of immediacy. But it is Tranter's two books, *The Young Montrose* and *The Captain General,* that combine deep understanding and serious intent with the total immediacy which only full fictional treatment can convey. In these two books, we are led by Tranter to re-experience the past as if it was new, and watch for ourselves from the sidelines as a real-life tragedy unfolds. Although some of his other books, notably the *Bruce* trilogy, had greater impact and were perhaps more intrinsically exciting, none are so moving, and the *Montrose* books are probably the best Tranter has ever written. He will be remembered for many books, for the popular impact they had at the time and the deeper impact they had on the national consciousness; but whatever books survive the test of time, those on Montrose should surely be among them.

XXIV

PHILIP

Quarry House, the drawing-room. Among all the mementoes of a happy and successful life, the Bannockburn chess set, the miniature Coronation Chair, a present from Frances May, with its crumb of the Coronation Stone beneath the seat, the model castles and ducks and presentation bowls of Caithness glass and the framed copy of the march composed for his 80th birthday and the family photographs, a little home-made Saltire droops. In uneven letters it bears the legend S H K E 1965. The Scottish Hindu Kush Expedition. Beside it, an ice-axe and a photograph of a young man in climbing gear. On the wall, a sketch map of high peaks. Infinitely sad, the little flag conjures up the wraiths of Scott and Amundsen, Mallory and Nansen, brave men planting their little flags in lonely places, and it is a shrine. Philip's shrine.

Philip was a climber. From those earliest beginnings at Maggie's Loup, he went on to hone his climbing skills on supervised school forays with the Ben Dorain climbing club, and on solitary expeditions to the Highlands after he had begun to outgrow the holiday outings with the family. At Edinburgh University he chose to read Civil Engineering because it would fit him for a profession where he could be out in the open air, and from the climbs with the University climbing club to the foundation of the Corriemulzie

Mountaineering Club in 1964 and the full-blown adult pioneering climbs in Turkey and the Hindu Kush, climbing was his life.

One annual engagement as an undergraduate had been Abergeldie Castle on Royal Deeside each August for the grouse-shooting, when the climbing clubs provided beaters and climbed every spare moment. Philip's first independent expeditions to the Highlands had been by bicycle, but he and Frances May both acquired motor scooters at the earliest possible opportunity, and it was while riding his scooter that Philip suffered a serious accident in August 1960 on his way north to Abergeldie, cracking his skull and requiring surgery and three weeks' hospitalisation. He travelled back to Abergeldie the day after he was discharged from hospital and the next day, while the rest of the party took time out to attend the Braemar Gathering, Philip was out on the hill again, toughening himself up. He had just graduated.

After university, he worked as a civil engineer with James Williamson & Partners, a firm of consultant engineers engaged in the design and construction of hydro-electric plants in the High-lands, and went on thereafter to build trunk roads for Ross-shire County Council. Both jobs allowed him considerable leeway as regards working hours and he was out climbing virtually every weekend. Friday after Friday he rushed away from work at the earliest possible moment and drove for hours in the battered little van that replaced the scooter, to rendezvous with other climbers who sometimes didn't turn up, or turned up hours late, in hotel bars, outside fish-and-chip shops, in hotel car parks, at road-ends at the back of beyond or in climbers' bothies, youth hostels or caves. He would dine off warmed-up soup, and suffer periodic stomach cramps from drinking too much hill water, play poker and talk into the night, often not getting to bed until four, five or even six in the morning, spend Saturday and Sunday climbing intensively and then get up again at four to drive hundreds of miles back to be in his office at nine on Monday for a full day's work. They were all doing it but none so intensively as Philip, who missed a weekend's climbing only for an occasional duty visit to his parents in Aberlady. Mainly he was climbing with the group that had originally coalesced at Abergeldie and later formed the nucleus of the Corriemulzie Mountaineering Club, which he founded. The Club was named for one of their favourite spots of which Philip once wrote "of all our camps, (it) was the most beautiful." In the Log of the Corriemulzie Club, from its inception in 1964 until first "Uncle" Park and then Philip died, their names are recorded as having attended virtually every meet. Much of the time they slept in tents whatever the temperature, and after the Corriemulzie Club was founded, in the big communal tent Philip designed and ran up himself on his landlady's sewing machine. The cars they used were an assortment of minis and little vans, always seriously overloaded with bulky climbers and their gear, and they drove and climbed in all conditions, snow, mist and black ice. An extraordinary amount of it, climbing included, was done in the dark, by moonlight and starlight and, when these failed, by the light of torches and miners' lamps. The season they looked forward to most was winter, when the ground was hard, the air clear and there was a chance at an ice-face. Philip kept detailed records from an early age, and much was documented in the articles he wrote for the Scottish glossies. With his tales of moonlight climbs and glittering, arctic conditions in lonely places, he was dispensing high romance for stay-at-homes and climbers alike and he had no difficulty in getting them published: by the time he was 25, he was publishing a mountaineering piece for general consumption every second month or so, sometimes oftener.

Despite their own wide knowledge of the Scottish hills, his parents knew only an edited version. But gradually they learned of the Munros conquered, the new routes climbed and the marathon non-stop walk from the Atlantic to the North Sea—another first—and they read his letters and the articles he published on climbing topics in *The Scottish Field* and *The Scots Magazine*, fast becoming Tranter house magazines. He was a gifted civil engineer, too, and the road he prospected along Loch Duich to Kyle in Wester Ross, with its inventive solutions to very difficult terrain, was known locally after its completion as "Philip's road": his parents were asked to go up and open it after his death. He seems to have been a natural leader, deploying his not inconsiderable charm to cajole his companions time and again to go out on yet another climb when they would rather have stayed put in the bothy. Gangling and bearded, with a robust sense of humour, he was a single-minded man, like his father, and he lived life right up to the hilt, accepted every challenge that came his way, and was incapable of taking No for an answer. He shared his charm with his father, but they also shared another vital attribute that marked them apart: a driven energy in pursuit of their own ends. If Philip was determined to cram in yet another climb and needed companions to go with him, it was usually easier, in the long run, to give in than to resist.

Philip Tranter was always interested in conquering new territory, pushing back boundaries, scaling new peaks and opening up new routes. By the time he was 22, he had climbed all the Munros twice and some three or four times. But his work took him into the far north and west of Scotland which was much less well known and this came to be his preferred territory when in Scotland. By 1963, however, with three close companions, Will Fraser, Gavin Johnstone and John Wedderburn, he was already contemplating bigger things. Everest had been done, but there were many peaks still unclimbed in the Hindu Kush range in Afghanistan. His own employers were generous as regards time off, two of the others were still at university and the third was a chartered surveyor, another independent job. There should be no difficulty about taking a couple of months out to climb in central Asia. The first tentative plans had been discussed in September 1963 and by 1964 they were ready to start preparing and organising an expedition in earnest. Finance was a problem, with halfway round the world to go before they even started climbing: and for the peaks over 20,000ft they were proposing to tackle they would need special equipment. But with a generous grant of £350 from the Everest Foundation, £50 from the Godman Exploration Fund and their own stake money, it looked feasible. They would bring back plant specimens and specimens of butterflies and insects to justify their claims to be a scientific expedition. Philip would be the expedition's surveyor and geographer, a major undertaking, since they were going into an area measuring some 800 square miles marked hitherto on maps only by a large white patch. They got contributions in kind from suppliers of equipment and provisions, and Philip expected to sell one or two articles to help recover some of the money expended. One major item of expenditure was a Land Rover, for they intended to drive across country from Edinburgh as far up the Bashgal Valley in Afghanistan as they could go. The Land Rover apart, they were, as usual, operating on a shoe-string, camping along the way, doing their own catering, and spending as little time as possible on the journey.

As might be expected of the son of such a father, Philip was a Scottish patriot. The Scottish Highlands, the remoter the better, were his happy hunting ground. His preferred dress as a young man was the kilt, and he even, improbably, wore it to climb in. They decided to call themselves, rather grandly, the Scottish Hindu Kush Expedition: the probability is that it never seriously occurred to them to call themselves anything else. In the best tradition, Liz MacLaren, Secretary of the Corriemulzie Club, sewed the flag. It could all be put down to youthful sentiment. But they were going where no man had ever gone before, and they would plant her little Saltire higher, probably, than any Scottish flag had ever been before. Not a bad memorial.

They reached Afghanistan 18 days out from Edinburgh, passing

Mount Ararat close to the Turkish border, some of the last stretches being done over atrocious roads, with some hair-raising near-misses, and progress down at times to 10mph. The Land Rover left behind, they had donkeys to take their gear up the next stage: finally they carried it themselves. Between them, in their three weeks in the Hindu Kush, they made nine first ascents of peaks around the 20,000ft mark, named them patriotically for the Scottish peaks they resembled, and Philip mapped and sketched them. Gavin collected plant specimens and John Wedderburn, the doctor of the party, monitored their physical condition. They were doing the climbs with the equipment available at the time, and all took time to adjust to the high altitudes. There was a lot of ice work to be done and Gavin had a very close call when a large portion of an ice cornice broke off within half an inch of his boot. All of them suffered stomach upsets from time to time and the physical strain was immense. Whenever he wasn't actually climbing, Philip was mapping: in one diary entry he records that he spent five hours mapping one afternoon, then woke early the next morning to finish off an article about climbing in the Scottish Highlands. He was also keeping a detailed diary, running to four or five closely written quarto pages a day, which he envisaged working up into a book in due course: this was the book subsequently completed by his father and published under the title *No Tigers in the Hindu Kush*. And he took hundreds of photographs. He was a keen photographer, and it was his habit to take photographs of every-one he ever climbed with: these photographs followed him around and he stuck them up in his various digs and the caravan he lived in for six months at Dornie. Climbing forms the closest of ties, and climbers' homes tend to be full of pictures and maps which keep the hills close even in suburban homes.

They returned to Edinburgh triumphant and invigorated by their experiences, and Philip, at least, was already toying with ideas for the future. In the meantime, there was a winter of climbing ahead in the Scottish Highlands. It was saddened by the death of one of Philip's oldest friends, Alastair Park, known to them all as "Uncle", who fell to his death on a pre-Easter Corriemulzie meet at Foinaven. Together they had pioneered many routes all over the North and West and co-authored a climber's guide to the North-west Highlands. Philip was involved in the recovery of the body and went with the others a few weeks later to scatter his ashes among the mountains he loved. It was terrible for all of them, and almost more so for the families worrying at home. Looking through old photograph albums of climbers with the survivors, it is striking how often they say, "He died". Although they were all experienced climbers and observed every precaution, the families were justified in their fears, for mountaineering is a dangerous sport, not because risks are taken, but because one slip can mean, not just a broken ankle, but death.

There were plans for climbing in Chamonix in the summer of 1966 and these went ahead. In the meantime, Philip's contract with Ross-shire County Council was coming to an end and he had applied for a job with the Livingston Development Corporation, starting the following autumn. It came as a surprise to his friends, for Livingston lies in the central belt of Scotland: was he thinking of settling down at last? The women closest to him could have made an educated guess. As far as the immediate future was concerned, the gap between jobs would give him an unusually long summer holiday and he meant to make the most of it. At 6'4" he was not only exceptionally tall, but, as all recall, had the longest legs they ever saw, and the little green mini van that went like a bomb had now been extended so that he would be more comfortable sleeping in the back. He would take it to Chamonix and then see what happened next. In the event, the group's time in Chamonix was not a wild success: the weather deteriorated sharply just after they arrived and they hung about, undecided whether to cut their losses and go home, or wait in hopes of an improvement. Hanging about was not in Philip's nature and he decided on the spur of the moment to make for Turkey and the Ali Doq range, persuading two of the others, both still at university, to go with him. Both were first-class climbers, in particular the girl, whom friends describe as a "seriously good rock climber".

This time they were really operating on a shoe-string, with the other two both still students and hard-up, and no financial backing: a £50 restriction was furthermore in force as far as currency for foreign travel was concerned, and they were dogged by car trouble, which delayed them and cost money not budgeted for. Although Philip had had the idea of climbing in Turkey in the back of his mind for some time, there had been no detailed planning, and he succeeded in leaving all his own climbing equipment behind. They followed the now established pattern of driving virtually round-the-clock, the two men taking turns at the wheel, while the other slept in the back, and it took them about ten days to reach their destination. Once there, they opted to concentrate on climbing the Lesser and Greater Demircazik peaks near Nigde, south-west of Ankara. The climbs were demanding and all of them suffered repeatedly from stomach upsets, but the diaries are consistently lyrical, with their descriptions of sleeping under the sky, watching wildfire lightning in the hills or lying on their backs counting shooting stars and talking of the universe. Again and again, he sums the day up as "the best ever", and they set off home again, sated and happy, on 11 August.

But the problems with the car continued, and there were some near-misses on the road to Ankara. There was trouble with the petrol gauge, the battery, and the windscreen wipers, serious overheating on the way up through the Balkans, and in Munich they ran the car into a hole in the road under some tramlines, only extracting it by the expenditure of much brute strength. They stopped on Wednesday 17 August to look up a hospitable friend in Leysin, who fed them and put them up for the night, leaving the next morning to make for Calais: they had just enough money left to pay the petrol to the ferry. Going too fast and trying to overtake a couple of slower vehicles, the van ran off the road and collided with a tree early on the morning of Friday 19 August, catapulting Philip, who was asleep in the back, straight through the windscreen, killing him instantly. The girl was in the passenger seat and was seriously injured and left, initially, for dead, and the driver sustained minor injuries.

His parents, who imagined him to be driving up through England, had been out all day, and returned home to find the house besieged by the carrion crows of the press, who had got the news from the tapes. The Police arrived later to confirm it. Nigel rang Frances May, who was with her family in England, to break it to her: her brother's last postcard, written in Ankara on the way home, reached her the next day. To compound their grief, there was a delay before the body was brought home, a Police investigation in France, and a long wrangle with insurance companies about payment of costs, including hospital and ambulance costs in France for the injured, which May gallantly dealt with.

It was a devastating blow for all of them, but most of all for May, who never really recovered. It was as though her nerves, already at full stretch following Uncle's death, had finally snapped. In the Scottish way, they had everyone back to the house after the funeral, and it was at this point that she broke down: her daughter found her in bed with the covers over her head. After all these years of worrying about accidents climbing, Philip had been killed, cruelly, on a back road in France. Nigel and Frances May both had ongoing lives that could not be ignored, Nigel his parallel world of the imagination and his public engagements, and Frances May her family, but the light had gone out for May, irrevocably.

They buried him in Aberlady kirkyard. An anonymous tribute in *The Climber*, which published his last article for them on the opposite page, had this to say of him: "Philip struggling to sew a ripped flysheet in a force 8 gale of a black winter's night; yelling defiance to the elements on a sleet-swept flog between camps; vigorously castigating would-be festerers, a blizzard raging outside; quietly philosophising on a long march back; making a 200 mile detour to give a lift home to a fellow climber. These are our memories . . ."

His parents did the best they could of course, although friends remember May as "terribly distressed", and Nigel decided to take up a long-standing suggestion from Hodder & Stoughton that he might do a new version of *The Queen's Scotland*. Although never completed, *The Queen's Scotland* was a hugely ambitious undertaking, originally rejected by Tranter as far too time-consuming and, from his own point of view, not commercial. An earlier version, *The King's Scotland*, edited, but not written, by Theo Lang, had covered the country region by region, telling the story of "the towns and villages of Scotland", and had been written in popular style and heavily illustrated, the entries varying in length according to the interest of the subject. The Tranter version was intended as a comprehensive account, covering the whole of Scotland parish by parish, each entry running to a minimum 1200-1500 words, with some of the longer ones as long as 10,000 words or more. It was envisaged as a kind of latter-day Statistical Account, only without the statistics, a snapshot of the present state, as well as the history, of each place.

It could never have been contemplated without May's assistance and Tranter only agreed to take it on as a form of therapy for both of them following Philip's death. They had worked successfully together on *The Fortified House*, with May making the notes while Nigel sketched. When they did *The Queen's Scotland*, they shared the preliminary research, May did the notes once more, and Nigel wrote them up. As usual, May also did the map-reading. In some cases May's notes have survived: they are unbelievably full, and the finished books contain a wealth of material not otherwise collected together in one place. Her notes for *The Queen's Scotland* are among his most precious possessions. There were over 1100 parishes in Scotland and they visited them all, averaging two a day on their research trips, working scientifically in order to try and keep costs down, and staying economically in commercial hotels. He was nevertheless considerably out of pocket on the deal. With *The Fortified House, The Queen's Scotland* constitutes the other major self-generated data bank on which he draws in his novels. Work tailed off as May became ill and was abandoned definitively after she died and never resumed, by Tranter or anyone else. Four volumes were published in all. Gamely, she had taken it on, and the magnitude of the undertaking ensured that as therapy it worked up to a point, and she struggled manfully to carry on with her life. But with Philip gone, Quarry House was doubly empty and she was too much alone with her thoughts. It was not an easy time for Nigel either, struggling with his own grief and desperately unhappy that there was so little he could do for May.

After Philip died, his father published two books based on the Hindu Kush expedition, an adventure story called *Cable from Kabul,* and another, *No Tigers in the Hindu Kush,* based directly on Philip's very full expedition diaries, and published under Philip's name, with Nigel credited only as editor. Philip had intended to write the book himself on his return from Turkey and his diaries, photographs, maps etc were all at Quarry House waiting for him to start. In addition to the pleasure and experience the expedition had given the four participants, their achievements were of course of some importance: between them, they had made nine ascents of hitherto unclimbed peaks, they had named a number of peaks, and Philip had mapped areas that had never been mapped before. It was with some hesitation, and only following consultation with his climbing friends, that Nigel undertook the task. He went ahead however and although it could never be other than heartbreaking, it was at the same time a labour of love, and together he and May set about the business of editing the diaries and preparing them in book form. As usual, May preferred her contribution to be anonymous and her name will not be found on the title page, but Nigel acknowledges her contribution in his foreword. It was May who got the last photographs developed and stuck them into the last of the dozens of climbing diaries, it was she who got them all identified and wrote the captions, and it was she who wrote across the bottom of the final page "He was killed early on Friday 19th and, please God, is now in the Heavenly Mountains". After discussing the matter with his closest friends, the dozen or so volumes of climbing diaries were divided up, Nigel and May keeping the last ones and the others going to other climbers.

The decision to publish *Cable from Kabul* was a little more surprising, in the circumstances, but it shows every sign of having been written before Philip died: his Hindu Kush diary on which it draws heavily for background was at Quarry House, waiting for him to work it up into what subsequently became *No Tigers in the Hindu Kush* and there is every reason to suppose that *Cable from Kabul* also drew on conversations between the two. Almost certainly they had discussed it together. It was furthermore written at a time when Nigel was worried about being able to sustain indefinitely the run of modern romantic adventure stories, and the switch to the historicals had not yet taken place. He would undoubtedly have discussed the matter with May, who read all his manuscripts, chapter by chapter. Presumably they came to the conclusion that since the work had been done, it might as well be published. At any rate, he decided to go ahead, although publication did not take place until 1968. It was a decision not everyone would have taken, but Nigel, who had felt himself once upon a time to be "sib" with his half-sister Dorothy, felt he was "sib", too, with Philip because Philip was also a writer, a fellow-practitioner of the same solitary trade, and perhaps in a way *Cable from Kabul*, too, seemed a kind of memorial. May was devastated because she had lost her only son, but Nigel had lost something closer than a son, a deep hurt that is with him for all time. Philip had been their own crusader, their valiant knight sallying forth, bearing their name out into the world and they had lost him, violently, on crusade.

XXV

THE BRUCE

A chess-board on a side-table, the pieces modelled with unusual care, the knights with surcoats and helms, the horses with shabracks, the King with the Lion Rampant on his breast, the royal circlet round his helm and his battle-axe in his hand. The King is Bruce and his knights are The Wallace and the Good Sir James Douglas. This is the Bannockburn chess-set presented to Nigel in 1992.

Measured by any standard—commercial success, critical acclaim, popular impact, personal satisfaction—the *Bruce* trilogy marks a high point in Nigel Tranter's career. Bruce was a key figure on the Scottish chess-board and here at last he had a subject capable of bringing out the best in him. The *Montrose* omnibus, which came immediately afterwards, surpassed it in quality of writing and had perhaps, in the last analysis, a nobler hero, if a less central one, but *The Steps to the Empty Throne*, published in 1969, was the defining book, the book which made him a household name. It was also the book that finally ousted the more minor causes from the forefront of his mind in favour of Scotland's story. Although he had gone on writing novels after Philip's death and was heavily involved in work on *The Queen's Scotland*, the books he had published since 1966 were a job lot of children's books and modern novels with two exceptions: Philip's book, *No Tigers in the Hindu Kush*, and *Black Douglas*. *Black Douglas*, published in 1968, might well have pre-empted the success of *The Steps to the Empty Throne* for it is an excellent book, rich in texture and full of action, with a meaty subject, the rivalry between the Red and Black Douglases, but Hodder misjudged sales and the print run was too short: for years afterwards, indeed until it was published in paperback in 1973, Tranter's papers are full of letters from readers wondering where they can get hold of a copy. As it was, it sold 85,000 copies. It was in fact the second of a three-book contract with Hodder, which seems never to have been completed, as sales took off, and sets of books supervened. But Bruce was the ultimate Scottish hero, which Douglas was not. Bruce was the victor of Bannockburn, whose heart had been carried to Jerusalem on crusade by the Good Sir James Douglas and hurled into battle at Tebas de Ardales with the words, "Lead on, Brave Heart, as thou wast ever wont to do". Encouraged by the success of the *MacGregor* and *Master of Gray* trilogies, Hodder signed Tranter in 1967 to a contract for all three books of the *Bruce* trilogy at an advance of £525 each. *The Steps to the Empty Throne* was an immediate, runaway success, selling half a million copies at first launch and notching up another half million over the years: even more extraordinary, the two succeeding books of the trilogy matched it in sales.

Tranter himself approached the writing of the *Bruce* trilogy with some trepidation, partly on grounds of its magnitude and partly because of the sheer importance of the subject, having thrust it from him for some years. Once started, it quickly became all-absorbing. When it was over, he wrote to a correspondent, "For the past four years, I have practically *been* Robert Bruce. The job is finished now and to some extent I feel quite lost." Tranter of course writes all his heroes largely out of his own experience, posing the question "What would *I* have done?" where the historical material fails him, but Bruce was a move up to a new dimension.

Rob Roy's saga had been played out essentially on a local scale and the *Master of Gray* trilogy was an odd mixture of palace intrigues and domestic preoccupations, the Master himself not a particularly familiar figure. Bruce however was a king and a general and the battles he fought were turning-points in Scotland's story, not local skirmishes. Above all, he was a national hero, the common property of the nation and as such, not to be tampered with injudiciously. It was a major triumph to depict Bruce with the verisimilitude and grandeur that Tranter achieved, and a triumph, above all, of the imagination. It was also a triumph as far as organisation of material was concerned, for the canvas on which he was working was vast and the supporting cast, like the hero, actors upon a national stage. Bruce, like most of the nobles, was also a Norman, which conferred a cosmopolitan dimension and involved the constant tensions between the loyalties of a ruling caste, many of whom had a personal stake also in England, and the deeper roots which tapped into the old Celtic blood. Tranter was not however making a book out of these tensions as Scott did of the struggle for supremacy between Norman and Saxon in *Ivanhoe*. The problem is deftly handled as a recurrent political complication: it is an element, but it is not the whole story, which is the fight for independence and unification under the crown. It is a measure of the skill with which he managed his huge canvas and how well he kept up the momentum over three long books, as well as of the enormous interest manifested in the subject, that the popular response was unprecedented, the most commonly expressed praise being "I feel as if I have lived myself through these turbulent years."

The reviews also were overwhelmingly positive, hailing *The Steps to the Empty Throne* as a remarkable achievement, "without a doubt, the most interesting historical novel of the year", but by and large most failed at this stage to spot the importance of the book or anticipate the huge sales. A few complained of some wooden-ness in the portrayal of Bruce, possibly attributable to the fact that Tranter was too much in awe of him, and the *Times Literary Supplement* noted that "We do not see his greatness except in fighting". Writing of the account of Bannockburn in *The Path of the Hero King,* the second book of the trilogy, the *Glasgow Herald,* which had thought Bruce himself a bit of a bore in the first book, noted with approval this time that the many battle scenes were given not only with a wealth of technical detail but with a restraint that would surprise some, and went on to say that to show Bannockburn, the climax of the book, as not a pitched battle at all, ". . . only a vast, horrible and unimaginable chaos of mud and blood and screaming frustration . . . is not the language of Barbour, but it reads like the truth."

When the third book, *The Price of the King's Peace,* came out, the critic H Forsyth Hardy wrote, "In choosing a phase of Scottish history familiar in superficial outline, he has . . . given a new depth and meaning to the story. . . . The trilogy gives the impression of a work long matured and deeply felt." Hardy's point about the choice of subject was an important one, as Tranter himself recognised: in taking on a subject of whom so much was known and concerning whom the preconceived ideas were so deeply rooted, he was taking on a momentous task. Had he failed, his future career might well have been very different: taking on the Bruce was risk-taking of a high degree. Any criticisms were not shared by the vast bulk of the reading public: as Hardy wrote, they knew the Bruce story in superficial outline but now at last Tranter had filled in the details and put into their hands a rich and wonderful story worthy of the great hero king, and, as Scots, they could walk tall. The *Bruce* trilogy was the point at which Tranter's re-telling of Scotland's story started to impinge on ordinary people's sense of their own identity.

The *Bruce* trilogy is a *tour de force* and deserved its success. From the shocking opening scene at Stracathro and the humiliation of

Baliol, the aftermath of the English sack of Berwick and the signing of the infamous Ragman's Roll, through the sacrilegious slaying of Comyn, Bannockburn itself, the dignified and courtly relationship with Elizabeth de Burgh and the warm comfort provided by Christina MacRuarie to the deathbed request to Angus Og to take custody of the Stone of Destiny, only one central scene fails: curiously enough, the one scene familiar to every school-child, the story of the spider, which he contrives to make tame. Although unlikely material, as a turning-point it needs to be dramatic, and indeed it is dramatic in the folk-mind. It is perhaps worth noting, too, that, although the *Bruce* trilogy is in essence as much a fictionalised life of Bruce as a set of three linked novels, the Bruce's story falls naturally into three parts: the gradual recognition of his role, the fight for independence, and the struggle to maintain it and establish royal authority, with plenty of action in all three. Not all the trilogies are as well balanced.

As it became apparent that the *Bruce* trilogy was going to sell and sell, minds turned to a successor. Once all three books were out, pressure began to build up for a book on Wallace, whom many felt had not had his due in the *Bruce* books and this Tranter agreed with. *The Wallace* was not destined to be the next book from his pen, but should be looked at in the context of the *Bruce*.

Tranter himself regards Wallace as the greater hero of the two, in that while Bruce fought for a throne, Wallace fought for a nobler cause, for liberty and the idea of nationhood; and many of Tranter's own ideas about nationhood are to be found spelt out when Wallace confronts the nobles at Mill of Fullarton and cries out: ". . . these noble lords—who do they speak for? Themselves, their lands, the power of the realm. But who speaks for the folk of Scotland, my lords? Does any here? The folk. The nation. This Scotland is more than a realm, my friends—it is a nation. A people, an ancient people. A people that has been betrayed and sold and spurned. All but forgotten by those who seek the power . . ." Throughout the book, we are constantly reminded that Wallace is a man of the people, just as we are constantly reminded of his great stature and physique, capable of severing a man's head from his body with a single blow of his sword. Although he never himself makes the connection, it is striking how both the great folk-heroes with whom Tranter deals—Wallace and Rob Roy—are men of extraordinary physical powers and presence, the very stuff of which folk-heroes are made, attracting to themselves semi-legendary feats, simply because their stature seems to render them possible. Such tales of Wallace, in particular, are to be found all over Scotland. In addition to being portrayed as the champion of the people, he is also of course the guerilla leader, with a deep understanding of how to use the terrain to his own advantage, and there is a striking scene at Abbey Craig, when he sits motionless on his horse, "staring out, as though he would imprint every fold, wrinkle and feature of that waterlogged plain indelibly on his mind". But in contrast to the Bruce, who plays the general's part, Wallace is shown as a natural hands-on captain, anxious to be in the thick of the battle, as when he gets in under the horses' bellies at the battle of Stirling Bridge. He is also depicted as a more human figure than Bruce, signalled by the opening line of the book, when he is shown weeping over the carnage at Carleith. Tranter is of course a master of the opening scene, and this one advances swiftly to the dramatic "shriek of steel" as Wallace pulls the great two-handed sword from its sheath behind his back, and upends it in a single movement to swear his silent vow of vengeance. As always, the opening scene tells us what the book will be about: the Bruce books open with the humiliation of Baliol by Edward Longshanks and its effect on Bruce, who was present at Stracathro, and *The Wallace* opens with the carnage wreaked on the common folk of Scotland by the English occupying forces and its effect on Wallace. The final scenes of the *Bruce* trilogy and *The Wallace* are both well-done, but the Wallace's shocking, brutal, dreadful end is unforgettable.

The complaint against the treatment of Wallace in the *Bruce* books had been that he was shouldered out of the picture and played too minor a role: in *The Wallace* both are given their proper place and the relations between them suitably developed. But though both are national heroes of equal stature, there are never-theless important differences between them, largely explained by their difference in rank: Wallace twice changes dramatically in emotional response to a situation, first at Carleith and later when he hears the news of Marion Braidfoot's death, whereas Bruce matures more gradually and rationally into the realisation that it is his destiny as monarch to lead his country to independence. Relations between the two men and their wives and lovers are also subtly differentiated: Wallace is shown as deeply and simply in love with his wife, compelled to visit her in secret, desolated and changed irrevocably by her death, and devastated also by his role in the death of Meg Drummond, the whore who provided him with valuable information at Perth. Bruce's relationship with Elizabeth de Burgh is more complex and more adult: Elizabeth a great lady with an interest in affairs of state, more accomplished in playing a waiting game, while Marion is still a girl, rushing to throw herself into her husband's arms when he suddenly appears at Lanark. It is also interesting that the relations of both Bruce and Wallace with their wives and lovers are tenderly drawn without recourse to explicit sex scenes, and the books are the better for it. (It is a curious fact that the few sex scenes in the earlier books, before his publishers allegedly asked him to spice them up a bit, are more satisfactory than the later ones, perhaps because they do not give the same impression of being pasted on.) Bruce is a great noble and a great king throughout and we admire him and thrill to him, but we are shown more of the inner workings of Wallace's mind and it is with Wallace that we empathise. It is noteworthy, too, that in *The Wallace*, written three or four years after the *Bruce* trilogy, Tranter slips in a couple of reminders of earlier books in depicting Lord James Stewart, with his slobbering mouth, an ancestor of Jamie Saxt of *The Wisest Fool*, and Glenorchy, an ancestor of Rob Roy, with the same massive stature. There are threads running backwards and forwards from all these central books: the links were beginning to appear which hint at the whole complex web Tranter would eventually weave in his dawning ambition to tell Scotland's story in its entirety.

From the publication of *The Steps to the Empty Throne* on, it began to be possible to detect a difference between the English and the Scottish reviewers. When *The Wallace* came out in 1975, the year of the Government White Paper on Devolution, the *Financial Times* wrote "Tranter treats history with respect . . . his account is detailed and dense, with names and places and a great feeling of authenticity". But the *Daily Record* described it as "a superb piece of work, filled with the smell and feel of history" and *The Scotsman* wrote that it was "the stuff that nationalist dreams are fuelled with". *Business Scotland* noted that "Patriotism of the kind shown by Wallace is becoming more important to us daily for complex psychological reasons" and the *Aberdeen Evening News* observed that it had been "launched at an ideal time to sail into the best-selling charts on the floodtide of Scottish Nationalism". A scribbled note from his publisher listing requests for newspaper, radio and TV interviews, profiles etc reflects the general excitement, "Clear the decks! A busy time ahead". *The Wallace* however sold rather less well than the *Bruce* books. Perhaps Wallace, man of the people as he was, had less intrinsic glamour; perhaps his career seemed more restricted; perhaps his dreadful end upset people; maybe the high tide of nationalism was on the ebb again.

Opinions are divided as to who first came up with the idea of a book about Montrose, but there were two weighty voices in favour: Hodder & Stoughton's own view, expressed by Tranter's editor Maggie Body, that the time was ripe for "a really full-blooded and dramatic re-telling" of the Montrose story and James

Thin, the influential Edinburgh bookseller, who in writing to Tranter to compliment him on the *Bruce*, also pressed for something on Montrose, and when he got it, wrote to Hodder & Stoughton "I really think Nigel has excelled himself. He has sent me . . . back to Buchan, but he has painted in the background . . . in so much greater detail . . ." Montrose is one of Nigel Tranter's own great heroes, because he had the courage to change his mind and change sides in the religious wars, and he had had it in mind for some time to write about him; but he would have preferred not to have done Montrose right on top of the Bruce books. He could see quite clearly, too, that Montrose was not going to be an easy subject, and has always regarded the *Montrose* books as the most difficult he ever tackled: the extraordinarily complex side-changing and inter-play of Scottish and English affairs involved in the civil and religious wars of the mid-17th century would call for the utmost skill and tact in writing, even three centuries on, and although there would be plenty of scope for military action, it would be of a different kind from the battles of the late mediaeval period at which he so excelled. There was also the problem involved in dealing with a figure who would offer so few opportunities for a lighter touch. However the temptation, as well as the pressure, to do something on Montrose proved in the last resort irresistible and he succumbed.

One of the problems with Montrose was how this "eternal type of the heroic" as John Buchan called him, was to be made human and comprehensible. Tranter did it through his portrayal of Montrose's relations with his wife and family. From the first, Magdalen Carnegie and her father the Earl of Southesk, under whose protection at Kinnaird Castle she wound up spending most of her married life, would have preferred to see him stand aside from his destiny, spend his life administering his estates and leading the life of a country gentleman, letting the religious passions that so ravaged the country pass him by. But Montrose was a man of conscience and of honour, and although snubbed initially by his King, he was a great noble with an overwhelming sense of duty to King and country, and could not stand aside: it was his misfortune that in the mid-17th century they were at odds as far as Scotland was concerned. As a staunch Presbyterian, disgusted by the King's high-handed policy towards the Kirk, he was the first to put his name to the Covenant at Greyfriars in 1638, and from then on, his rank and qualities as a general ensured that he would be drawn ineluctably into a struggle from which there was no turning back and which would end in death on the scaffold. His few subsequent confrontations with Charles I, while still committed to the Covenant, are marked by Montrose's heart-felt declarations of loyalty and assurance that the Covenanters do not seek to undermine the throne. Charles, although ill-advised and paralysed by court convention and the baleful influence of his wife Henrietta Maria, was disbelieving and he was proved right. As he watched the excesses of the extremists grow, and the Kirk itself grow increasingly ambitious and dictatorial, the most fanatical seeking to establish a theocracy, and others bent less gloriously on personal power, Montrose's misgivings increased and he eventually entered into a Bond, or agreement, with other like-minded moderates, which in the end proved his undoing. He went over to the King in 1641 and spent some months in prison thereafter without trial, suspected of conspiracy against Argyll. Argyll's dark and sinister figure lurks and sidles right through the books, and is there, half hidden at the back of Moray's balcony on the High Street, to watch Montrose being carried to his death, head bared that the mob may see him. In 1644, Montrose rallied the royalist Highland clans in support of the King and defeated the Covenanters at Tippermuir, Inverlochy and Auldearn, but his efforts to raise the Lowlands were unsuccessful and after a crushing defeat at Philiphaugh in 1645 he went into exile in Norway. He was in the Low Countries when he heard of Charles's execution. He returned in 1650 with too small a force and was easily defeated at Carbisdale by Leslie, the brilliant turncoat general of the Covenanting armies who was prepared to fight for Charles against the Parliamentarians if the terms were right. Montrose was eventually betrayed to the Covenant by Macleod of Assynt.

Montrose, like Bruce, was known as a great general, but Tranter achieves more insight into the personality of Montrose and gives a moving picture of the personal sacrifice and the strains imposed by his constant campaigning in the King's cause, the pain caused by the loss of his young son on campaign and his ultimate rejection by his wife Magdalen. The rivalry with Argyll is felt as a constant menace and the reader watches with growing apprehension the progress of the quarrel to its inevitable end on the gallows. Tranter's handling of the two most familiar scenes, Jenny Geddes throwing her stool in St Giles' when the Book of Canons is introduced in 1637, and Montrose's execution in 1650, the two events which bracket together Montrose's public career, is superb. Between these two scenes the tragedy of his personal, as well as his public, life, is played out. We have an early glimpse of him, tenderly stroking Magdalen Carnegie's hair but within weeks of marriage, he leaves this wife to whom he was devoted to set off on an extended search on the continent of Europe for his wayward sister Kate, and from then on, they have only brief interludes together. Time and again, she pleads with him to stay: before Tippermuir, she pleads to go with him. She pleads with him not to accede to young Johnnie's request to go campaigning with him, and Johnnie eventually dies of a fever with the army. She suffers the loss of another son at home, alone, and eventually she rejects him. It was perhaps his greatest sacrifice in his country's cause, for by the time his life was required of him, it had lost much of its meaning. He comes across as a truly noble figure, whose tragic end seems pre-ordained in Tranter's portrayal.

The critics were overwhelmingly positive, although *The Scotsman* thought the King seemed more like a tailor's dummy than a man—which he may well have been in reality—but *Scotland's Magazine* wrote of the scene in St Giles when the Prayer Book was introduced, "Such an oft-told tale might well have fallen flat, but the colourful scene is cunningly built-up against the grey backcloth of the church—the gathering of the notables, the shattering of the silence by the throwing of the stool and the subsequent pandemonium . . ." There was also praise for his handling of the execution scene.

Two sets of books of the magnitude and importance of the *Bruce* trilogy and the *Montrose* omnibus one on top of the other was punishing and not what Tranter would have chosen, but he went straight from the Montrose books to *The Wallace*—an extraordinary feat of endurance, made the more remarkable by the fact that the first of the books were written in the immediate aftermath of his son Philip's death and all of them were written in tandem with the huge labour involved in producing *The Queen's Scotland*.

Tranter had written for the first time about James VI & I, his all-time favourite character, in the *Master of Gray* trilogy, and he was an obvious choice of subject to provide some relaxation, some undiluted enjoyment, after the strain of writing the *Bruce* and *Montrose* books. In *The Master of Gray* books, James is not yet assured of the English succession and his physical cowardice combined with extreme political caution show him perhaps as more of the traditional poltroon than the great comic figure he later becomes in Tranter's expert hands. But all the comic features are already there, waiting to be developed: the lolling head and knock knees combined with the beautiful Stewart eyes, the combination of puritanism and timorous lewdness, the sudden swings from informality to regal dignity, the keen eye for the main chance, the liking for Latin tags, the pawky wit, the use of the Doric, even the "Ooh, ayes" are there already, just waiting to be brought to full fruition in *The Wisest Fool*.

The Wisest Fool, published in 1974, nine years after the last of the *Master of Gray* books, is a comic masterpiece, not because it has us chuckling all the way through, but because it makes of a rather obscure and unattractive figure a great comic personality, great because it contains also seriousness and tragedy to underscore the comic elements. Tranter's Jamie Saxt is a figure in the tradition of Falstaff or *Le Malade Imaginaire*, but his undoubted qualities of kingship—a rare example for the age of a king who kept first Scotland, then the combined kingdoms of Scotland and England out of war for the whole of his reign—are never lost sight of. He is of course also most recognisably Scots: homespun, pawky, canny, cautious, scheming, sharp, shrewd, devious, inventive, serious-minded, full of curious ideas, some of them strongly-held, possessive, unexpectedly affectionate and forebearing with his long-suffering Queen, Anne of Denmark, despite his weakness for young men, taking a hand in everything from court entertainments (we are told his taste was for percussion and loud noises, provided he knew they were coming) to the translation of the Psalms, licentious and disapproving by turns. He also has a devastating capacity for deflating the pompous as when he responds to the High Sheriff of York's elegant and well-turned words of greeting, seeking his "gracious goodwill for duchy and city, and royal confirmation of our ancient charters and privileges" with "Is that so?"—the pure, distilled essence of the Scot's native determination not to be impressed. Through all, he is highly individual and totally unpredictable: from the moment he crosses the border at Berwick, complaining loudly that the bridge is "shoogly", to our last sight of him, telling Geordie Heriot to get out his kist so that he can hand over his winnings at cards, suddenly announcing that the Master of Gray is ". . . deid . . . Deceased. On his way to hell, belike!" and adding unexpectedly "Mind you, I'll miss him", the great thing about Tranter's Jamie

Saxt is that you never know what he'll say next. Not much wonder he kept his English courtiers guessing: they thought him a country bumpkin on arrival and for some time thereafter, but learnt better.

Geordie Heriot, goldsmith and banker to the King, and founder of Heriot's School, is of course the other great creation of *The Wisest Fool,* solid, stocky, sober, reliable, another archetypal Scot of a different kidney, and it is in the contrast between the two and the confidential conversations with Heriot that much of the King's character is revealed. Heriot also presents one of the few instances of mature love in the books and his sedate courtship and eventual marriage to Alison Primrose is wholly in character and gives particular satisfaction to the reader because Heriot is at the same time such a thoroughly estimable and sympathetic character. Tranter did well here by his old school.

Mail Royal, published in 1989, also written by way of relaxation, this time following *Columba,* which Tranter regarded as his greatest challenge, is another of the Jamie Saxt books, but more obliquely. It deals with the Casket Letters, allegedly written by Mary Queen of Scots to Bothwell and supposed to contain an admission that James was the son, as many believed, of her secretary David Rizzio, who had been murdered before her eyes at Holyrood before he was born, and thus that James was illegitimate and not entitled to either the Scottish or the English throne. The Letters appear to have disappeared after the execution of the Earl of Gowrie in 1584, but the possibility that they might once more come to light and be used to oust him preyed on James's mind and was used periodically to blackmail him. In Tranter's story, young David Gray, an illegitimate grandson of the Master of Gray, thought to have been one of the blackmailers, is recruited by his father, the Lord of Gray, to search for the letters at Fast Castle on the Berwickshire coast. He finds the letters, but not the feared incriminating information about James's parentage, and the conclusion is that it never existed. The scenes with James are as diverting as ever and the mystery of the Casket Letters resolved—even if it seems a bit of a let-down—but the book itself is slight, and essentially the love story of David Gray and Barbara Home of Bilsdean.

Poetic Justice, published in 1996, is a much meatier follow-up to *The Wisest Fool*, and deals with James's absorbing interest in poetry and consequent interest in fellow-poet William Alexander of Menstrie, whom he brings to London with him in 1603 and appoints tutor, first of his elder son Prince Henry, Prince of Wales, and after Henry's death of Charles, later Charles I. Alexander is eventually roped in to mastermind the King's arrangements for the Plantation of Ulster and the colonisation of Nova Scotia, both settled by grants of baronetcies under an extension of one of the King's favourite money-making schemes. Tranter had taken a close interest in Menstrie nearly forty years before, when the local county council clapped a demolition order on the castle because of its ruinous state. Aware of its interest far beyond the shores of Scotland, he fired off letters to the Premier of Nova Scotia and the Mayor of Halifax as well the National Trust for Scotland appealing to them to have the order lifted. His campaign was successful, Menstrie was saved and in due course the Commemoration Room at the castle, which is dedicated to these baronetcies of Ulster and Nova Scotia, was opened by the Queen in May 1963.

XXVI

CHEVALIER

In Edinburgh, a chapel hung with green and white banners, the ceiling and choir-stalls thick with armorial escutcheons, huge heraldic windows of stained glass, the whole carpeted in the distinctive emerald green of the Order of St Lazarus. In East Lothian, an open door in the new Phrontistery and inside, the black velvet cloak and green shoulder cross of a Knight Commander of the Order.

Nigel's grandchildren call him "Chevalier" and sometimes "Chev" for short. The background is that, having married young, he found himself a grandfather at the age of 53, which he thought was much too young. As usual, it was May that came up with a solution: he was entitled to call himself "Chevalier", so why not settle for that? And Chevalier he became. The name has a highly romantic connotation in Scotland, for "The Young Chevalier" was the name—commemorated in song and story familiar to every Scot—by which the Young Pretender, Bonnie Prince Charlie, was popularly known.

In Nigel's case, he actually *was* a Chevalier. In 1961 he was appointed a Knight, or Chevalier, of the Order of St Lazarus of Jerusalem and was one of the first two Scots to be dubbed knight by the Duc de Brissac, international Grand Prior of the Order.

Since the Order of St Lazarus is a knightly order, all its members are knights, so Chevalier is the lowest, not the highest, rank. But he advanced in time to become a Commander of Merit, and became, first, Vice-Chancellor of the Order in Scotland in 1982, and then Chancellor in 1986. The Order of St Lazarus of Jerusalem, founded by St Basil in the 4th century as an order of hospitallers, was reconstituted as a military order in 1098 and is the second-oldest order of chivalry in Christendom, pre-dated only by the Order of St John of Jerusalem, which was founded in 1070. It had a special mission to minister to Crusaders who were lepers. Bruce believed himself to have leprosy, although doctors nowadays think it was more likely to have been a form of dermatitis, but some knights *did* go down with leprosy, and had to be totally isolated from the rest of society: lepers were also regarded as being outcasts of God, who ceased officially to exist, and were therefore considered objects of particular compassion. The Order of St Lazarus was founded to provide a house for them in Jerusalem, and lepers, although fewer nowadays, still top the Order's list of charities and they still maintain a presence in Jerusalem.

Originally a Papal Order, the Order of St Lazarus continued to be so, in more or less unbroken succession, until it passed in the 16th century under the protection of the Kings of France. It was banned by the Papacy in 1789 following the French Revolution. There seems to have been a considerable lapse of time before it was resuscitated under the patronage of the high nobility of France towards the end of the 19th century after the collapse of the post-Napoleonic monarchy, and in the early 20th century it experienced a resurgence of vigour also in Britain. The Scottish and English branches of the Order are separate—there is a Grand Priory in England and a Grand Bailliewick in Scotland—and by the time Nigel Tranter was appointed a Chevalier, as one of the first under a new dispensation, the Scottish branch was already riven with schism, and close to splitting. In the absence of either royal or papal patronage, feuding broke out between the different factions as to which was the true successor order. (The Vatican, if consulted, would have said neither. Orders of Chivalry, it seems, are a bit like the Apostolic Succession: once the chain is broken, it cannot be repaired.) Tranter's papers contain copious references to the problems which beset the Order in Scotland. The majority view was that the true faith remained in the custody of the French chapter and its Grand Master, the Duc de Brissac, but the Scottish Grand Baillie held differently and Eugene Cardinale, historian of the Papal Orders, records that the Vatican was bombarded during this time with such a barrage of letters demanding re-admission to Papal patronage that it was eventually compelled to issue a definitive statement to the effect that the Pope had no intention, then or ever, of re-admitting the Order of St Lazarus as a Papal Order. For good measure, it went on to say that acceptance of membership by distinguished individuals, even bishops and cardinals, however innocent, was only an indication of their gullibility, and in no way implied official status. The Order continues, however, to flourish in both England and Scotland, making new knights and going about its charitable business, and Tranter is still a knight, although scarcely an active one, and takes some pride in it: the letters KStLJ will be found printed on his visiting cards and in his entry in the Scottish *Who's Who*. And the insignia and ceremonies which go with membership are dignified and colourful. Among other things, they address each other as *confrère*. Sadly, although recognised as an international order of chivalry, the Order enjoys no more official status in Britain than it does in the Vatican, the ground-rule apparently still being that laid down by Elizabeth Tudor, "My dogs shall wear no collars but mine". But it is pleasant to think that Nigel Tranter, who has written so much and so vividly about the days of chivalry and the institution of knighthood, should have taken his knightly vows in the Order of St Lazarus and pledged himself to continue a true knight to his life's end.

The concept of knighthood has of course long interested him and there are frequent references to it in his books. Writing in *The Scots Magazine* in April 1971, he spelt out his views at some length, stating that the three essential conditions of knighthood are that a knight shall be male, that he shall be selected, and that he shall be honourable. In contradistinction to all other honours carrying titles, an earldom, say, it confers rank independent of social standing, and it has its origins in Roman times. It was the Normans who first introduced the idea of armed service owed to a superior in exchange for tenure of land. With the coming of the Crusades, however, the link between armed service and land tenure began to be eroded: since not all were prepared to abandon management of their lands to others for years at a time in order to go off on crusade, the Crusaders in fact included many younger sons who were landless and the link between land tenure and military service was lost. It was at this period that the quasi-religious, chivalric concept of knighthood crept in. By tradition, only a knight could make a knight and there are frequent references to this in the books. When James VI introduced his new baronetcies, which carried social precedence, it cut right across the concept of knighthood and since the sovereign is the fount of all honour in modern times, the conferral of knighthood is now associated with conferral by the monarch who happens at the present time to be a woman. Tranter therefore poses, without answering, the interesting question whether this means that knighthoods conferred by the present monarch are technically invalid. To which it must be said that, in that case, the knighthoods conferred by other women monarchs, notably Elizabeth Tudor, must have been invalid, too.

The whole operation and status of knighthood fascinated him, and he was particularly intrigued by the way it cut across other considerations of rank. He also uses the conferral of knighthood to advantage in the books, as a means whereby to transform overnight the status of the humbly-born illegitimate half-brothers of whom he makes such play, so as to enable them to participate in great events rather than merely witness them, or aspire to the hand of a lady otherwise above their station. The young Jamie Douglas in *Lords of Misrule* is a good example. Called into service to keep the tally of men volunteered to King Robert II at Stirling, he acquits himself well and is rewarded by his father, the Earl of Dalkeith, with the little estate of Aberdour, which in its turn enables him to maintain a modest dignity when he rides with the King's armies into England as esquire to the Earl of Douglas: conspicuous gallantry in the field earns him a knighthood from Dunbar at Otterburn, and that in its turn enables him to wed Mary Stewart, a King's daughter, even though illegitimate like himself. The young David Gray in *Mail Royal* is another: knighted unexpectedly by James VI & I to enhance his authority as member of an embassy, he suddenly sees the way open to pay his suit to Barbara Home of Bilsdean.

But the most dramatic knighting of all comes in *The Wallace*, when Bruce suddenly knights Wallace as he stands there at Selkirk among the commonality in his old chain-mail and leather arm-guards, to enable him to become Guardian of Scotland, a real-life event of the utmost importance, for it makes the link between Bruce and Wallace and is the first act of Bruce's coming kingship, but enhanced in Tranter's telling, for not only does he vividly underline Wallace's former humble station but he tells us as well what is going on his head: "he had, in these few moments, become something other than he had been, a man on a different level, a knight . . . By one brief and simple rite, in that chivalric age, he had been made dignified, eminent, transferred to the ranks of the men of honour."

The *Scots Magazine* article prompted a response from fellow-writer Donald Sutherland who wrote at length giving his own views on the subject of honours, and the two men settled down to a cosy little correspondence in which they let their imaginations run riot constructing an alternative honours system, with some new orders of their own devising, Tranter enlarging on the abuses of the present system, and, being totally opposed to any political patronage whatsoever as far as honours were concerned, coming up with a proposal that Life Peers be automatically reduced to the ranks, or at least removed from the House of Lords, when the Government that appointed them lost an election. They toyed with the idea of confining knighthoods to the military and the diplomatic service: in general Tranter wanted to see knighthood "cleaned up, not abolished", adding "I'd like to see an Order of St Andrew established for Scotland, with a Grand Master and Chapter General whose duty it would be to advise on admission and promotion" (a borrowing, presumably, from the Order of St Lazarus). Interestingly, for this was 1971, he tended to see it all in terms of a future independent Scotland. In fact, of course, after all these years of writing about castles and great nobles with historic names, Tranter dearly loves a lord, certainly a hereditary one, and indeed knows a good many by now, and when he celebrated his 80th birthday in 1989, Lord and Lady Lothian had the inspired idea of assembling at Ferniehurst for a birthday lunch as many of the descendants of the heroes of his books as they could find. From the Duke of Buccleuch down, the guest-list read like a roll-call of the peerage of Scotland and few gestures could have given greater pleasure.

Public honours of a more conventional nature started to pour in from around 1970 on. One of the first was an honorary MA in 1971 from the University of Edinburgh. The citation which accompanied it makes interesting reading viewed from a later perspective, for it postdates publication of *The Fortified House* but not completion of the *Bruce* trilogy, and runs "it is above all as a guardian of the Scottish heritage that we . . . honour him today", and goes on to refer first to his campaigning work to save and document Scottish castles, only turning thereafter to the historical novels, of which only two of the *Bruce* books had yet been published and the

Montrose and *Wallace* books had yet to be written. In 1989 came an award which gave particular pleasure, since it was the result of a popular vote: Radio Scotland's listeners voted him "Scot of the Year". There were also a number of humbler honours which gave pleasure, among them, appointment as an honorary vice-president of the Scottish Association of Teachers of History, a clear indication that whatever doubts their grander academic colleagues at the universities might occasionally voice—mainly because of a gut objection to blurring the line between fiction and history—the people in the front-line of history teaching admire and appreciate his work. In 1990, the University of Strathclyde made him an Honorary Doctor of Literature.

In 1982 he received the signal honour of an invitation to lunch with the Queen at Holyrood Palace, an occasion made memorable *inter alia* by knocking over his finger-bowl and telling the story of how Holyrood got its name, and this was followed up in 1983 by an OBE for services to literature. Commanded to appear at a morning Investiture at Buckingham Palace, he elected for unfathomable reasons to fly down from Edinburgh to London the same morning, when Lady Douglas of Kirtleside, whom he had invited to accompany him, volunteered to pick him up at the airport and take him to the Palace. In the event, the plane was on time but Lady Douglas and her Rolls Royce got stuck in the traffic and they were seriously late, necessitating much telephoning and causing no doubt a considerable flurry behind the scenes. He was, however, duly invested with the insignia of an Officer of the Order of the British Empire—which he found an anachronism, but wears with pride.

Throughout the years, the stream of books continued, too many to do justice to, some aspiring no higher than his original storyteller's aim—to entertain—but others with a deeper purpose. *MacBeth the King*, published in 1978, was a deliberate work of rehabilitation, and none too easy: Shakespeare's Scottish play had seen to that. But Tranter believed MacBeth had been seriously traduced by Shakespeare, who based himself more or less exclusively on Holinshed and gave us a great play, but not about the real Macbeth. Scott, too, in his *Tales of a Grandfather,* had followed Holinshed. In particular, Tranter believed that MacBeth deserved recognition for his qualities of kingship, his long tenure of the throne, and the legitimacy of his claim to it. He believed the play's Lady Macbeth was another travesty: it was through her that the stronger claim lay, their rule was a partnership, so why should she not be accorded her rights as Queen? Why should we know her only as the Lady Macbeth of the play, remembered only for egging her husband on to the murder of Duncan? Why did we not even know her name? In his own book he set about putting things right, and he paints a picture of responsible and successful government, a convincing relationship, and a sensible, attractive, even motherly Queen Gruach. But without a doubt, the most memorable characters in the book are MacBeth's half-brother Thorfinn Raven-Feeder, another full-blooded, roistering giant in the mould of Roddie Roy MacGregor of *The Freebooters* and *Ducks and Drakes,* and his hefty, jolly Norse wife. He wrote again about the Norsemen and their dragon-ships in *Lord of the Isles,* published in 1983, with another character in Somerled who can measure up to Thorfinn; and in *High Kings and Vikings,* published in 1998, both Thorfinn and MacBeth return, with many fine sea-scenes and a narrative that manages to do almost entirely without dialogue for the first sixty pages.

Another book worth singling out is *The Patriot,* published in 1982, and one of Tranter's best books, although, untypically, dense with discussion rather than warfare. It deals with the difficult and confusing religious wars, the Darien scheme and the negotiation of the Treaty of Union, all seen through the eyes of Andrew Fletcher of Saltoun, member of the Scots Parliament—"the parcel of rogues"—but resolutely opposed to the Union. With two periods of exile on the Continent, it includes a good picture of the various parties, English and Scottish, scheming and plotting in the Netherlands for Monmouth and the Succession, and allowing Fletcher to pick up some hints about modern Dutch farming methods in the bygoing, and there are notable appearances by Graham of Claverhouse, Rob Roy MacGregor and William Paterson, founder of banking and a central figure in the Darien Scheme. The quarrel with Alderman Dare, which leads to Fletcher pulling out his pistol and shooting him, is well done, with an immediate and irrational enmity springing up between the two at first meeting, and Fletcher's own abortive romance with Margaret Carnegie, who marries his brother Henry, is neatly handled and not mawkish, although a bit marred by "wordless claspings" in the early stages. Fletcher himself comes across as a true patriot, not driven by sentiment alone, a more solidly-drawn figure than some of Tranter's other heroes—but then of course, he has the benefit of a fairly full historical record. But the book is most notable for its masterly treatment of a complex and difficult subject, taking us clearly and lucidly through the legal points, the arguments for and against, the religious differences and what the Test Act was about, the ignorance of Scottish affairs in London, the decisions facing Scotland from the death of Charles II on, the recurrent problems of the Succession, the adverse conditions affecting Scottish overseas trade, the Darien disaster, and the readiness of some of the grasping Scots Lords of Parliament to sell their parliament for gold, all through the words of his characters, with many dramatic confrontations in the Scots Parliament and elsewhere.

The sets of books also continued to pour out: a trilogy on the rise of the House of Stewart, another on James V, two books on Mary Stewart, elder sister of James III, more to come on the Cospatricks. They all have their merits, but perhaps *The Stewart Trilogy* is the best of them, meaty, colourful, action-packed, a tangled tale of family rivalries and ambitious nobles, child kings and regencies, with memorable characters in King Bleary, the all-powerful Wolf of Badenoch in his mountain fastness at Lochindorb and a brilliant, impudent, arrogant young Prince David. The battle-scenes are real and immediate, with touches everywhere that enhance the sense of being present, as in *Lords of Misrule*, when he writes of the smell of "sweat and leather and horse and unwashed humanity" and the young Archie Douglas suddenly vomiting among the "screaming horses and bellowing cattle, weeping women and cursing men, priests and friars on their knees praying" as Finchale Priory burns. There is drama too in confrontations off the battlefield, like the clash between Prince David and the Douglas in the Great Hall in Stirling over who is to command, when the Prince suddenly shouts "Remember who will be King hereafter" and hurls his goblet the length of the dais-table, scattering all in its path, to crash to the floor beside the Duke of Albany.

XXVII

GONE ON AHEAD

Silence, save for the crunch of a pebbled path beneath the feet. Beyond a low stone wall, the Bay. The tide is on the ebb, the water the merest film of glass, fretted with the emerald of the St Lazarus cross. The stillness has a softness, a Hebridean feel, we might almost be standing on the machair. Among the graves, the last resting place of Philip and May; Phyllis is here, too. The stone reads "Gone On Ahead". Always, Philip had gone on ahead. The air is sharpening now, the grass damp with dew. The sun slants low across the Firth: soon it will set.

To others, May Tranter, so central to her husband's life, seems to have been an elusive personality, coming alive only with close members of her family, her real life lived mainly within the confines of her own home. Only 22 when she married Nigel in 1933, and only 16 when she met him, she had had no other suitors and appears to have had time, as a young woman, to make few friends other than family friends: the two of them quickly became all in all to each other to the exclusion of all others, and seem indeed to have had no need of others, apart of course from fellow-members of the Mansfield Place Church, but were perhaps unconsciously distancing themselves from their contemporaries. Nigel was already self-sufficient, poised at that invisible door into

Silent and grim before the battle of Aberlady Bay

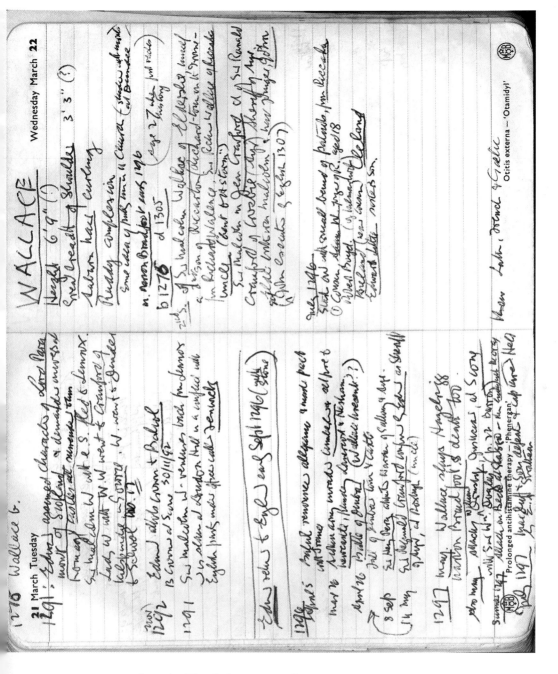

Opposite: The daily routine—leaving Quarry House for his day's work, with Philip looking on

Above: A typical entry in Tranter's notebook

Above: Frances May's wedding to Robert Baker, with a kilted Philip standing behind

Opposite above: Philip relaxing after a tough climb, resplendent in his kilt

Opposite below: Philip with Will Fraser and Chris Doake on Aonach Eagach ridge in 1965

Left: A summer outing for Nigel and May, at the top of Ben Damph

Above left: Knight Commander of the Order of St Lazarus of Jerusalem

Above right: Joan Earle, Nigel's close friend and companion

Opposite: Before & after—Little Tarrel Castle restored to its former glory, one of the many historical transformations in which Nigel Tranter has been instrumental

Left: Nigel on the footbridge to Aberlady Bay

Nigel Tranter at Quarry House, his home for nearly fifty years

the parallel life of the imagination through which he would slip so easily back and forth throughout his life. For whatever reason, possibly because of the strong hold his church had on him, providing another self-sufficient life, they turned into rather an old-fashioned couple, turned a little in on themselves. Possibly the absence of the usual dense network of young friends led them to replicate more exactly the mores of their parents, possibly it was the all-pervading influence of the church's teaching. Certainly May appears to have been an old-fashioned girl, regarding marriage as a woman's proper end in life, her role that of home-maker, her husband the provider. She accepted that her husband's personal and professional status would be hers, she would do what she could to enhance it, and with that she was content. She would provide the secure home base from which he would go out and conquer the world, in whatever form. From the start, she seems to have had an absolute confidence in his abilities. And to the end of her life, despite her independent existence during the war years, she seems to have assumed automatically, as her mother clearly did, that she would always be entitled to rely on some male member of her family to look after her: if Nigel died, then Philip, after Philip was killed, presumably Rob; but that her own life would be lived inside her own home. Nigel, however, was equally old-fashioned, assuming his wife would play the stay-at-home role, busying herself with house and garden and children while he dealt with the outside world. It was his good fortune that there was very much more to May Grieve than that, and she was to prove an able helpmeet, an essential adjunct to his life as a writer, even though always in the secondary role. Outside the family circle, she was retiring, silent and self-effacing in company, while Nigel occupied the centre-stage. Only occasionally, when she put him right about a date or restrained his wilder flights of fancy, did she give a hint that within the privacy of their home she might be more of a force to be reckoned with: only occasionally, when dealing with a tradesman or a shop assistant, did she show that she was not to be trifled with. But generally speaking, she seems in any case to have been ill-at-ease with strangers and happiest in the company of her children and grandchildren. In this she seems to have been exhibiting a family trait, possibly attributable to her family's Highland blood, the innate distrust of strangers often manifested by people who live in lonely places.

Nigel and May also applied old-fashioned standards to the upbringing of their children, frowning on waste, encouraging thrift and decidedly strait-laced as regards morals. Nigel in particular was inclined to be austere, demanding a high standard of behaviour, bringing them up to be considerate always of other people, not to mistake money for wealth. But they were not a couple to whom you could take home a wilder university acquaintance or a casual girl-friend with impunity: by the time Philip was in his twenties the liberated Sixties were getting into their swing, but any hint of carnal relations would have shocked them immeasurably; or so at least, their children thought. There was no question however even when they were young of banishing the children from adult company: on the contrary, all remember them as an unusually united family in which the children were treated as equal partners from an early age, all enjoying each other's company on equal terms. Both, perhaps Philip in particular, however gradually developed lives of their own, not concealed exactly from their parents, but not entirely revealed either: areas of Philip's climbing life, for example, were unknown to them, like some of his friendships, and they would have been startled to learn of the beer-drinking and poker playing that was an integral part of his climbing weekends. Nevertheless they remained extremely close: Philip wrote copious and frequent letters home whenever he was abroad and made a point of visiting frequently. Although living and working hundreds of miles away he still regarded Quarry House as "home" and it was Quarry House he always longed to get back to when journeying abroad.

In the first couple of decades of their marriage, May's retiring nature and the presence of young children in the house, combined with Nigel's deliberate encouragement of his outside interests in public affairs, led to a situation in which he developed a full and busy life of committees and public meetings in which May did not share, or could only share vicariously, and which regularly took him away from the house in the evenings: she occasionally took him to task about it, complaining that she never saw him, but it had no very noticeable effect. She once counted up that he was chairman of eleven different organisations, a story he is fond of recounting, with a hint of pride in his achievement. But it must have looked somewhat different to May, sitting at home by the fire, and she must have felt at times that she had to share him with half Scotland. When great success came to him in the 1970s after the publication of the *Bruce* trilogy she of course rejoiced for him, but she had no taste for the public exposure and razzmatazz that went with it, nor did she enjoy the invasion of their private life. She was a willing accomplice when it came to composing letters to the press, but she would have preferred not to have them about the house. And she fiercely protected Quarry House as his workplace as well as her home, barring the way to the importunate.

After their children had grown up and left home, however, she travelled regularly with him on research trips, sitting alongside him in the car reading the maps, seeking out castles, going with him to talk to ministers and teachers and librarians and post-mistresses in connection with *The Queen's Scotland*, making the notes while he asked the questions or sketched the castles, joining him when they were asked in for a cup of tea by the local minister or the laird, packing the picnic and staying in cheap hotels. But she shrank from the book-launches and the self-publicising aspects of his success, and she remained all her life a very private person:

few indeed are the surviving friends who claim to have known her really well. Apart from the War years, her sorties outside Quarry House were made with Nigel, on a highly selective basis, and she never learned to drive a car, a seriously limiting factor, living where they did. But exceptions were always made in deserving cases: an old lady in need of help, a relative struggling to look after a sick mother, the provision of a second home for Nigel's sister Phyl. Unable to express her emotions in words, she was yet a deeply compassionate and caring woman. In the unstinting and unquestioning old-fashioned way, she stepped in unbidden and helped where she could. Both his children were to inherit Nigel's unforced charm, but it was their daughter Frances May who inherited May's quality of inwardness, for Philip was gregarious by nature, like his father, and, because he was a climber, and climbers must function in partnership with others, he lived a great deal of his adult life in the closest physical proximity to others. It wouldn't have done for May.

She was old-fashioned in another sense, for she adhered, no doubt unconsciously, to a fairly widespread behavioural pattern among artists' wives, in that she accepted sacrifice and a secondary role because she believed absolutely in her husband's special gift. Artists, be they painters or poets, are not like other men. They live, quite literally, for their art: they believe, because they must, or they would never survive, absolutely in what they are doing. They are artists, of whatever degree or kind, precisely because they are more perceptive, which also means more sensitive, than the rest of us. If they are to flourish, their lives must be lived according to their own rules and priorities and, mild-mannered though he may seem in most things, Nigel Tranter is no exception to this general rule and can deploy a ruthless streak where his work is concerned. All this May instinctively accepted: some things she drew the line at, but by and large all danced after his tune, and when she took him to task occasionally, it was in defence of his own interests and he took it like a lamb. But in all other respects she deferred to him outside the strictly domestic sphere. She had absolute trust in his qualities as a writer, and he relied absolutely on her in all other aspects of his life.

It made for a quiet life—some would say, a dull one: but it was a life to her taste and of her own choosing and after they moved to Quarry House she had the compensation of a spacious establishment, a beautiful garden and the privacy she craved. Nigel's real life was lived largely inside his own head, and when he moved on to write the historical novels, he walked and talked daily, on his solitary expeditions around the Bay, with Bruce and Wallace and Montrose. But even when he was writing the humble Westerns, he was already living a life apart from the life of the real world, that was completely satisfying to him and made him supremely happy, but in which May could share only at one remove, after he had written it down. Frances May married young and moved away. But Philip continued to live at home as long as he was at university, kept his gear at Quarry House and visited regularly. He grew up to be an enormously attractive personality, the attraction enhanced by his great height, and they both came close to idolising him, May perhaps even more than Nigel. They worried about his climbing and waited anxiously for the call from some lonely Highland call-box when he rang to let them know he was safely down off the hill. Although they didn't know it, he, too, worried; worried about worrying them. Not that it stopped him: Philip, too, had a ruthless, single-minded streak in pursuit of what he really cared about, in his case, the high tops. But May was nervous by disposition and pre-eminently a worrier: she worried about Nigel driving home late at night from meetings in Edinburgh and Glasgow and Aberdeen, she worried about Frances May and her babies, and she worried above all about Philip. It was fortunate, perhaps, that they never knew about the marathon drives he was undertaking on climbing weekends with far too little sleep.

Common to all who remember May, her husband apart, is an obscure feeling of compassion. They feel sorry for her, sorry, above all, for the loss of Philip, which so devastated her, and sorry that May, who had struggled in the early days to make ends meet, who worked so hard on his behalf, May who stayed home when Nigel went adventuring abroad, May who worried about them all, sitting alone by the fire in Quarry House, with its four outside doors, had died unable to share in the rewards of his success, and enjoy the comfortable old age together that was their due. It shouldn't be a sad story, for they were idyllically happy together, but somehow it is: after Philip died, she was too much alone.

May herself was struck down by illness early in 1978 and became increasingly unwell. The eventual diagnosis was myeloma, a cancer of the bone marrow, for which there were palliatives but no real treatment. She went into hospital from time to time for blood transfusions, but most of the time she was at home up to the last, and it was now that Frances May stepped in. By this time she was back in Scotland with her family, for her husband Rob, also a Scot, had retired from the Navy and was now working in Edinburgh. To Nigel's great joy, they had settled in the old manse at Athelstaneford, only a few miles away, and Frances May now came over daily to visit her mother and keep the household going, singing as she went about the eleven-room house, so that her mother would know where she was. Like most young people, she realised that her mother was very ill, but did not fully comprehend that she was going to die: it was an enormously difficult time for her, too, torn as she was between the two households.

May died on 23 October 1979. Nigel buried her with Philip in Aberlady kirkyard. May, too, had gone on ahead. They had been married for 46 years. He stayed on at Quarry House, which had been May's creation and where May continued to be a presence and a comfort: because of his faith, he had no doubt he would be reunited with her some day, as he would be reunited with Philip.

During her illness, because he was more tied to the house, he wrote *The Story of Scotland*, which was not published until 1987. After she died, he wrote *Nigel Tranter's Scotland*, a retrospective look at his life and the causes on which he had lavished so much energy. It was the book he wrote instead of an autobiography, and it was a time for taking stock personally as well as professionally. But quite soon he had taken refuge again in the life of the imagination and was at work on another novel. Frances May looked in occasionally to keep an eye on things domestically and see that he was all right, and he spent Sundays at Athelstaneford, but writing was his real solace and, surprisingly, perhaps, to the outside observer, he was doing some remarkably good work. His own explanation is simple: he had nothing else to do. But it is testimony to how important his other life had become to him.

The year that May died, he published *Margaret the Queen*, the first of two major novels he would write about Scottish saints. The book presents the reader with a problem. In the first place it opens with a brutal scene of rapine and pillage into which Margaret steps, apparently without noticing it, when she first comes ashore at Northumbria. And in the second place, we are presented with a personality which is inherently self-contradictory, for she is both beautiful and sexually attractive—so reeking indeed with sex that Malcolm cannot wait to get his hands on her, even at the expense of poisoning his wife—and at the same time a saint, who demonstrates her saintliness by relentless good works and relentless proselytising on behalf of the church of Rome at the expense of the homegrown Celtic church. Since Tranter's sympathies so obviously lie with the national church, we are left with a feeling that as well as being relentlessly saintly she is also hopelessly wrong-headed. She was obviously loved for her good works— although good works do not always inspire love in the beneficiaries—and was the object of the King's lust and subsequent devotion, but somehow she does not come across as a particularly lovable person. And national saint though she later became, she clearly did her best to destroy the national church utterly. Yet again, she has a worldly acceptance of the realities of her situation and her beauty's due in accepting the hand of the King she categorised at first sight as a "brute-beast". Tranter's defence is that this is how she is presented in the chronicles. But his version verges on hagiography, which suggests that his primary sources were also hagiographical and that he did not apply his customary critical approach in assessing them. Ingebiorg, whom Malcolm poisons to clear the way for marriage to Margaret, is much more sympathetic. However, the book was presumably written when May was already dying and she may have been too much in his mind.

Columba, which he regarded as his greatest challenge, presents none of these problems. Although from the modern point of view, Columba's story contains as many inherent contradictions, if not more, than Margaret's, they give the impression of being better-digested, better-imagined. Columba, unlike Margaret, is convincing, without internal contradictions, now one aspect, now another aspect of his personality coming to the fore, a mature, rounded, real, thinking, sentient man. Prince of the royal house of Ireland who turned down election as High King, and soldier as well as Abbot, we see how his qualities as statesman and general lead him to fight at Cooldrevny for the survival of Irish Christianity; we see how as churchman he fights the symbols of the Druid faith by sending his Psalter into battle at the head of his army; we see his subsequent horror at the slaughter and the crisis of conscience which takes him to Scotland. We see how attractive he is towards women and how much he enjoys their company; we see him warm towards Bridget, who is a good woman and not a temptress, and yet resist, not because his church imposes celibacy but because he must not allow himself to be distracted from his mission; we see his trembling weariness and physical fear when he climbs the Sgurr nan Cu-Chulinn to scotch the story of the Fell Hound; we see his terrifying encounter with the wild boar brought vividly to life with the spurt of blood when he cuts the brute's throat; we see his worries that some of his gambles on miracles will not succeed; we see him suddenly losing his temper and banging on the door to gain admission to Craig Phadraig; we see him pull rank when he needs to. We read descriptions of Iona that have the freshness of Eden; we hear the cuckoos calling again and again through the book. And we find an endearing likeness in one respect to Tranter himself, for Columba, too, is an impatient man, "never one for delay once a course was decided on".

After the Irish years, the book lacks action in the usual Tranter sense of action in battle, but it is hardly noticeable because the various encounters with pagan or otherwise hostile magnates contain sufficient tension of themselves: it is only after his mission is established, that the book turns into a bit of a travelogue as he roams the length and breadth of Scotland preaching the faith (and no doubt material gleaned from *The Queen's Scotland* played its part). But the more pedestrian passages are wholly redeemed at the end by his deeply moving meditations on old age, his sense that his friend Moluag has stolen a march on him by dying first, imbued from first to last with the joyous confidence of Tranter's own faith. Columba's leave-taking and death are deeply felt and honestly expressed, without sentimentality: the last twenty or so pages of *Columba* are among the best he has ever written. The book, which carries the dedication "For Joan, who greatly helped" (the only such), was published in 1987 and written probably a year or eighteen months earlier. The dedication presumably marks a point at which the loss of May was becoming less vivid but there can be little doubt that these last pages represent Tranter's own working through the meaning of death. Columba is real because he taps into some deep roots in Tranter himself.

The early 1990s also saw the publication of another little book outside the general run: *Footbridge to Enchantment,* many people's favourite, a hymn to the saltmarsh and the Bay and the bents and the happy years at Quarry House. It is well-named for the little timber bridge he crossed each day to reach his enchanted world, for it was a poor day when he was not already scribbling before he was over the bridge. All who read it have their own favourite passage that they read over and over again, but few can fail to warm to the wonderful portrayal of the relationship between a man and his dog, Tess, who surely belongs among the immortals.

With May gone, he was of course miserably lonely and missed her dreadfully, missed her physical presence and missed her counsel: but May had been released from pain and he knew she was waiting for him, and his absolute certainty that they would eventually be reunited gave his grief a different quality. His professional life had always been a solitary one. May was no longer there with his lunch waiting when he came home from the Bay, but the hours spent walking were no different from what they had been before: by the time he was across the footbridge his imagination was busily at work and he quickly picked up the threads again. The parallel life of the imagination he had already been living for the past 40-odd years was a kindly retreat, which stood him in good stead in his widowhood. But he still sensed May's presence in the house and he continued to take her views into account in everything he did. And, since he believed that marriage is not for life, but for eternity, he continued to think of himself as a married man.

There was one respect however in which he changed. From a child, he had been accustomed to the company of women, and, in addition to missing May as a person, he was missing a female presence in his life. As a famous name, a public figure, he was accustomed to a certain amount of female adulation, which May had kept firmly at bay. He was accustomed to being solitary, but now he was lonely, an important difference, and although no one could replace May, he needed someone else: now he was alone, not a few were interested. No one was surprised when he started to see women friends again: they were, however, surprised by how many there were. Since few knew the unusual nature of his thinking about marriage, no one would have been surprised if, having enjoyed a happy marriage with May, he remarried after a decent interval. They were, however, a little taken aback by what in fact happened.

XXVIII

INDIAN SUMMER

A golden day of sun on autumn leaves, with a touch of chill in the air, just enough to sharpen the focus and give everything an edge. In the distance, a woman in cords, sweater and wellies, swinging a stick, preceded by a black labrador dog. A luxuriant shock of grey hair that once was black, a girlish figure. She has a very distinctive, dark, throaty voice and an upper-class accent. She is smiling to herself, turning her face this way and that, enjoying the sun, in no great hurry to get home. Her name is Joan.

Although his co-religionists are few and the churches closed, Nigel Tranter still considers himself a member of the Catholic Apostolic Church in which he grew up and he still holds the beliefs they preached. Chief among these is the belief that they have been granted a privileged insight, through revelation, into the purposes of God for man. Their faith in the reality of God and the reality of a life after death is absolute, and this faith Nigel shares. For most of us our faith, or the lack of it, is a private matter, no longer, whatever the teaching of religion, an all-pervading influence on the conduct of our lives. We go to church or stay away, we pray or don't pray, we continue out of habit to celebrate our personal rites of passage—birth, marriage, death—in a religious context, we call on our God *in extremis*, we try to practise the virtues and believe in the common worth of our fellow-men. But few could claim convincingly that they walk with their God in their daily lives. In this one vital respect, Nigel Tranter is different from most of the rest of us, and this means that his attitude to some of the central relationships of his life is also different.

The faith in which Nigel Tranter was brought up is a joyful faith, because it is based on absolute certainties. He believes with absolute certainty that his gift of storytelling is not just a gift but a gift from God, which he has a duty to exercise to the best of his ability: for this reason, if for no other, he will continue to exercise it as long as he is able. Another certainty which he holds absolutely is that we will be reunited with our loved ones after death. In the language of his faith, they are the sleeping Saints, asleep in the Lord, and waiting, like their brothers and sisters on earth, for the Second Coming. The Catholic Apostolic Church believes that we will be translated from a physical to a spiritual body on death but continue to be clearly identifiable as the individuals we were on earth. It therefore follows that he expects to be reunited after death with his wife May. He believes, as one might expect, that marriage is for life. But he also believes—and this seems to be an extrapolation of his own, since his father took a different line— that since husband and wife are "made one body" in marriage, in the conventional term, and the body continues in spiritual, if not in physical, form after death, marriage is not just for life but for eternity. It follows that May is still central to his life: he dreams of her, he talks to her in his waking dreams, and he still says, with great simplicity, "I'm in love with her still". These beliefs are unshaken and unshakable; but they present a problem—to which he appears oblivious—in their repercussions on the other close relationship of his life, that with Joan Earle.

Joan Earle came into Nigel's life on New Year's Day 1982. Both of them were relatively recently widowed, but over the worst, and they were invited to spend New Year with mutual friends, Andrew and Dorothy Haddon, at Denholm in the Borders. It was not the first time they had met, for when May was still alive, the Haddons had taken Joan and her husband to visit, but the acquaintance didn't take off. Probably it was the two men who had little in common. Basil was hail-fellow-well-met, a great games-player with an expansive personality: not anathema to Nigel exactly, but nothing to attract his interest either. Nigel, furthermore, has little small-talk and is inclined at times either to sit mumchance and silent with people he doesn't know or launch forth into a mild history lesson connected with whatever it is he is currently working on. Anyhow, for whatever reason, the relationship failed to develop. But both couples continued to see the Haddons, who were hospitable and caring people, and when first Basil and then May died, they kept an eye on the survivors. They were not the only guests at the Haddons' house that New Year but there may have been an element of match-making in inviting the two of them together as singletons. If so, it was a success. Nigel has always enjoyed female company and had other women friends, but Joan was to be different. In a comparatively short space of time, the relationship had developed far enough for her to ask him to drop the others: she was not interested in being one among many.

Joan's life had been vastly different from Nigel's. The War years always excepted, Nigel's life has been spent in Edinburgh and Aberlady, a mere seventeen miles apart. Until her late fifties, Joan's life was spent roaming round India and Pakistan, and commuting back and forth to Britain from the sub-continent. Her siblings were on the other side of the Atlantic. It has taken her seventy years to attain her present settled home in East Lothian. Born Joan Isobel Esslemont Paton in 1920, she was the daughter of a doctor in the Indian Medical Service, who was spending a year's home leave in Edinburgh working towards fellowship of the Royal College of Surgeons. She was born in Coates Crescent, in Edinburgh's West

End. Her younger brother and sister were both born in India. Her father's career is of some interest, for membership of the Indian Medical Service carried Army rank and as his career prospered he fetched up a Major-General. On the way to these heights, the family moved from station to station, and in the first ten years of her life, Joan lived in turn in Madras, North India, Kasauli, Lahore, Coonoor and Ootacamund, to which she would return: Ooty in particular was a highly-prized posting, with balls, the club, the hunt, and golf, amateur theatricals, tennis parties and all the advantages of a comfortable life in the Home Counties. At ten she came home to school in Scotland, first at St Katharine's and then at St Leonard's, both in St Andrews. As the custom was in those days, her mother came home to see her settled in, bringing the younger children with her, taking a house in St Andrews for the summer term, during which Joan, and later her brother and sister, were day-pupils for the first few years. In the winter, they boarded. Her father had six months' home leave every three years and that was all she saw of him until she finished school in 1938, when she went out to India for a year of partying before university. By 1939 war-clouds had gathered, and she stayed on in India. Her younger sister Dorothy was in Canada that summer on a school trip and they wired to her, too, to stay put. Dorothy finished her schooling in Canada, went on to university there, married a Canadian and became a Canadian citizen. In the fullness of time and for quite different reasons, the youngest child, Bruce, who became a doctor like his father, settled in the United States.

When war broke out in 1939, Joan volunteered as a nursing auxiliary, and it was while nursing up on the Afghan border that she met Basil Earle, whom she was to marry. He had gone out to India before the War as a shipping agent with Binny & Co, had volunteered for the Indian Army immediately war broke out, and was now up on the frontier with the South Waziristan Scouts engaged in intelligence work. They married in January 1943.

Because the Scouts didn't take married officers, he obtained a posting in Delhi, and Joan gave up nursing and joined the Censor's Office. Their first daughter was born in Simla, in the hot weather in July 1944. A second daughter was born in Madras and a third back home in Inverness.

They came back to Britain on a troopship early in 1945, travelling in convoy, and Joan vividly remembers the passage through the Mediterranean, zig-zagging to avoid the submarines, hearing the boom of depth charges going off in the dark, wearing a life-jacket day and night and never moving without the baby under her arm, listening in the darkness to the eery sound of the Polish Army Choir, also on board, which burst into song to keep up morale when the danger was at its most acute. Basil however was soon posted back to India, and she made the passage back again through the Mediterranean, travelling this time with other wives and children, in an antique converted passenger liner known—not affectionately—as The Squeaking Chitral. After he was demobilised, they resumed civilian life in India and embarked once more on a peripatetic existence, living in turn in Madras, where the seasons were "hot" and "hotter", and Cochin, with its associations with Vasco da Gama, where they sat on the verandah watching for the "green flash" as the sun went down over the ocean. In 1969 Basil came home for good and they settled, first in the Borders, moving from place to place for a couple of years, and then in East Lothian. Basil then launched himself belatedly on legal training, and Joan took a job at the Scottish Office, working on an Open University degree in her spare time. He died, as he would have wished, suddenly and violently, on the squash court in 1979, and the gypsy life was over.

Joan Earle is a stout-hearted and independent lady whose energy matches Nigel's own, if it does not surpass it: in addition to being a highly-involved grandmother, she has a string of lame ducks she keeps an eye on in the discreetest possible way. More unusually, she started her own little business in her seventies and is currently mastering the art of internet sales. And for the past seventeen years or so, she has read Nigel's books chapter by chapter as he writes them, advising and counselling and generally keeping company with him.

It is an unconventional relationship: their friendship is close, but there has been no question of marriage. They meet most days, go most places together, travel together, but they do not share a house. Despite the fact that Joan now reads his manuscripts for him, keeps track of his papers and tries to make him eat his vegetables and take his vitamin pills, it is not a re-run of his relationship with May: nor is Nigel a substitute for Basil. They have a loving friendship, not a marriage. As it settled into this form, it came as a surprise to most of their friends, not all of whom understood it or were prepared, unquestioningly, to welcome them as a couple. For their families a new partner might well in any case have presented problems, but this departure from the accepted norm was particularly difficult to come to terms with: it says much for all concerned that they have settled down with it and are grateful that Nigel and Joan are happy together. It is a romantic relationship and the attraction between them is clearly strong, Nigel protective and possessive, and Joan happy to relax into the warmth of his affection. It is easy to see how it would come about: in addition to being very attractive, she is quite small, and he must have wanted to pick her up and put her in his pocket. He had almost certainly never met anyone like her before, and Joan, after roaming all her life, had found safe haven at last. At this stage in their lives, she provides the stimulus he needs, and he provides the fixed point, the father figure she had lost. Both are quietly content within the limits they have themselves imposed.

If May's personality was elusive, so too is Nigel's, but for wholly different reasons. Where all seemed to be withdrawn, concealed, tamped down in May Grieve, Nigel appears, at first glance, all on the surface. A quiet, douce man, you would say: affable, friendly, generous, courteous, cautious, open, modest, unassuming, unselfish, frugal and quietly open-handed at the same time, prudent, level-headed, intelligent but not much interested in ideas, diligent, industrious, devout, honest, temperate, loyal, patriotic, his devotion to Scotland complete. At ninety, all these appear to be constants, and consistent.

When we look at the record however, it immediately becomes apparent that the list is inadequate to describe the man: there is something missing. For one thing, it is too simple. Would a prudent man have given quite so many hostages to fortune throughout his life in pursuit of his causes? Would a temperate man have used the impassioned language he poured out on the unfortunate Mr Carse? Would a cautious man have to be forcibly restrained at ninety from climbing up on his garage roof? Would a sensible man have taken that early morning plane to his Investiture? Would a shrewd man have so incensed the Lords Lieutenant and the Tweed Commissioners? Would a canny man speak quite so freely to the press every time they ring him up? What is missing from the list is the impatient side of his nature, familiar to all who know him well, and carried all too frequently to the point of rashness, and, more unexpected in a man who greatly enjoys intrigue, a certain quality of guilelessness: he does not guard against, because he does not see, the possible repercussions of some of the things he says and does. It is an engaging fault. Assuredly, he is not streetwise: he does not cover his back.

And what of the darker side? If, as he claims, he lives his characters as he writes them, from what hidden depths does he dredge up the passion and terror and brutality that go into so many of his scenes? Where do the torrid scenes of rape and pillage come from, the scenes of debauch? It can scarcely be from the dry history books he reads to research them. There are secrets inside

Nigel Tranter, perhaps inside all men of powerful imagination, that are beyond our understanding and perhaps also beyond his own.

XXIX

LOCAL PATRIOT

A winter evening, a dusty village hall, crammed as for a protest meeting about bus-stops. A rickety table at the front and a man behind it, his glasses slightly askew, holding forth, gesturing with both hands as though conducting an orchestra. In his hand are the familiar postcard-size slips of paper. There is a warm, relaxed feel to the hall, despite the institutional chairs: the audience has come out, knowing it will enjoy itself, and it has not been disappointed. Every so often it laughs happily, comfortably, looks round and gives an appreciative nod of recognition. This is Nigel Tranter on his home ground, talking to a local history society about what he knows best, East Lothian.

With the passage of time, Nigel Tranter's role as national gadfly has shrunk and his platform narrowed: he takes pleasure in retaining his connection with the various organisations to which he has devoted so much time, but in an honorary capacity, not an active one. He takes a benevolent interest in what they get up to, but not more. There is one area however in which he remains as active as ever: he continues to find it well-nigh impossible to resist an invitation to give a talk, and, since no one who has read his books with any attention can be in any doubt about his abiding affection for East Lothian, it will come as no surprise that the organisations which can always call on his time with impunity are the local history societies of East Lothian, of which there are many. He is universally popular as a speaker, always producing some new titbit of information about the history of their own community they have never heard before. And the people who come to his talks are not necessarily the people who buy his books, or indeed many books at all. It is his great knowledge and his accessibility that draws in these catholic audiences. As a speaker, he is completely natural: he has no side, and there is absolutely no reason why even the most diffident should feel shy about asking a question or going up afterwards to shake his hand. By now, most of his audiences have heard him speak before and regard him as an old friend. He has the gift of being totally approachable.

Closest of all to his heart, however, is the St Andrew Society of East Lothian, which is his own creation, since it was he who founded it in 1966. He has been its chairman ever since. There was already an East Lothian Antiquarian Society, but he felt there was a need for something a little broader. He was a member of the Saltire Society, established in 1936 to preserve the Scottish heritage and foster Scottish culture generally (and he is now an Honorary President of the Society) and toyed for a time with the idea of establishing a local branch in Haddington, but decided eventually against it: better not to lay themselves open to policy swings in Edinburgh, and to go it alone. But the general pattern would be roughly the same: broadly cultural with a strong patriotic tinge. It goes without saying that it has a strong historical list. The timing of the launch in autumn 1966 however could not have been more unfortunate from a personal point of view for in the event it was in the immediate aftermath of Philip's death and May felt unable to be present at the first, or indeed any other, meeting. Indeed, there seems to have been some difference between them at this period about accepting outside engagements, May feeling that all should be declined, while Nigel insisted on fulfilling engagements already entered into. The St Andrew Society however went ahead and continues to flourish, with Nigel a most active chairman, always present at meetings, taking a keen interest in the programme, presiding genially over its annual St Andrew's Day dinner and clambering happily aboard bus or boat for summer outings.

He is as generous with his time to correspondents. His postbag is enormous and until recently, he replied promptly and punctiliously to every letter he received, often at surprising length, to the point at which correspondence began to usurp time and energy that should rightly have gone into the books. In fact, he enjoys the feedback from readers and a glance through his files reveals many exchanges with total strangers going back sometimes over decades. The bulk of them are sparked by his seemingly inexhaustible knowledge of Scotland and Scottish history: readers write in looking for help in tracing their ancestors, in the case of the exiles of the Scottish diaspora the names and whereabouts of the places their grandfathers emigrated from, sometimes centuries ago, their coats of arms, and their long-lost relatives. In some cases they are looking for an Open Sesame, in others the last piece to complete a jigsaw lovingly built up over the years. Some of these exchanges are fruitful also from his own point of view, producing more family history and traditions of the kind that came to light in researching the castles books. Many come from hopefuls searching for a link with a noble house. Some are looking for free research, others only for a way in to do their own research. Many send manuscripts for advice: all writers' postbags contain letters from would-be authors looking for a magic formula. Some are simply looking for tourist tips; others for an autograph or an excuse to call. Some are looking for castles to restore. Some are looking for romance. And there is the usual quota of letters most public figures receive from the sad, the mad and the lonely in search of comfort and a sympathetic ear. Often they want simply to tell him a story of their own. All receive a sympathetic hearing:

Nigel Tranter is in the business of communication and the material he is communicating is Scotland. But eventually a line had to be drawn: now some who send fan letters receive a polite standard note regretting the impossibility of a more personal reply, or a card with a photograph.

XXX

THE AULD SANG MADE NEW

Edinburgh, 1 July 1999. The Assembly Hall. Scotland's Parliament, the Scottish Crown in place before the Queen, the new Mace waiting to be unveiled, Mrs Winifred Ewing, presiding, "The Scottish Parliament, adjourned on the 25th of March 1707, is hereby reconvened." An auld sang taken up again. Ian Hamilton, commenting, "I have waited for this day all my life . . . the cringe has gone."

Although the Covenant Association for which Nigel Tranter had worked so long and so faithfully had long since withered and died, the devolution issue had not, and the Scottish National Party continued throughout the 1960s and 1970s to gather strength. A shock SNP win in a hitherto safe Labour seat in Hamilton in 1967 jolted the Labour Government into appointing a Royal Commission on the Constitution, which duly reported in 1973, recommending assemblies, with limited powers, for Scotland and Wales. By this time all the major parties had moved in the direction of a measure of self-government (although the Conservatives later changed their minds). The thrust of the Royal Commission's recommendations was blunted however by a couple of dissenting opinions and the Labour Government was in any case no longer in power, and although SNP representation in the House of Commons advanced by leaps and bounds, progress thereafter was slow. By 1976, however, Labour was back in power, the Government was ready to publish a White Paper and it was announced that a referendum would be held in Scotland, with another in Wales.

With hindsight, the 1979 referendum was a botched job, despite its long period of gestation. At the time, Britain had little experience of referendums and since Britain has no written constitution, there were few rules to follow. People knew what it was about—devolution—but they had no clear understanding of the connection between cause and effect. They knew that devolution would mean change, fundamental change, but they had no real understanding that fundamental, irreversible change of this nature perhaps needed to be hedged around with safeguards to prevent it being undertaken on a whim. The Government envisaged the referendum as advisory only, a means whereby to test the will of the Scottish people, but many people saw it more in terms of a form of direct democracy which would *decide* the issue. Their only experience of voting—in parliamentary elections and elections to local government assemblies—after all produced instant, direct results. A last minute amendment to the Devolution Bill came as a shock and was widely criticized. In effect, it produced a hybrid. Now a simple majority would not be enough: instead, it would be necessary to win the assent of over 40% of the registered electorate as well. If the referendum was to be *advisory* only, this was superfluous: had it been *binding,* some such safeguard would have been regarded as essential in most democratic countries. In the event, people felt the goal-posts had been moved back and they had been cheated: when the results came in, even more so, for the turnout was low, higher than in most local elections but decidedly lower than the average for parliamentary elections and a vote in favour of devolution by more then 40% of the electorate had not been achieved. The result was a three-way split: one third for, one third against and one third abstaining. It was a serious disappointment.

The Government, and England in general, felt justified in saying "so much for Scottish interest in devolution" and supporters of devolution in Scotland were badly bruised. The Scottish Nationalists in the House of Commons contributed their mite by voting against the Callaghan Government in the 1979 No Confidence vote, but the defeat of the Callaghan government brought Mrs Thatcher to power instead and she promptly took devolution off the agenda. Next time round, in the 1997 referendum, after another twenty years of non-devolved government, the Scottish electorate made sure self-government would stick. But it had been a long wait.

In 1999 was achieved the ultimate goal Nigel Tranter had worked for over a lifetime: the resumption of the Scottish Parliament. Like Ian Hamilton, he had been waiting for it all his life. He has always believed that a nation that allows itself to be governed by another nation is no nation at all. Now that the Parliament is here, like most other people, he feels a sense of satisfaction, even if he still regrets the failure of the Covenant to achieve it a generation earlier. His only doubts now relate to the naturally argumentative nature of the Scots, his only fear that inability to agree will trammel action. Behind every Scottish campaign in which he engaged, the Covenant, the Road Bridge, even Aberlady Bay and the Salmon War, there had burned the sense of frustration that Scotland was hamstrung by not having a parliament of her own: behind the long series of historical novels, and in particular books like the *Bruce* trilogy, the *Montrose* books, *The Wallace*, *The Patriot*, a burning desire to give Scotland back her sense of identity. In all his campaigns, it was the quality of his anger that distinguished Nigel Tranter: in all his books on Scottish history, the quality and enduring nature of his love of country. But he was not in the

Assembly Hall that first day of July 1999: instead, he watched the ceremonial at home on TV. As with the opening of the Forth Road Bridge, as with the ceremonial return of the Stone to Scotland, so with the opening of the Scottish Parliament, they didn't invite him.

TRANSITION

Cardboard boxes all over the place, lists, an odd collection of objects on the dining-room table for the grandchildren to choose a keepsake. Joan's felt-pen is working overtime. Nigel is leaving Quarry House. One morning quite soon, he will walk out of the old Phrontistery and set off across the timber bridge and, when he reaches Gullane, just keep going: that evening, he will type up in a new Phrontistery, to which the Imperial typewriter and all the old familiar books have miraculously been transferred, seamlessly as ever, with no interruption to his routine.

In 1998, he moved to golfing Gullane, where he had gone to church for sixty years, to a modern little house, with central heating and a bright new kitchen and a miniscule garden and neighbours who look in. It was Joan, of course, who engineered it, identified the moment, spotted the advertisement, made the first, anonymous inquiries, took him to see it and sold him the idea, Joan who organised the move, Joan who dashed about and fell over and broke her wrist so that he had to read the Riot Act, Joan who took everyone by surprise yet again. In less time than it takes most people to select a postage stamp, Nigel had gone firm on the deal, bought the house—cash, of course—and was all set to move in. Many of their friends now assumed that the affair would come to a satisfactory (to them) conclusion and Joan would move in, too. But they were wrong: Joan is a very self-contained and independent lady and she has remained her own woman. But she has made a lovely home for him, where he is transparently happy. He yearned of course at first for Quarry House, brooded about it lying there for a time empty and unloved, when it had been loved so much for so long. But the transition was remarkably painless. The mementoes have been pruned a bit and re-disposed, but the walls are still lined with the evidence of his extraordinary industry, the 130 hardbacks and half as many paperback editions that mark his path through life. The side-tables are still heaped with the books that people send him, and all the really important talismans are still there, the photographs of the grandchildren, Frances May in her wedding dress, the Bannockburn chess set, Philip's ice-axe and the SHKE flag, the models of castles and the doll of James VI, the pictures of May, the painting of Joan. A modest car stands in the garage. Except as a means to get about, it does not greatly interest him: to Tranter a car is an aid, necessary to extend the range of his own busily striding legs, not a fetish. He has had one for over seventy years. He can no longer see the Bay from his new windows, no longer step from his own front door straight out into his enchanted land, but five minutes takes him to the Bents and the sand and buckthorn of Gullane and he walks the familiar coastline from here now instead, east to west instead of west to east, his appetite for life undiminished.

END-PIECE

Goose Green Mews, a Tuesday in June. It is four o'clock and, sitting side by side on the little sofa, we are having tea, the tray balanced on the stool in front of us, the tape recorder switched off. "You've gone to an awful lot of trouble, lass," he says, wonderingly, and pats my knee. No one has called me "lass" for a very long time. Writing about someone who is still very much alive is not an easy process for either party, and some of the material I have dug up might have been better left where it was. Not all of it appears in this book. But together we have followed one man's path through epic struggles in Scotland's cause, through public triumphs and private sorrows. Both of us know more about Nigel Tranter now than we did before and the time has come for me to bow out. In any case Joan will be in later. And tomorrow, he will be out again, striding along the shoreline, this man who has given us back our past, walking with Wallace and Bruce, his mind far distant from the petty concerns of everyday.

Gullane, 1999

NIGEL TRANTER
BIBLIOGRAPHY

1935   *The Fortalices and Early Mansions of Southern Scotland 1400-1650*
        (The Moray Press)

1937   *Trespass* (The Moray Press)
        (re-issued by Ward Lock & Co, 1940)

1939   *Mammon's Daughter* (Ward Lock & Co)

1940   *Harsh Heritage* (Ward Lock & Co)
        (paperback edition by B&W Publishing, 1996)

1941   *Eagle's Feathers* (Ward Lock & Co)

        Watershed (Ward Lock & Co)

1942   *The Gilded Fleece* (Ward Lock & Co)
        (paperback edition by B&W Publishing, 1993)

1944   *Delayed Action* (Ward Lock & Co)

1945   *Tinker's Pride* (Ward Lock & Co)
        (paperback edition by B&W Publishing, 1994)

1946   *Flight of Dutchmen* (Ward Lock & Co)

1947   *Man's Estate* (Ward Lock & Co)

        Island Twilight (Ward Lock & Co)
        (paperback edition by B&W Publishing, 1992)

1948   *Root and Branch* (Ward Lock & Co)

        Colours Flying (Ward Lock & Co)

1949   *The Chosen Course* (Ward Lock & Co)
        (re-issued by Molindar Press, 1980)

1950   *Fair Game* (Ward Lock & Co)

        High Spirits (Ward Lock & Co)

        Thirsty Range (Ward Lock & Co)
        (pseudonym: Nye Tredgold)

1950   *The Freebooters* (Ward Lock & Co)
             (paperback edition by B&W Publishing, 1997)

1951   *Tidewrack* (Ward Lock & Co)

             Fast and Loose (Ward Lock & Co)
             (paperback edition by B&W Publishing, 1994)

             Heartbreak Valley (Ward Lock & Co)
             (pseudonym: Nye Tredgold)

1952   *Big Corral* (Ward Lock & Co)
             (pseudonym: Nye Tredgold)

             Bridal Path (Ward Lock & Co)
             (paperback edition by B&W Publishing, 1992)

             Cheviot Chase (Ward Lock & Co)

             Trail Herd (Ward Lock & Co)
             (pseudonym: Nye Tredgold)

1953   *Ducks and Drakes* (Ward Lock & Co)

             Desert Doublecross (Ward Lock & Co)
             (pseudonym: Nye Tredgold)

             The Queen's Grace (Ward Lock & Co)
             (paperback edition by B&W Publishing, 1992)

1954   *Rum Week* (Collins)

             The Night Riders (Ward Lock & Co)

             Cloven Hooves (Ward Lock & Co)
             (pseudonym: Nye Tredgold)

1955   *There are Worse Jungles* (Ward Lock & Co)

             Rio d'Oro (Ward Lock & Co)

             Dynamite Trail (Ward Lock & Co)
             (pseudonym: Nye Tredgold)

1956   *The Long Coffin* (Ward Lock & Co)

             Rancher Renegade (Ward Lock & Co)
             (pseudonym: Nye Tredgold)

1957   *Trailing Trouble* (Ward Lock & Co)
             (pseudonym: Nye Tredgold)

1957   *MacGregor's Gathering* (Hodder & Stoughton)
        (Book I of *The MacGregor Trilogy*)
        (paperback edition 1974)

        The Enduring Flame (Hodder & Stoughton)
        (Reprinted by Remploy, 1979)

1958   *Balefire* (Hodder & Stoughton)
        (paperback edition by B&W Publishing, 1992)

        The Stone (Hodder & Stoughton)
        (paperback edition by B&W Publishing, 1992)

        Bloodstone Trail (Ward Lock & Co)
        (pseudonym:Nye Tredgold)

        Spaniard's Isle (Brockhampton Press)

1959   *Border Riding* (Brockhampton Press)

        The Man behind the Curtain (Hodder & Stoughton)

        The Clansman (Hodder & Stoughton)
        (Book II of *The MacGregor Trilogy*)
        (paperback edition 1974)

1960   *Nestor the Monster* (Brockhampton Press)
        (paperback edition by B&W Publishing, 1992)

        Spanish Galleon (Hodder & Stoughton)

        The Flockmasters (Hodder & Stoughton)
        (paperback edition by B&W Publishing, 1994)

1961   *Kettle of Fish* (Hodder & Stoughton)
        (paperback edition by B&W Publishing, 1994)

        The Master of Gray (Hodder & Stoughton)
        (Book I of *The Master of Gray Trilogy*, title later altered
        to *Lord and Master*)
        (paperback edition published as *Lord and Master*, 1973)

        Birds of a Feather (Brockhampton Press)

        The Deer Poachers (Blackie)

1962   *Gold for Prince Charlie* (Hodder & Stoughton)
        (Book III of *The MacGregor Trilogy*)
        (paperback edition 1974)

        Drug on the Market (Hodder & Stoughton)

1962   *The Fortified House in Scotland: Volume 1: South-East Scotland*
(Oliver & Boyd)
(revised edition by The Mercat Press, 1986)

Something Very Fishy (Collins)

1963   *The Courtesan* (Hodder & Stoughton)
(Book II of *The Master of Gray Trilogy*)
(paperback edition 1973)

The Fortified House in Scotland: Volume 2: Central Scotland
(Oliver & Boyd)
(revised edition by The Mercat Press, 1986)

Give a Dog a Bad Name (Collins)
(US edition published as *Smoke Across the Highlands*
by Platt & Monk, 1964)

1964   *Silver Island* (Thomas Nelson)

Pegasus Book of Scotland (Dobson Books)

Chain of Destiny (Hodder & Stoughton)
(paperback edition 1977)

1965   *Pursuit* (Collins)

The Fortified House in Scotland: Volume 3: South-West Scotland
(Oliver & Boyd)
(revised edition by The Mercat Press, 1986)

Outlaw of the Highlands: Rob Roy (Dobson Books)
(re-issued as *Rob Roy MacGregor* by Lochar Publishing, 1991)
(re-issued as *Rob Roy MacGregor* by Neil Wilson Publishing,
1995)

Past Master (Hodder & Stoughton)
(Book III of *The Master of Gray Trilogy*)
(paperback edition 1973)

1966   *The Fortified House in Scotland: Volume 4: Aberdeenshire, Angus and
Kincardineshire* (Oliver & Boyd)
(revised edition by The Mercat Press, 1986)

A Stake in the Kingdom (Hodder & Stoughton)
(paperback edition 1995)

1967   *Lion Let Loose* (Hodder & Stoughton)
(paperback edition 1993)

Tinker Tess (Dobson Books)

1967   *Fire and High Water* (Collins)

        Cable from Kabul (Hodder & Stoughton)

1968   *Land of the Scots* (Hodder & Stoughton)

        To the Rescue (Dobson Books)

        Black Douglas (Hodder & Stoughton)
            (paperback edition 1973)

1969   *Robert the Bruce: The Steps to the Empty Throne*
            (Hodder & Stoughton)
            (Book I of *The Bruce Trilogy*)
            (paperback edition 1971)

1970   *The Fortified House in Scotland: Volume 5: North and West Scotland
        and Miscellaneous* (W & R Chambers)
            (revised edition by The Mercat Press, 1986)

        Robert the Bruce: The Path of the Hero King (Hodder & Stoughton)
            (Book II of *The Bruce Trilogy*)
            (paperback edition 1972)

1971   *The Queen's Scotland: The Heartland* (Hodder & Stoughton)

        Robert the Bruce: The Price of the King's Peace (Hodder & Stoughton)
            (Book III of *The Bruce Trilogy*)
            (paperback edition 1972)

1972   *Portrait of the Border Country* (Robert Hale)
            (revised edition published as *The Illustrated Portrait
            of the Border Country* by Robert Hale, 1987)

        The Queen's Scotland: The Eastern Counties (Hodder & Stoughton)

        The Young Montrose (Hodder & Stoughton)
            (Book I of *The Montrose Omnibus*)
            (paperback edition 1973)

1973   *Montrose: Captain General* (Hodder & Stoughton)
            (Book II of *The Montrose Omnibus*)
            (paperback edition 1974)

1974   *The Queen's Scotland: The North-East* (Hodder & Stoughton)

        The Wisest Fool (Hodder & Stoughton)
            (paperback edition 1976)

1975   *The Wallace* (Hodder & Stoughton)
            (paperback edition 1992)

1976   *Lords of Misrule* (Hodder & Stoughton)
              (Book I of *The Stewart Trilogy*)
              (paperback edition 1978)

1977   *A Folly of Princes* (Hodder & Stoughton)
              (Book II of *The Stewart Trilogy*)
              (paperback edition 1979)

            The Captive Crown (Hodder & Stoughton)
              (Book III of *The Stewart Trilogy*)
              (paperback edition 1980)

            The Queen's Scotland: Argyll & Bute (Hodder & Stoughton)

1978   *MacBeth the King* (Hodder & Stoughton)
              (paperback edition 1981)

1979   *Portrait of the Lothians* (Robert Hale)

            Margaret the Queen (Hodder & Stoughton)
              (paperback edition 1981)

1980   *David the Prince* (Hodder & Stoughton)
              (paperback edition 1982)

1981   *True Thomas* (Hodder & Stoughton)
              (paperback edition 1996)

            Nigel Tranter's Scotland (Richard Drew Publishing)
              (Penguin edition 1983)

1982   *The Patriot* (Hodder & Stoughton)
              (paperback edition 1984)

            Scottish Castles: Tales and Traditions (Macdonald Publishing)
              (revised edition by Neil Wilson Publishing, 1993)
              (US edition by Barnes & Noble, 1993)

1983   *Lord of the Isles* (Hodder & Stoughton)
              (paperback edition 1985)

1984   *Unicorn Rampant* (Hodder & Stoughton)
              (paperback edition 1986)

            The Riven Realm (Hodder & Stoughton)
              (Book I of *The James V Trilogy*)
              (paperback edition 1987)

1985   *James by the Grace of God* (Hodder & Stoughton)
              (Book II of *The James V Trilogy*)
              (paperback edition 1988)

1985   *Traveller's Guide to the Scotland of Robert the Bruce*
        (Routledge & Kegan Paul)
        (US edition by Historical Times Inc, 1985)

1986   *Rough Wooing* (Hodder & Stoughton)
        (Book III of *The James V Trilogy*)
        (paperback edition 1989)

1987   *The Story of Scotland* (Routledge & Kegan Paul)
        (re-issued by Neil Wilson Publishing, 1992)

        Cache Down (The Scotsman Publications Ltd)

        Columba (Hodder & Stoughton)
        (paperback edition 1990)

        Flowers of Chivalry (Hodder & Stoughton)
        (paperback edition 1990)

1989   *Mail Royal* (Hodder & Stoughton)
        (paperback edition 1991)

        Warden of the Queen's March (Hodder & Stoughton)
        (paperback edition 1991)

1990   *Kenneth* (Hodder & Stoughton)
        (paperback edition 1992)

1991   *Crusader* (Hodder & Stoughton)
        (paperback edition 1992)

1992   *Footbridge to Enchantment* (Lochar Publishing)
        (revised edition by B&W Publishing, 1993)

        Children of the Mist (Hodder & Stoughton)
        (paperback edition 1993)

1993   *Druid Sacrifice* (Hodder & Stoughton)
        (paperback edition 1993)

        Tapestry of the Boar (Hodder & Stoughton)
        (paperback edition 1994)

1994   *Price of a Princess* (Hodder & Stoughton)
        (Book I of *The Mary Stewart Omnibus*)
        (paperback edition 1995)

        Lord in Waiting (Hodder & Stoughton)
        (Book II of *The Mary Stewart Omnibus*)
        (paperback edition 1995)

1995   *Highness in Hiding* (Hodder & Stoughton)
           (paperback edition 1996)

           Honours Even (Hodder & Stoughton)
           (paperback edition 1996)

1996   *A Rage of Regents* (Hodder & Stoughton)
           (paperback edition 1996)

           Poetic Justice (Hodder & Stoughton)
           (paperback edition 1997)

1997   *The Marchman* (Hodder & Stoughton)
           (paperback edition 1997)

           The Lion's Whelp (Hodder & Stoughton)
           (paperback edition 1998)

1998   *High Kings and Vikings* (Hodder & Stoughton)
           (paperback edition 1998)

           A Flame for the Fire (Hodder & Stoughton)
           (paperback edition 1999)

1999   *Sword of State* (Hodder & Stoughton)
           (paperback edition 1999)

           Envoy Extraordinary (Hodder & Stoughton)

PHILIP TRANTER:

1968   *No Tigers in the Hindu Kush* (Hodder & Stoughton)
           (Edited: Nigel Tranter)

INDEX